ALL THINGS POSSIBLE

ALL THINGS POSSIBLE

*My Story of Faith, Football,
and the Miracle Season*

KURT WARNER

WITH MICHAEL SILVER

HarperSanFrancisco

Zondervan

ALL THINGS POSSIBLE: My Story of Faith, Football, and the Miracle Season. Copyright © 2000 by Kurt Warner with Michael Silver. All rights reserved. Printed in the United States of America. No part of this book may be used or reproduced in any manner whatsoever without written permission except in the case of brief quotations embodied in critical articles and reviews. For information address HarperCollins Publishers, Inc., 10 East 53rd Street, New York, NY 10022.

HarperCollins books may be purchased for educational, business, or sales promotional use. For information please write: Special Markets Department, HarperCollins Publishers, Inc., 10 East 53rd Street, New York, NY 10022.

HarperCollins Web site: http://www.harpercollins.com
HarperCollins®, ✦®, and HarperSanFrancisco™ are
trademarks of HarperCollins Publishers, Inc.

FIRST EDITION
Designed by Joseph Rutt

Library of Congress Cataloging-in-Publication Data
Warner, Kurt
    ALL THINGS POSSIBLE : *my story of faith, football, and the miracle season /*
Kurt Warner with Michael Silver.
    p. cm.
    ISBN 0–06–251717–1 (cloth)
    ISBN 0–06–251718–X (pbk.)
    1. Warner, Kurt. 2. Football players — United States — Biography.
3. Faith. 4. Title.
GV939.W36A29   2000

00 01 02 03 04 ✦/QW 10 9 8 7 6 5 4 3 2 1

To Brenda, Zachary, Jesse, Kade,
and to the little one I don't know yet—
you have made me want to be the best Christian father and
husband I can be. You are my life. I love you all.
—Kurt Warner

To my parents, Stephen and Susan Silver,
for giving me unlimited love, teaching what's right and wrong,
and letting me fall on my face a few times.
—Michael Silver

CONTENTS

INTRODUCTION

On the morning of May 23, 2000, when I was in a clouded state of consciousness, my world turned wacky, and I had what some might regard as an out-of-body experience.

While recovering from surgery at Missouri Baptist Hospital in St. Louis, I began to break out of my Demerol-triggered delirium and started focusing on a small television set in the corner of a post-op room. A voice was talking breathlessly about a matter of great importance, and as I squinted my eyes to make out the figure on the screen—a man in a white, blue, and yellow jersey throwing a football while being clobbered—I realized that the cause for the commotion was me.

"Rams quarterback Kurt Warner was rushed to emergency surgery, where his appendix is being removed as we speak," the newscaster reported. "There's still no word on his condition or what impact this appendectomy may have on his football future . . ."

If I hadn't been so groggy, I'd have burst out laughing. A little more than nine months earlier, I could have bungee jumped from atop the St. Louis Gateway Arch, and it's questionable whether anyone would have even noticed. Back then, I was as anonymous as any player in the National Football League, a guy whose career path included a Division I-AA college, the University of Northern Iowa, and a pair of low-prestige pro leagues, Arena Football and NFL Europe. Even the previous summer, after having ascended to the number two quarterback job while heading into my second year with the Rams, I could roam the aisles of my local supermarket and be recognized by exactly no one.

Heck, only five years earlier, I *worked* at a supermarket, stocking shelves on the graveyard shift for minimum wage at the Hy-Vee in Cedar Falls, Iowa.

Now, here I was, interrupting soap operas, Jerry Springer, and other daytime programming because of a relatively innocuous surgery. After all, I had driven myself to the hospital before the procedure, and the doctors later told me my appendix had never been in danger of bursting. I'd been nauseous on and off for the previous sixty hours, but I didn't even have any lower abdominal pain at the time I was examined.

Still, after our miracle season of 1999, when I emerged from obscurity to throw forty-one touchdown passes, win the league's Most Valuable Player award, and lead us to our first Super Bowl victory, the Rams weren't taking any chances. Following my Tuesday morning workout at our facility, I was examined by our team physician, and he sent me to Barnes-Jewish Hospital for a precautionary CAT-scan. I was supposed to fly to New York later that day to tape some promotional spots for *Monday Night Football,* so I figured I'd get the test and jump on a later flight.

My wife, Brenda, got a babysitter for our youngest child, Kade, and met me at the hospital. Brenda used to work as a nurse, so she knows a little something about normal hospital protocol—and she was amazed by what happened next. We went into a tiny room for the CAT-scan, and five hospital employees followed us inside. The last guy had to press his shoulder against the door to squeeze his way into the room. I've been in pileups after fumbles with more breathing room.

"Your appendix is inflamed," one of the technicians told me shortly after the test. Brenda and I looked at each other and shrugged, because we didn't know what that meant. A doctor then entered the room and said, cheerfully, "Hey, we've got you set up for surgery in an hour or two." My jaw dropped, and we drove to Missouri Baptist for the operation. Shortly thereafter, television watchers all over St. Louis shared my surprise.

Our two other children, Zachary and Jesse, were in school at the time, and one of their teachers told them I was having an operation, because I guess she had heard about it on the radio. Obviously, they were a little concerned, and the massive news coverage that followed the surgery didn't help. When I looked out the window of my room in the maternity ward, where I was being stashed to keep away fans and media members, I saw a bunch of news trucks clustered in the parking lot—like someone really important was there. Even though I was loopy from the morphine in my IV, I knew this was too weird not to be true.

"This is ridiculous," I said. I asked Brenda to go outside and calm everyone down. She did, and the reporters were yelling questions in frantic tones until Brenda finally said, "You guys need to relax and stop freaking our kids out."

Eventually, the storm died down, and I resumed my offseason routine. My family and I have been on quite a whirlwind since I became the Rams' starting quarterback, and our definition of *normal* changes by the day. We've tried to stay as rooted as possible, which is tough when useless body parts are treated as regional treasures. Yet as silly as it seemed to me that people cared so much about my appendix, I'm flattered that I've touched them in a way that provokes their concern. Further, I hope that my improbable success story gives me a forum from which to share the values, lessons, and faith that made it all possible.

ALL THINGS POSSIBLE

CHAPTER ONE

SUNDAY DRIVE

Just before I threw the biggest pass of my life, the sideline bomb that won the Super Bowl and completed one of the wildest slingshot rides you'll ever see in sports or anywhere else, I closed my eyes, savored the moment, and felt nothing but sincere, honest-to-goodness joy.

It was a strange feeling to experience at the time, because my St. Louis Rams teammates and coaches were nervously pacing the sidelines, and there wasn't a whole lot of exhaling going on around me. By all rights, I should've been a stressed-out mess. The dream I've had since I first got out of diapers was slipping away like a football caked in Vaseline, but for some crazy reason, I couldn't stop smiling.

I had helped give my team a 16–0 advantage in Super Bowl XXXIV, but now the Tennessee Titans had made up the deficit, and 72,625 fans at the Georgia Dome—and about 800 million watching TV across the world—were wondering whether we'd fold. The Titans had a bounce in their step, and for good reason: they had stopped our offense cold on the previous two drives, and for the third consecutive possession their offense had ripped through our extremely tired defense. As my teammates and I watched Al Del Greco's forty-three-yard field goal sail through the uprights to tie the game at 16–16 with two minutes and twelve seconds remaining, the oxygen on our sidelines grew dense, and the mood grew extremely tense.

Everyone looked at me to see how I would react, but I was eleven years and thousands of miles away, daydreaming about Joe Montana and the greatest Super Bowl finish of all time. As the world waited for a worthy encore, I stood there smiling, alone in my thoughts, a gleam in my eyes, head held high to the heavens.

One mistake, and our incredible, worst-to-first season would be obliterated. It was a daunting situation, but I wasn't worried about the possibility of pulling the biggest choke job in Super Bowl history. For one thing, I'd been confronted with far more intimidating circumstances in the past. When you've helped your soul mate throw her parents' ashes to the wind after they were killed in a freak tornado, when you've walked alone through the snow, digging your freezing hands into your pants pockets and trying to dredge up quarters for gas money while the woman and young children you love sit stranded and shivering alongside a freeway on-ramp, losing a football game—even *that* football game— doesn't qualify as a disaster.

By the time that chilling conclusion was playing out, most people watching knew that five years earlier I'd stocked shelves at the Hy-Vee Supermarket in Cedar Falls, Iowa. But those long nights on the graveyard shift were hardly the lowest moments of my life; at least then I didn't have to worry where the next meal would come from, because I knew whatever goodies my co-workers and I dropped and damaged would go straight into our stomachs. Back then, I was struggling not only to resuscitate my football career but also to help provide for a young woman, Brenda Meoni, and her two young children, one of whom was mentally disabled. Brenda, who was my girlfriend at the time, did her shopping at the Hy-Vee—and paid for her groceries with food stamps.

One snowy Sunday afternoon, when the four of us were holing up in the cold, dank basement of her parents' apartment, we decided to get into my GMC Jimmy and go for a ride. The Jimmy, purchased with the signing bonus I'd received from the Green Bay Packers a few months earlier, was the one luxury item I owned, and taking a drive seemed like the cheapest form of entertainment.

A few miles into our outing, two problems developed. The gas gauge hit empty, and we had no money to fill up the tank. It was one of those times late in the month when we were trying to stretch the pennies while waiting for a paycheck to come in, and now we were out in the cold. We figured we had enough gas to make it home, so we headed back toward Highway 218 and pulled onto the on-ramp. The car coughed, wheezed, and made that horrible noise, then chugged to an inglorious halt on the shoulder. The kids were in the backseat, shivering and crying. It was car-cleaning time.

We scrounged around the vehicle, searching the floors and digging through the glove compartment, and scraped together as much change as we could—about a dollar ninety-five. I grabbed a gas can and hiked back toward the nearest filling station while Brenda and the kids froze their tushes off in the car. Fortunately, we were only a few blocks from a gas station, and I was able to buy enough fuel to get us home. But I'll never forget that walk, because I didn't have any gloves with me, so here I was, getting snowed on, shivering, with numb hands, rushing back while worrying that the kids were going to catch pneumonia.

Thankfully, we escaped from that predicament—and so many other trying times—with an even stronger sense of what our faith, priorities, and motivation should be. It's all about perspective, and when you've walked a few miles in my cleats, blowing a sixteen-point lead in the Super Bowl is nothing to get freaked out about. Besides, it wasn't as though I was a helpless bystander. The ball would be in my hands, and ever since I became the reluctant quarterback of my freshman team at Regis High School in Cedar Rapids, Iowa, that has usually been a good thing.

Long before people became captivated by my out-of-nowhere success story, I knew I was a pretty good quarterback, especially when it counted most. And though I was overlooked and underappreciated at every level after high school, I made the most of my

opportunities and played exceptional football for winning teams.
That I had risen from the ranks of the Arena Football League and NFL
Europe—two C-list enterprises viewed with scorn and condescen-
sion by NFL scouts, coaches, and fans—wasn't such a miracle to me.

Cinderella? Heck, no. When I get out there on that field, any
field, I'm more like the big bad wolf.

Still, I can see why *you* were surprised to see me in position to
give the Rams' fairy-tale season its "happily ever after." Five
months earlier, the few sports fans who even knew who I was
regarded me as a marginal journeyman who was lucky to be in the
NFL. Then our starter, Trent Green, went down with a knee injury
in the preseason, and I stepped in and became the league's Most
Valuable Player. I had thrown forty-one touchdown passes in the
regular season, the third-highest total in history, and seven more
in the playoffs.

One more, I told myself, *and the dream will be complete.*

This was all I'd ever wanted—a chance to prove myself under
fire—and I wasn't going to let nerves get in the way of glory. I
started grinning like a guy who figures out the ending to a thriller
before anyone else in the movie theater.

Here it is, I thought. *Here's your dream, the way you've always
imagined it, the ball in your hands and the chance to lead the winning drive in the biggest game of all.* Then I had a vivid flashback.
Suddenly it was 1989, and I was back in the family room of the
small house in Cedar Rapids that I shared with my mother and
older brother. We were watching Joe Montana, maybe the greatest
quarterback ever to live, work his two-minute magic in Super
Bowl XXIII in Miami. I remembered him hustling onto the field
with time running out and his San Francisco 49ers trailing the
Cincinnati Bengals by three points. Montana was so cool on that
drive, he paused in the huddle to point out John Candy, an over-
sized actor who was sitting in the front row. Then Montana pulled
off one of the sweetest endings in history, giving the Niners the
victory on a perfect slant to John Taylor in the back of the end
zone with thirty-four seconds remaining.

Now it was time for me to pull a Montana and produce a fantastic finish. Cool, I thought, but let's get on with the show. After a career of patiently waiting my turn, it was time for some instant gratification.

As I surveyed the stands, John Candy, God rest his soul, was nowhere to be found. No problem. I spotted a small woman with spiked hair and a metallic blue shag blouse and felt warm and fuzzy inside. Over in the corner of the far end zone the former Brenda Meoni, now my wife, was on the edge of her front-row seat. I thought about all we had been through together—the joy we'd shared with our three children, the time I'd foolishly broken up with her to search for something better, the way God had used her to strengthen my faith. Looking at the love of my life, not to mention one of the strongest people I know, I felt a surge of power rush through my veins. For a split second, football was the furthest thing from my mind.

Brenda was there for me when I excitedly joined the Packers in 1994 and got fourteen measly plays to prove myself in five weeks of training camp. She was supportive after I got cut and went back to Cedar Falls to work out with my old University of Northern Iowa teammates by day and stock shelves at the Hy-Vee by night. Back then, when I talked about making it to the NFL, she was probably the only person on earth who didn't think sleep deprivation had sapped me of my sanity. Now, more than anyone, she understood the sacrifices I'd made and the inner fire I'd displayed to get to the brink of an NFL championship. As remarkable as people think my story is, Brenda's story, in my eyes, is far more compelling and incredible. Winning this game would be a triumph for both of us, and I relished the opportunity to do it.

Then I began to pray—for focus, for strength, for protection. I'm a man who is driven by faith, and any power or peace I feel, on the football field or otherwise, is because of my faith and my relationship with Jesus. A lot of people are turned off when athletes talk like this, so let me come right out and clarify my position: I'm not trying to preach or be overly judgmental, and I'm not in any way claiming that God is some sort of football grand pooh-bah who hands out touchdowns and sacks to the faithful like winning lottery tickets. I'm just trying to give people a sense of what works for me and how it has helped me achieve success in sports and in much more important endeavors. To put it simply, any sharpness, clarity, and grace under fire I'm able to summon are a result of faith and God's presence in my life.

All season long, I had sensed that my efforts were part of God's plan—that he wanted to use me to give him glory and spread his gospel to others. That doesn't mean that God would call plays, go through progressions, and throw passes for me, just that he would help give me the confidence and focus to tap my potential and go after my dreams. Week after week, situation after situation, I'd tell myself, *God is faithful; he finishes what he starts.*

As I stood on the sidelines, waiting for the final act of a sensational drama, I looked up to sky—well, okay, the top of the dome—and said it again: *He's gonna finish what he started. He has finished it in every other way, and now this is my moment. It's time for me to win this game.*

The Titans kicked off, and Tony Horne ran it back to our twenty-seven yard line. Dick Vermeil, our amazing and emotional head coach, was darting up and down the sidelines, making sure each and every player was overcoming the shock of losing the lead, keeping the mood upbeat and positive. "This is how it ought to be," he was saying, over and over. "The world championship game, tied 16–16, with two minutes to go. This is great! Let's go win it right now."

When he got to me, he put his hands on my shoulders and sized me up. Dick's belief in me, even before Trent Green got hurt, was a major reason I was in this position, and now I had a chance to repay him. He had been jumpy, even a little chippy, all game long, but he could tell I was ready for the biggest moment of all, and I think that calmed him down some. "Hey," he told me, his eyes shining, "you couldn't ask for a better script. Now go out and give it that perfect ending."

"You've got it, coach," I said.

The next thing I heard was Mike Martz, our offensive coordinator, barking out, "Kurt, you ready?" I nodded. Mike was upstairs in the coaches' box, and I was on the sideline phone. Back in August, before Trent got hurt, the mere sound of Martz's voice made me feel about two feet tall. If Trent was the golden boy, I was the whipping boy. It seemed like nothing I did was good enough for Mike, and he made a point of reaming me in front of everyone if I made the slightest screwup, even if Trent had done the same thing a play earlier. I later learned that he was testing me, seeing whether I'd buckle under constant pressure, but we were way beyond that now. Mike's an aggressive coach, and I'm a bold quarterback. When I heard the play call, 999 H-Balloon, I nodded and smiled.

We hadn't called that play a single time all season long, and this was a great opportunity to let it rip. On first down, we figured they might be sitting back in single coverage, loading up against the short pass or run, so it made sense to take a shot. It's one of our riskiest passes, with four receivers bolting straight down a field and a minimal amount of protection for the quarterback. This last part was a bit dicey. One of my strengths is my willingness to hang tough in the pocket and calmly deliver the ball to the proper target while 280-pound pass rushers are threatening to smack me into never-never land, but now there were mitigating circumstances. I had suffered a painful rib injury shortly before halftime, and every time I moved, let alone absorbed a vicious hit, it felt like a serrated steak knife was jutting through my torso.

Strained rib cartilage aside, I was one tired quarterback. At halftime, though I didn't realize it, I had thrown a record thirty-five passes—thirty-five passes!—and now that total was up to forty-four. The Titans, as usual, were blitzing like madmen, and they had pounded me into the AstroTurf® on many of those throws. In the fourth quarter, I had misfired on all four of my attempts, including a deep ball to our rookie wideout, Torry Holt, that I desperately would have liked to have had back. The Titans were playing a coverage that had their cornerbacks covering our wideouts one-on-one on the outside. Torry went streaking down the left sideline, and he got bumped a little bit by Titans cornerback Samari Rolle. I might have overthrown him a touch, and we misconnected by inches. That would have given us a 23–7 lead and pretty much decided things; instead, we punted, and the Titans continued their comeback.

Now, as I ran on the field with two minutes and five seconds left, and as I called "999 H-Balloon" in the huddle, I thought back to that earlier play and stared into the eyes of our All-Pro wideout, Isaac Bruce. After the near miss to Torry, several of my teammates and coaches, including Mike Martz, had made a point of telling me that Ike, who'd run a streak down the opposite sideline, had been wide open. Wow, I thought, what a shock. For one thing, trying to cover Isaac one-on-one is like trying to stop a brushfire with a garden hose. And like all truly great receivers (and some not-so-great ones, too), Isaac, in his own mind, is *always* open.

Ike and I hadn't talked much during the game, which wasn't unusual. For all that we have in common—mostly, our ultracompetitive natures and our intense faith in God—we really haven't gotten as close as I hope we can in the future. Isaac is a headstrong, private person who plays by his own rules, and I know he doesn't need any pep talks from me. What he wants is the ball, and with our season on the line, I was determined to get it to him.

We had run so many plays during the season with Isaac and Torry going deep on opposite sides of the field, and for some reason I'd thrown to Torry on most of them. Usually, Isaac is on the wide side of the field—the one where we line up two or three receivers in our multiple-receiver sets—and getting it to him is a longer throw, so it's a little bit tougher to be accurate. This time, with all due respect to Torry and our other excellent wideouts, Az-Zahir Hakim and Ricky Proehl, there was no question where I wanted the ball to go.

All four wideouts were going long: Torry, who lines up alone to the left, would run a streak down that sideline; Ricky, the inside man to the right, would run a post to the middle; Az, in the slot between Ricky and Ike, would run a "go," and Ike would do his thing on the outside.

I broke the huddle, walked up to the line of scrimmage, and surveyed the Titans' coverage. It was identical to what they ran on the earlier incompletion to Torry: they had their two safeties, Anthony Dorsett and Perry Phenix, lined up high in the formation to try to make it look like a "Cover-2" defense, which means a two-deep zone in which each cornerback would have help from a safety on the outside. But I wasn't fooled: instead of playing Cover-2, Phenix, the safety on Isaac's side, would drop into coverage as kind of a "robber" type, trying to take away anything that came through the middle; Dorsett would shift from the backside and drop deep into the middle of the zone, leaving the corners isolated on the outside.

All week long during our film sessions, we had noticed that in such situations, the Titans' corners played what we call a "high-shoulder technique," which means they run with the receiver and try to stay alongside the shoulder farthest from the quarterback. Theoretically, you can't throw a deep ball over the top of them, and they're positioned to defend a slant to the inside, but it leaves them susceptible to any stop or comeback route. This bit of information came in handy, because a couple of seconds after I snapped the ball, as I was getting ready to go up top for Isaac, The Freak suddenly appeared in my line of vision.

The Freak is what people call Jevon Kearse, the Titans' fantastic defensive end who wreaked havoc on the league during his rookie year. The Freak is a 260-pound terror who, when he isn't sacking quarterbacks, knocking down passes, or recovering fumbles, is chasing down speedy halfbacks and receivers from behind. He was the last person on earth I wanted to see bearing down on me and my aching ribs as I took the snap from center, went into my drop, and reared my arm back to throw. But that's one of the chances you take when no one stays home to block.

I knew as I released the ball I was going to get smacked. It's part of being a quarterback; it's why we make the big bucks, even though I technically played for the NFL minimum in 1999 before the Rams gave me a year-end bonus. I wasn't worried so much about the pain as about how the blow would affect my follow-through. Ideally, I would've hummed the ball over the top for Ike to run under, because he had Denard Walker beat. But if Jevon's blow caused me to under-throw it, I still figured that with Walker playing high-shoulder and Ike being one of the best in the business at adjusting to the ball in flight, we'd have a chance to hit it for a big gain.

Fortunately, The Freak's tweak didn't thrash me that badly. I was off balance as I released the ball, and he just kind of came down with his arm on top of me and knocked me down. After I fell, I looked up in time to see Ike come back and catch the underthrown pass just in front of the off-balance Walker. Then there were bodies in front of me, but I could tell from the way the fans were screaming that something good had happened. Ike made a beautiful move, and that was it. I got to my feet just as he was charging into the end zone, and I started sprinting down there to join the celebration.

Time to rock and roll: our guys had this end-zone dance called the "Bob and Weave" they had patterned after Muhammad Ali's boxing moves, and even though I'd never so much as practiced it, I had told everybody I was going to join in if we scored in the Super Bowl. On our first touchdown, the nine-yard slant pass I threw to Torry Holt in the third quarter, I figured there would be more to come, so I let the receivers dance alone. Now, here was my chance to shed my milk-and-cookies image and show the world the John Travolta lurking on the inside. The only problem was, by the time I got down there, it seemed like our whole team was on the field mobbing one another, and nobody thought to do the dance. How typical: I'm finally ready to boogie, and I can't find a partner.

At that point, I remember looking over at the gorgeous dance partner I put the moves on seven years earlier at Wild E. Coyote's in Cedar Falls. Brenda saw me pointing right at her, and she pointed back, and we acknowledged the end of an incredible climb no one else in the stadium could truly appreciate.

Only, it wasn't over. Not by a long shot. My teammates were bouncing up and down in the end zone, and even though it was the two-minute warning, I worried that we'd receive a fifteen-yard penalty for excessive celebration. I tried to get everyone off the field so we could kick the extra point. As it went through, giving us a 23–16 lead, I wasn't aware that I had broken Montana's Super Bowl record with 414 passing yards. All I could think was that we were one big defensive play away from the sharpest turnaround in league history.

Then came the longest 114 seconds of football you could ever imagine. As much as I love the Rams and what we accomplished last year—going from the last-place laughingstocks of the league who hadn't made the playoffs in a decade to the top of the NFL— we were battling a bunch of guys who have as much heart and competitive spunk as anyone I've ever played.

Steve McNair, Tennessee's gutsy quarterback, started marching his team down the field. I stood alone on the sidelines, my heart racing. When I was in control, when I knew I'd have the ball in my hands, I felt so peaceful and secure. But now there was nothing I could do but watch as our extremely exhausted defensive players tried to hang on.

As the Titans crossed midfield, Isaac Bruce sidled up next to me. It's funny, but he said the same thing I had said to myself a couple of minutes earlier.

"The Lord is gonna finish what he started," Ike said confidently. "It's all part of his plan."

Then, bam: McNair took off around right end, and Todd Lyght, our All-Pro cornerback and inspirational leader, nailed him after a two-yard gain. Second and three from our thirty-eight. The clock went under the one-minute mark and kept ticking.

Suddenly, I wasn't quite as certain as Isaac. I fully expected to win the game, but at that point it sure looked like the Lord's plan included the first ever Super Bowl sudden-death overtime.

Besides, as much as anyone in the Georgia Dome, I understood how dangerous it can be to count someone out prematurely.

It's a subject I know well, from a generous helping of personal experience. Trust me, I could write a book on it.

CHAPTER TWO

FIRST THINGS FIRST

Steve McNair went down, I jumped up, and for a couple of glorious seconds, I thought we were sitting pretty. Only a Hail Mary, it seemed, could keep us from winning the Super Bowl, and I couldn't wait to start celebrating. I waved my arms and let out a gleeful scream as I landed on the edge of our sideline bench area . . . and then my stomach dropped. Somehow, astonishingly, McNair was still running with the ball in his hands, and the Tennessee Titans were far from dead.

Like everyone else, I was having trouble believing my eyes in the waning seconds of history's most thrilling Super Bowl climax. With twenty-two seconds to go and Tennessee trailing 23–16, McNair, on third and five from our twenty-six yard line, took a snap from the shotgun formation, scrambled away from pressure, made a 360-degree turn, and was run down by two of our defensive linemen: six-foot-five, 280-pound Kevin Carter, the NFL's sack champion, and six-foot-three, 280-pound Jay Williams. Each player had a firm grip on McNair, and each drove the determined quarterback toward the turf. But McNair didn't care. The guy just laughed in the face of gravity, fought his way back upright, and kept on running. It was an awesome, awesome play, one of the best I've ever seen.

By the time I realized what was happening, McNair had released the ball to Kevin Dyson, the Titans' speedy receiver, for a sixteen-yard gain. Time-out, Tennessee, with six seconds remaining. Instead of a forty-yard heave-ho into massive coverage, the Titans were ten yards and an extra point away from forcing overtime.

Over on our sidelines, everyone was stunned. Some negative comments were flying around—"Come on, defense, you're not doing it"—but I tried to look on the bright side. Worst-case scenario, I figured, they tie it up, and I get a chance to lead us to victory in overtime.

Technically, my theory wasn't airtight. However unlikely, they could've beaten us on a two-point conversion; more plausibly, they might have won the coin toss, gotten the first possession of overtime, and scored to end the game, but it was enough to comfort me as our extremely weary defense dug in for what I hoped would be one last stand. How winded were our defenders? Some have since said they were giving one another hand signals on that last drive, splitting up portions of the field, because they were too tired to deal with the defensive coverages being called by the coaches.

As McNair jogged back onto the field, I remember asking God, *The Bible says you will finish what you've started. I've believed that all season. Are you gonna finish this now?* I wasn't asking in an entitled way, more a curious one. Would this miracle season end in a narrow Super Bowl defeat, or would it be even greater?

McNair took the shotgun snap and the middle of the field cleared out. He threw underneath to Dyson, who crossed the five yard line and headed for the end zone. From where I was, the space in front of him seemed wide open, and it looked like he was going to walk in easily for a touchdown. Out of nowhere I saw Mike Jones, our middle linebacker, burst into the frame. Then, with no one else in the vicinity, Mike made a tackle that every high school football coach in America should show to his players.

I've seen the replay a few dozen times by now, and the more I watch it, the more I appreciate the beauty of Mike's stop. Nine times out of ten, Dyson's momentum would have carried him into the end zone, but Mike just made an unbelievable tackle. Right place, right time, right technique: he grabbed one foot and then kicked the other knee out from underneath, so Dyson had no feet left. If Mike had missed that second foot, I think Dyson would've taken another step and reached that extra yard to cross the plane of the goal line, but Mike managed to take him straight down.

As our magical season unfolded, so many players got a ton of attention, starting with me, the guy who, as a former grocery store clerk, went from bags to riches, as one of my business associates put it. Obviously, guys like Marshall Faulk and Isaac Bruce and Kevin Carter and Todd Lyght played a huge part in our championship season. But there were so many other great warriors on our roster who were largely overlooked, and I like to think Mike Jones symbolized those unsung heroes. He's a great player who until that tackle hadn't gotten the credit he deserved. He's also a quality guy, a fellow Christian who does a lot of valuable work in the community and is as solid as they come. On and off the field, he's not necessarily flashy, but you can always count on him to do his job. That last tackle was the perfect snapshot epitomizing what he's all about.

It's a play that will be talked about for decades, and like everyone else, I've wondered whether the Titans made the right call in that situation. Ideally, you want to throw the ball into the end zone, but I also know what it looks like from McNair's perspective, and the middle was so open and inviting. As I said, Dyson probably scores nine times out of ten. After the game, the Titans were saying the play was designed to go underneath. But then, a couple of weeks later, I went to Kansas City to receive a player of the year award from the 101 Club, and I had a chance to talk with Tennessee coach Jeff Fisher, who was there to present one of his players, Jevon Kearse, with the AFC Defensive Player of the Year award. To my surprise, Fisher told me that Frank Wycheck, the Titans' Pro Bowl tight end, had expected the ball to come his way. Wycheck, who ran a little inside seam route to the end zone, figured that Dyson would be double covered, and he was fully prepared to be the hero.

All I know is, I'm glad it happened the way it did, though there were a couple of restless seconds before I was sure we had won. From our angle, it looked like Dyson might have reached out over the goal line with the ball, but then I saw one of our defensive players, Jeff Zgonina, gesturing "No good" with his hands, and then I watched the ref wave it off. I looked at the clock and made sure that time had expired, and then the inside of my body exploded with rapture, and I rushed onto the field to join the party.

Instinctively, I glanced over toward my wife in her front-row seat, but Brenda was hugging everyone around her and didn't notice me, so I went looking for someone else to hug. I embraced Ernie Conwell, maybe my closest friend on the team, a courageous tight end who had fought back from one of the most brutal knee injuries imaginable to become a key contributor to our offense. Then I hugged Coach Vermeil and congratulated him, and we told each other, "I love you." He got teary eyed—Coach Vermeil cries more often than a Barbara Walters interview subject—and said, "You are special." Since Dick had shown so much faith in me when he made me our starter after Trent Green's injury, I added, "Thanks for the chance." That's when I started crying, too.

The rest was a blur. Everyone started flocking toward me, but I swept past the mob and made a beeline for Brenda. She leaned over the railing to kiss me. "We did it, Momma," I told her, using the pet name I've favored since shortly after we met. "I know, Kurtis," she screamed, "we did it!"

A wave of euphoria washed over me, and it's really hard to put that feeling into words. It's just complete joy and happiness, similar to what you experience when you fall in love or when you get married or when you watch your child being born. I don't want to get too carried away—obviously, those other events are greater and more special. But in terms of football, there is no better set of emotions. That's the joy of playing sports, the plateau you dream about from the time you're a little kid, and when it actually happened, it felt as monumental as I'd always hoped it would. So many times during my football career it had seemed like I'd never have a chance to *attend* a Super Bowl, let alone win one. Now, resoundingly, I had reached the pinnacle, and nobody could ever take that away. I just wanted to share it with my teammates and hug everybody I could find.

Unfortunately, I was about to face the fiercest rush I encountered all day—from a barrage of people I didn't know. The mob scene on the field was so overwhelming that I could barely get to my teammates. I felt like screaming, "Get out of my way and let me celebrate!" But I was too ecstatic to quibble with the masses.

All through the celebration, I was being trailed by the people from Disney, and they were harassing me almost as badly as Jevon Kearse and the other Titans defensive linemen had for the previous four hours. I had agreed to do one of the "I'm going to Disneyland" spots if we won the game, which was cool, but they needed one version for Disney World and one for Disneyland, and I guess they wanted to make sure they got the perfect rendition. I'd give them what I thought was a decent take, and then a few seconds later they'd flag me down and grab me, and I'd have to do it again. I felt like the Road Runner being chased by Wile E. Coyote. After the fourth time, I was pretty annoyed. "I just want to celebrate," I told them. "Can't you just find one that works?" Something tells me that Phil Simms didn't have to go through all of that when he did the first "I'm going to Disneyland" commercial back in 1987.

Finally, I broke free and got to the middle of the field, where a bunch of my teammates were congregating. The guys whose reactions I really remember being touched by were the veterans, the ones who had been through so many losing seasons and now finally had a taste of glory. Todd Lyght, Isaac Bruce, Keith Lyle, Ricky Proehl—you could just see the emotion in their eyes. I also remember getting a big bear hug from Mike Martz, our offensive coordinator, who told me, "Kurt, you were awesome. You're an awesome, awesome player." We were both crying, and then all of a sudden I almost started laughing: as he continued to praise me,

I flashed back to the first few weeks of training camp, before Trent got hurt, when Mike put me through the wringer and chewed me out like I was the least prepared quarterback he had ever seen. In less than six months, I'd gone from "the stupidest player ever" to "awesome," which tells you all you need to know about my story.

Eventually, some security guards escorted me up to the victory podium, where ABC's Mike Tirico was presenting the Lombardi Trophy and doing interviews. He was talking to Dick and our owner, Georgia Frontiere, and that's when someone told me I had been named Super Bowl MVP. All I was thinking was, *praise the Lord.* Throughout the year, I had joked around with Ernie Conwell and the pastor of our church in St. Louis, Jeff Perry, that if we won the Super Bowl and got the opportunity to proclaim our faith for Jesus in front of such a huge TV audience, we would totally ham it up: "Thank you, Jesus, I'm going to Disneyland!" or something like that. I didn't know if I'd get quite that silly, but I figured that this would be my big chance to assert my faith and to thank God—not just in terms of winning that game, but in much more important ways that go well beyond football.

So Mike Tirico said, "Kurt, first things first—tell me about the final touchdown pass to Isaac." And I said, "Well, first things *first,* I've got to thank my Lord and Savior up above—thank you, Jesus!" I didn't mean to be disrespectful to Mike. I just wanted to use the opportunity to point out that the Lord does come first in my life, and I'm not shy about sharing that with the world.

In the days after the Super Bowl, when I went to Disney World, then to our victory parade in St. Louis and then to Hawaii for the Pro Bowl, a lot of Christians came up to me and thanked me for speaking out so boldly. That's partly because they're used to seeing Christians who seem self-conscious discussing Jesus in that context. It's weird how that works: a lot of times, a Christian athlete will approach me and tell me how much he admires me for being so outspoken about my faith. But he'll whisper when he says it, or he'll pull me aside where no one else can hear us rather than just saying it loudly in front of a group. Even in Hawaii, a bunch of the other Pro Bowlers told me they appreciated my will-ingness to express my Christian beliefs, but they did it when no one else was around.

I'm well aware that an athlete who thanks Jesus after a victory turns some people off, but as I hope you'll learn in the pages to come, I'm not thanking him so much because I threw a lot of touchdowns or my team won the game, but because of the incred-ible effect he has had on my life. If anyone would ask, I'd gladly thank him after every bitter defeat, too, because the feelings I'm expressing are far bigger than football.

I want to be as clear as I can here: God is not Santa Claus. I don't ask God to direct my passes into the hands of my receivers the way I'd order a three-egg omelet at a diner. I think he does care about football, because he is powerful and almighty and loving enough to care about every facet of everybody's life, but I'm not saying he chooses one team over another depending on whose faith is strongest. To me, speaking out is a no-brainer. Even before I made the Rams, I came to believe that God's desire for me was to put me in a situation where I could touch lives. I always felt like he had something significant in store for me, and I used to pray that he would use me in big ways. Maybe it's Des Moines, because I was getting a fair degree of attention as the Barnstormers' quar-terback. But as I look back now, I see that God spent years and years preparing me for a much bigger opportunity.

The cool thing is, "First Things First" has become a little catch-phrase for me, and the more I think about it, the more I realize that it works on several levels. The first is obvious. As a kid, I remem-ber reading a book by Gale Sayers, the Chicago Bears' Hall of Fame running back, entitled *I Am Third*. The title referred to the fact that he put his God first, his family second, and himself third. I always wanted to be a person who could say the same, and thanks to Brenda and some other people who have helped me grow as a Christian, I believe I'm on the right path.

Another meaning of "First Things First" has to do with the jour-ney I took to get to where I am today. Before I could devote myself to Jesus and start living my life for him, I had to go through a lot of personal struggles, including a period a few years ago where I got a little caught up in things that aren't important—fame, money, lust—and risked everything I had, including my relationship with Brenda. Also, before I could realize the success I did with the Rams, I needed to grow as a football player. Even though I felt rejected by the NFL during the time I spent in the Arena League, even though there were so many moments when it seemed I was ignored or shooed away by people who I thought could've helped my career, I realize now that I would not have been prepared for my big chance had it happened before it did.

Finally, to me, "First Things First" is a reminder that glory is a matter of perspective—that even when you experience a joy as intense as winning a Super Bowl, there are millions of people who don't care, because they have a much different set of priorities. I know, because my son Zachary is one of them.

Zachary is a walking miracle, a beautiful boy who exudes love on a pure and undiscriminating level. He was accidentally dropped into the bathtub when he was four months old, and doctors told Brenda and her ex-husband that their son would almost certainly die. Their best-case scenario had him existing as little more than a vegetable, but Zachary fooled everyone. Now eleven years old, he has his disabilities—he's legally blind, and he has some developmental irregularities—but he's able to live a rich and happy life.

Through all the drama that has played out during my career, from the frustrating lows to the Super Bowl, Zachary, whom I adopted along with his sister, Jesse, in 1997, shortly after marrying Brenda, has been my instant perspective. I don't have to worry about getting caught up in my football achievements because he keeps me grounded without even trying.

After I got off the victory podium and headed back to our locker room, I plunked myself down on a table in the training room so a doctor could examine my ribs, and then I made one of the most satisfying phone calls of my life. Jesse, my eight-year-old daughter, came to the phone first; she'd been watching the game at our house in St. Louis while her one-year-old brother, Kade, thrashed his way about the room. "Congratulations, Daddy, you won!" she said. I told her I loved her, and then she went to get Zack.

It took what seemed like forever for him to come to the phone. "Hi, Dad!" he said. "I'm watching *Veggie Tales!*"

"Hey, Zack Man. Did you see the game?"

"Uh-huh. Hey, Dad, I'm watching *Veggie Tales!*"

"Great. I love you," I told him.

"I love you, too. Gotta go watch the movie."

I'm going to Disney World, and he's watching *Veggie Tales.* Now *that's* a commercial I'd like to see.

You have to love Zack's indifference. He was excited to talk to me, but he would have been just as pumped up if I'd said, "I got the car washed," or "There's a piece of hot dog caught in my teeth." What's so great about him is that he doesn't care about winning, losing, or any of that stuff. When people at school come up to him and make a big deal about me or the Rams, Zack just lets it all bounce off him. The only attention he pays to football is that it takes me away from him. He knows I have to go to work every day and that sometimes I have to get on an airplane. He'll ask me, "You have to go to football *again?* When's football going to stop?"

You worry about your kids getting affected by all this madness, but Zack really doesn't care. He's excited because I'm excited, but he couldn't care less what I'm excited about. The neat thing is that when all this is over and somebody asks him about his dad, he might tell them I was a football player, but that's the most he'll say on the subject. It won't be, "He won this many Super Bowls," or "He was a star quarterback." Instead, he'll remember the stuff that to me is the most important—the time we spent together, the experiences we had.

I love him so much because his love is so pure. It's not what we buy him or what he gets to do, it's the experiences we have and the time we get to share. And even though Jesse's more aware of what's going on, I don't think she understands the magnitude of what happened last season, because she thought my games with the Barnstormers were a big deal, too. I've heard stories about kids coming up to Jesse in school and saying, "Your dad plays football for the Rams; he's going to win the Super Bowl," and her responding, "So what?" One time recently, someone asked Brenda for her autograph, and afterward Jesse looked at her mom and asked, "What does that do for them, getting you to write your name on a piece of paper? Why does that mean anything?" So I think she has a pretty good perspective on the whole situation, which is a huge load off my mind.

By the time I hung up the phone with Zack and Jesse, I was crying again. Some security officials took me out to a small podium, where I answered questions for what seemed like hundreds of reporters, though I have no memory of what was asked or what my responses were. I remember seeing Coach Vermeil at a podium down the row and yelling out something to him like, "Yeah, coach, we did it!" I was pretty loopy—and that was *before* the doctors gave me the painkilling injection for my ribs, a shot I'd refused to take until the game was over, because I didn't want anything to mess with my mind.

The rest of the night was a blur. I went to the victory party, where I sat at a table with many of the people closest to me—my mom, Sue; my father, Gene, and my stepmom, Mimi; my brothers, Matt and Matt (don't worry, I'm not a distant relative of George Foreman: one of the Matts is Mimi's son from a previous marriage); Brenda's sister, Kim, and her husband, John Hawley; Lynn Cowell, a childhood friend of Brenda's who played an important role in her spiritual life, and Lynn's husband, Greg; and my pastors from the St. Louis Family Church, Jeff and Patsy Perry. Oh, and the little lady in the electric blue shag blouse whose romantic advances I'd been rebuffing for the past several days.

Brenda and I had finally realized our dreams, and our lives would never be the same. While the celebration continued around us, we clasped hands and said a little prayer of thanks. Certainly, having the opportunity to win the Super Bowl was a great blessing, and we were humbled by the magnitude of the achievement. But if there was one thing we'd learned during our improbable rise to professional fulfillment, it's that winning a football game is a small part of God's equation. Reaching my potential as a person, learning to be a good husband and responsible father, and accepting the unconditional love of God—those were the real victories.

If you sit back and delve into my story, you'll understand why I couldn't really be a winner until I figured out the rules of the game.

CHAPTER THREE

PLASTIC SHEETS AND TOILET PAPER

Looking back on my childhood, sometimes I wonder why the geek patrol didn't come to my house in Cedar Rapids and take me away to the goofy farm. I was a chubby kid who wore the same pair of green jeans almost every day for about two years, didn't stop wetting his bed until he was in middle school, and in high school thought it was more fun to toilet-paper friends' houses than to make out with girls.

Thank goodness for sports, or I might still be looking for my first date. Sports were my refuge, my social life, and for a long time my salvation. I didn't have much money or fashion sense, but on the football field or baseball diamond or basketball court I was the coolest dude there was. Part of the reason I excelled is because I was blessed with athletic ability, but the biggest secrets of my success were the obvious ones: I worked my butt off, and I cared more about being the best than anyone else I knew. I learned to be self-motivated, to ignore the obstacles you can't control, and above all to treat people with kindness and respect along the way.

There are so many kids who are good at sports, maybe the best of anyone in their neighborhood. But talent alone guarantees you nothing. To get to the pros, even to make it to the Arena Football

League, takes an incredible degree of drive, desire, and discipline. When you have the right attitude, your skills can be developed. But intensity is something that can't be faked, and I definitely had it from the start.

I wasn't just the guy who kept shooting baskets when his mom was calling him inside for dinner, I was the guy who shot the ball at an *empty backboard,* just trying to hit the sweet spot of the painted square. Rain, sleet, snow, darkness, or whatever, I'd be out in our backyard shooting the ball—usually, one of those rubber kickballs because we couldn't always afford a basketball—at the hoop over our garage. It wasn't the sturdiest rim in the world, and over the years it kept getting lower and lower, until I could finally dunk on it, which was cool until I ripped the sucker down when I went up for a jam and the rotten wood gave way. So from then on I would go out and shoot the ball against the backboard, just pretending I was hitting the rim, I guess.

No matter what else was happening around me, I was always up for a game. If my older brother, Matt, and I were the only kids around, we'd play each other in one-on-one football in our front yard. You know, football where you pass the ball to yourself, the other guy can't touch you when the ball is in the air, and you run and try to catch it and then get clobbered. If Matt wouldn't play, I'd go out and throw the ball to myself, staging mock games between my beloved Iowa Hawkeyes and one of their Big Ten rivals or pitting my favorite pro team, the Dallas Cowboys, against the Washington Redskins.

When it came time for real games, I was a tad bit competitive. Okay, I was ridiculously competitive. You might say I was the Bobby Knight of our grade school basketball league, except that might be a little insulting to Coach Knight.

I'd be playing for All Saints in our games against other Catholic grade schools, and when a referee's call would go against me, I'd go ballistic. I mean, I was out of control. It wasn't so much that I yelled at the refs, I would just rant and rave and jump around and scream my displeasure so everyone in the gym could hear. As far as I was concerned, I never, ever fouled anyone, but of course I got fouled nearly every time I shot the ball. I was irate and intense, and I don't think the refs appreciated that a whole lot. I picked up technicals like Dennis Rodman, and I got tossed from games a couple of times, too.

Fortunately, I was good, or I wouldn't have gotten away with any of it. I wasn't trying to be rebellious toward the refs. I just couldn't stomach the notion of losing, and if a call went against me I felt the officials were keeping me from what was rightfully mine. That relentless pursuit of victory didn't make me the most pleasant person to interact with during a game, and sportsmanship was something I developed gradually. I wasn't trying to be a jerk; it was just that I cared so much and was so passionate about what I was doing, and I wasn't mature enough to consider the effects my behavior might have on others. All I knew was that my teams almost always won, on every level, and on the rare occasions when we did lose, no one could say it was because I didn't want it badly enough.

When I became the Rams' starting quarterback, it seemed all anyone focused on was that my credentials were small-time, but nobody bothered to check my record. Other than my junior year of football at Regis High, I never played on a losing team in any sport, in any league. And as great as the Rams were in 1999, and as awesome as I hope we'll be over the course of my career and beyond, they were hardly the most dominant team I ever played for and certainly not the biggest underdogs.

Both of those distinctions belong to the Jane Boyd Community Center flag football dynasty I was part of before I reached puberty. From the third through the fifth grades, my teammates and I didn't lose a single game. It was great, too, because we were total outsiders, sort of the like the Bad News Bears. Most kids played for YMCA teams, but we lived in a lower-income area, and joining our group didn't cost any money. So when we would play the YMCA teams, they'd have really cool, matching uniforms and nice equipment. We might have T-shirts that were the same color, but that was it. The only thing uglier than our uniforms were the scores we'd put up on our spiffy competition. We were unbeatable, and some of the adults in town weren't too thrilled. By the time we ripped through the league for the third consecutive year, the powers that be had had enough. When it came time for the trophy presentations that last year, they ignored us and gave the championship trophy to the YMCA team that had the best record, even though we had whipped that team and everyone else we played. We just sort of laughed and said, "Whatever."

Playing sports allowed me to feel like a kid, which was nice, because in some ways I had to grow up quickly. My parents divorced when I was four, and the way I remember it, I didn't see my dad for a while after that happened. It was a tough transition for me, as I'm sure it is for all kids in that situation. The divorce made me feel extremely protective toward my mom, and I became very self-motivated. Even today, I don't depend on other people to tell me how well I'm doing because I measure myself against my own standards.

My mom, Sue Warner, is a strong woman whom I love very much. She sacrificed a lot to raise my brother and me in a positive manner, and I believe that she gave us the best life she could under the circumstances. She sometimes worked more than one job to make sure we'd be able to have a few luxuries from time to time, and she managed to walk the fine line between being a strong disciplinarian and a warm, loving caregiver. It's funny, I can be such a passive person, a guy who longs for peace, love, and happiness and assumes that everything will work itself out. My mom, conversely, is strong willed, stubborn, passionate, and assertive. Because of that, she has often clashed with Brenda, both before and after I got married. But when I think about it, Brenda is so much like my mom, it's scary. I don't think it's a coincidence that I fell for a woman who has so many of the same qualities that I admire in my mother.

Not only did my mom support the family, she also fostered an atmosphere of togetherness. She made sure my brother attended my sporting events. Similarly, she got me involved in his activities, such as music; Matt played the saxophone in the high school band. And when I blossomed as an athlete and started getting lots of attention, she made certain that my brother always knew he was just as important.

After the divorce, Matt and I had sort of an us-against-the-world mentality. He wasn't into sports like I was, but he did play with me some, often at great risk of verbal abuse. I was ultracompetitive, and if I felt my brother wasn't giving 100 percent effort, I'd jump all over him: "I can't believe I have to play with someone so lazy." I was probably harder on him than on anyone. But the minute someone else criticized Matt, well, that's my *brother* you're talking about, buster. Matt likes to tell this story about the first time he got into a fight, when he was in the second grade and I was a year behind. He and another kid squared off in the schoolyard, and everyone gathered in a circle around them as they prepared to slug it out. But before any punches were thrown, I barreled in from behind, jumped on the kid's back, and took him down—I was bigger than Matt or the other kid, even though they were older—and that was that. The funny thing is, that guy, Brian Hafer, ended up being a teammate of mine in basketball and football throughout our time in Cedar Rapids; he was one of my tight ends in high school.

Matt and I were especially close throughout our childhood, sometimes a little too close for comfort. We shared a room all our lives, and in high school we even shared a waterbed. By then, at least, I didn't need plastic sheets, because I had a problem wetting my bed only until I was, oh, eleven or twelve years old. The bed-wetting thing was an issue for me, because when a friend would invite me to spend the night, I'd worry that I would wet the bed at his house and embarrass myself to no end. I remember times when I'd stay up half the night at someone else's house stressing out about the possibility. At home, we'd just use plastic sheets and do the wash every day, but I didn't have much interest in sleepovers until the bed-wetting finally stopped.

If people think that I tend to get a little overly emotional, I tell them, "You should see my brother." Matt makes me look like Al Gore. The guy sobs at the drop of a hat, and I love him for that. Think Dick Vermeil, only even more raw. When I was with the Iowa Barnstormers and we lost the 1996 Arena Bowl, I was naturally somewhat disappointed. But when I emerged from the locker room, I was amazed to see Matt, who is definitely my biggest fan, bawling like a baby. He can be watching a TV segment in which I talk about Brenda and the kids, and he'll burst into tears. A few months after the Super Bowl, he came down to watch my kids, Zack and Jesse, perform in a talent show, and that sent him into another crying spell. You can imagine how he is around his own daughter, Amber.

Until I met Brenda, Matt was my right-hand man in life. As kids, we competed against each other in everything. We even picked different favorite teams in each sport, so we could continue our battles through them. But we never let the competition carry over into our relationship; we were always friends when the game ended.

Eventually, Matt and I found a third Musketeer: our stepbrother, Matt Post, who's about three years older than I am. Sometimes I feel like such a hillbilly when I tell people I have two brothers named Matt. It's like the gag from that old sitcom *Newhart:* "This is my brother Darrell, and this is my other brother Darrell." Here's the deal: when I was in the first grade, my father, Gene, got remarried to Mimi, and though it was a little awkward at first for me, she always loved us and was very good to us, so that made the transition easier. Matt Post, Mimi's son from a previous marriage, lived with her and my dad, so when Matt Warner and I spent weekends there, we got to hang out with him. The three of us got along great. We'd play hide-and-seek and other games around the neighborhood, and of course we'd play every sport you can imagine. We had a Nerf hoop down in the basement, which led to some high-contact battles, and my dad would take us to the park and set up games of one-on-one-on-one football, with him playing quarterback for all three of our teams.

Then there were these friends up the street who lived on a bunch of land and loved football. These guys were so dedicated they would mow out a bunch of weeds to form a football field—how Iowa is that?—so we could have a lot of room. Our homemade gridiron wasn't quite as nice as the baseball diamond in *Field of Dreams,* but to us it was pretty sweet. We also had a neighbor two houses down who loved basketball. He and Matt Post were the two oldest and best players, so naturally they played together as a team, and they beat me and my brother about a hundred times in a row. Then, after I grew up a little and got pretty good, we started dominating them. Once that happened, believe me, we showed no mercy.

I'll never forget the hoop wars that my dad, my brothers, and I used to wage inside the equipment shed of one of my dad's friends. The shed had a hoop inside, but the rafters weren't very high, so we learned to fire up our three-pointers at an extremely low trajectory. The floor was always dusty, and we'd be slipping and sliding all over the place. The cool thing was that even in the dead of winter we had a place to play.

The stepbrother thing was tough at first, especially on Matt Post. He was the guy who had to live with my dad and Mimi during the week and get disciplined as such, while we were the guys who blew in on the weekend and did mostly fun stuff. But eventually, everything between us clicked, and it was as if we'd all been together from the start. The fact that Matt Warner and Matt Post live together now, as men in their thirties, should give you an idea of how close we all became.

Matt Post was one of those older brothers who could do anything—at least, that's the way he portrayed things to us. I remember him telling me that he could run a forty-yard dash in 4.5 seconds or that he could throw the ball fifty yards or some ridiculous distance. There was never any confirmation, so we believed him for a while. We'd say, "Wow, Matt must be a great athlete." We went to a different school than Matt Post did, and he was the backup quarterback for his school team. One day he finally got into a game, and, the way the story goes, he totally panicked after he took the snap. He lobbed the ball to a lineman on the other team, who ran it in for a touchdown. When Matt Warner and I heard that story, we were pumped, because we finally had some ammunition to fire back at our big brother.

It's amazing how fortunate Matt Warner and I were with our dad's new family. In contrast, my mom's second attempt at marriage wasn't so pleasant for us. When I was about ten, my mom married a guy who didn't treat her, or us, very well. He and I never got along, and the weird thing was, it seemed like he wanted me to like him, maybe because he thought it was cool that I was into sports. He didn't get very far with me, because I didn't like the way he was treating my mom. My brother was the opposite: he tried to do whatever he could to make his stepdad like him, probably in the interest of harmony, and he got almost no attention in return.

It took my mom five years to dump the guy, and the whole episode made me grow up fast. I remember having long conversations with her, trying to convince her that she should leave him and move on. I had always felt very protective of her and now even more so. I matured quickly out of necessity, because with things being so bad I put a lot of pressure on myself to try to straighten them out. Or maybe I'm just trying to make a lousy chapter of my past sound good after the fact.

Money was also an issue. My mom had a job making plastic plates for a company called Cryo-Vac, and though she never was out of work, we were hardly living large. I don't want to make it sound like I was too deprived—I know a lot of pro athletes who had it much worse as kids than I did—but my mom was basically living paycheck to paycheck, and there were plenty of times I got angry because there was something I wanted that she simply couldn't afford, like cool high-tops or other athletic gear. However, once I got old enough to understand our situation, I became extremely money conscious. Even now, when I make a generous salary and, hopefully, am on the verge of getting a contract that will pay me beyond my wildest dreams, I'm still very selective about what I spend. Obviously, I want nice things for myself and for my family, but I'm also still a guy who won't buy cereal at the supermarket unless it happens to be on sale, because I think the regular prices are outlandish.

One lesson my mom helped instill in me is that it's no use moping about your circumstances because self-pity will get you nowhere. If you want to rise above the hardships and carve out a better reality, the worst thing you can do is concern yourself with things that are out of your control. The only thing you can control is yourself—what *you* do. For me, this outlook went beyond monetary issues. For example, if I wanted to play basketball and there weren't any other kids around to join me for a game, I'd shoot baskets by myself.

Similarly, if you want to succeed in sports or anything else, I think it's important that you find a way to be self-motivated. All kids seek approval, but in my case that was never the driving force. Not only did I love sports, but I also had an internal fire that caused me to push ahead and develop my skills. I wanted to be as good as I could possibly be, and I wasn't going to let anybody tell me I couldn't do something. And, believe me, there were plenty of naysayers, not just when I was growing up but throughout my football career. Yet no matter what I was trying to accomplish, I always knew that it wasn't about how many times you get patted on the back. The key is to push yourself to the upper limits of your abilities and to do it regardless of the impediments that confront you.

In our family, whining wasn't tolerated, and we didn't spend a whole lot of time worrying about what we didn't have. In fact, part of the way I tried to be a caretaker toward my mom had to do with saving money. We'd go to the supermarket, and I'd point out the items that were the best value because I knew we had to pinch pennies. As kids, we usually got one pair of shoes to wear everywhere, though sometimes I'd get a second pair for sports. When I was about eight, I noticed that I'd worn a hole through one of the soles in my main pair of shoes, and rather than telling my mom, I just took a piece of cardboard and covered up the hole so I could keep wearing them. The foot odor got pretty brutal, but at least I made them last until the next school year started.

Still, I wasn't in rags—though the grade school classmates who called me "Mr. Green Jeans" in honor of my ever-present pair of Sears Toughskins might beg to differ—and I certainly wasn't in danger of starving. I was a chubby kid, and that was partly because of my eating habits. I loved fast food and hated vegetables, two preferences that have followed me into adulthood, I'm ashamed to say. I have a hard time getting my kids to eat vegetables now because I have very little credibility on the subject.

My diet may have been lousy, but my demeanor was pretty good—at least when I wasn't playing sports. I had respect for my parents and teachers, and I rarely talked back. I'd get into the typical kind of kid mischief, and I definitely wanted attention. When I was really young and my mom would take me and my brother to Kmart, she'd drop us off in the toy department while she shopped. I'd always go up to the people at the register and tell them I was lost so they'd announce my name over the loudspeaker, which I thought was really cool.

Like every kid, I had my mischievous moments. One time I pulled all these clean sheets off the clothesline in our backyard and passed them out to the neighborhood kids so we could play Batman; that earned me a *biff* and a *pow* from my mom, who used to spank me with a wooden spoon when I was really naughty. Another time, Matt and I were over at our dad's house one morning getting ready to go to school, and I decided to get into the driver's seat of his Datsun pickup truck. Matt showed me how to work a stick shift, and I moved the car out of gear and pulled down the parking brake. All of a sudden we started rolling down the steep driveway, across the street, and onto the neighbors' lawn. The truck probably would've have smashed into their house, but it hit a tree first, and we escaped with a big dent and a very angry father.

As hard as it was for me when my parents first got divorced, I give my dad a lot of credit for doing the right thing and remaining a big part of my life. I respect him for the way he stayed involved, especially as Matt and I got older. He could've disappeared, like so many fathers do in that situation, but he helped us out in every possible way. Even though at first it was tough to deal with him leaving home, I don't think a father and son could have a better relationship than we have now.

Of all the great things I can say about my dad, the most striking is the way that he treats people. He's a guy who wants to make everybody feel good and accentuate the positive, and I think I'm similar. Like me, he's not confrontational and isn't afraid to show people how much he loves them. Instead of getting caught up in being a man's man, he'll give another man a hug without worrying about how people might perceive it.

This, above all, is the message I hope to pass on to my children—and any others who might be interested. The golden rule, *Do unto others as you want others to do unto you*, really is golden. When you're growing up, there's so much pressure to fit in and be cool, and it's easy to get caught up in that at the expense of others. Doing so might give you some short-term satisfaction, but in the long run that's not the way to get to the top. If you go through life being afraid to show your emotions and reveal your true feelings, you'll end up cheating yourself as well as the people close to you. Similarly, if somebody does something to hurt you, it's far better to forgive that person and move on rather than hold a grudge.

During childhood, I had my surly moments like everyone else, but I do think I usually treated people with respect and compassion. Even though I guess I was a "cool" guy, because I was good in sports, I think I always related to everyone in the same manner. Treating people equally was important to me, because the way I saw it, you never knew when you'd be the one in that situation. Ultimately, I learned that being a nice, sincere person is far more important than being cool.

My dad worked for the phone company and still does. He's more of a foreman now, but back then he used to spend a lot of his days climbing poles and working as a repairman. Mimi also worked for the phone company when they met, but she now has an interior decorating business. Over time, she and I have also gotten close so that now I regard her like a second mom. She didn't have to do much disciplining when we were kids, because my dad handled most of it. But in other ways, I never saw a discrepancy in the way she treated her own son, Matt Post, and the way she did me and my brother. We were just very fortunate that our dad found a wonderful wife and stepmother who loved and cared for us and made us feel like we were all part of the same family.

I was raised in the Catholic church, and though I don't remember having much passion for my religion back then, I was an altar boy, and I went to confession and Sunday school. I don't ever remember getting much out of it, though it was obviously good to learn about Jesus and how you should live your life like he did. My spiritual training never emphasized the Bible or the meaning of a personal relationship with Christ, and so I never understood much about the two things that would become cornerstones of my faith years later. Still, I credit my mom for being so adamant about keeping God in our lives and instilling the discipline that kept me on the right path.

On Sundays, I'd go to church, then come home, turn on the TV, and worship at the altar of America's Team. Yes, like so many other kids back then, I was a huge Dallas Cowboys fan, mostly because of Roger Staubach, whom I admired greatly as a player and as a person. His career was cut short by naval service and concussions, but he was truly one of the greatest, most clutch quarterbacks in history, and I absolutely loved watching him. When I was about nine or ten, my dad bought me a regulation Cowboys helmet for Christmas, and I used to walk around the house wearing it and pretending I was Roger the Dodger.

The funny thing was, I never wanted to be a quarterback. I had so much more fun playing receiver and scoring touchdowns. It seemed like a drag to be the guy who took the ball from center and dropped back. I started playing tackle football in the seventh grade, and my chubbiness became a problem. That first year I was a tight end, which was okay, but in the eighth grade, because I weighed more than 140 pounds, the league rule was that I had to play on the line, which meant I never touched the ball.

Then, as a high school freshman, I showed up for football try-outs, and the coach was looking for a quarterback. He asked everyone to throw the ball, and I could throw it the farthest, so he gave me the job. I was totally bummed out, but once I learned the position a little bit, I fell in love with it. It was great having the ball in my hands every play, and we played on a team that went unde-feated.

Actually, not everything about playing quarterback was fun. Our coach, Jim Padlock, came up with this sadistic drill called "Kill Kurt" that I quickly learned to dread. The point of the drill was to make me a more disciplined quarterback. Early on, because I was new to the position, whenever there was any pres-sure at all I'd bail out of the pocket and start running all over the place. Coach Padlock's idea was to have me take a snap, drop back a few steps, and stand there like a human tackling dummy while our fired-up defensive players licked their chops.

So every day in practice I'd have to take five or more snaps of "Kill Kurt" and prepare to get pummeled. I wasn't allowed to throw the ball; the only thing I could do was move within the pocket to avoid people, but that could only last so long. Eventually, the pass rushers would beat their blockers, and I would just get drilled.

I can't overstate how much I hated this. My teammates would openly laugh at me, and I couldn't really blame them. I just had to sit in there and take it. But here's the thing: it made me a better player, and it formed good habits that are still with me today. Now one of my strong suits is that I stand there under pressure and deliver the ball accurately, even if someone's in my face and I'm about to take a shot. That's what everyone talks about now—that no matter what's going on in front of me, I don't ever move. You can smack me in the face and I'll make the throw.

After that disastrous season we had when I was a junior—my first year as the varsity's starting quarterback—I came back and led us to a 7–2 record as a senior. We tied for the league title before losing in the first round of the state playoffs. I was named All-State, and I thought I had it made.

For one thing, because of sports, I didn't have to get a job during the school year. My brother, Matt Warner, worked in the produce department of a grocery store in high school. I'd make up for that later, during my infamous stint at the Hy-Vee in Cedar Falls. He was the laziest kid I've ever seen when we were at home, or at least I thought so because he didn't want to run out and play sports at every waking hour. But he was a hard worker at the grocery store, and he ended up buying his own car. The only time I had to do anything tough was in the summers, when I did what pretty much every Iowa kid does for spare cash: I detasseled corn. For those of you from the other forty-nine states, or from anywhere else in the world, the tassel is the fringe on top of the cornstalk, the part of the corn that gets pollinated. To detassel, you pull that fringe off and throw it onto the ground. You do this over and over and over until you reach the end of the row, and then you start in on the next row.

It's not a very glamorous pursuit: you and a bunch of other kids meet somewhere in the early morning—I'm talking before it gets light, like 5:30 A.M.—with your packed lunches, and a bus takes you out to the field. You pull and separate all day long in the boiling sun and get all scratched up by the cornstalks because the leaves are long, thin, and rough. One time, some of my friends and I spent a day detasseling corn that must have been infected, because we ended up with horrible rashes. A couple of my buddies had it really bad. They had pus pockets all over the place and chafing all over their inner thighs.

Because detasseling can carve up your body, a lot of people choose to wear long sleeves and pants. But when the temperature is in the nineties, with maximum humidity, that's not a very enticing option.

In Iowa, the summer heat is just unbearable. It wasn't uncommon for a worker to pass out from heat exhaustion, and when one did, it took a long time to notice that he or she was missing because the rows of corn were so thick. Short people, especially, tended to fall by the wayside, because the act of reaching up and pulling just wore them out. When someone hadn't turned up for a while, we'd have to go back into the rows and pull them out.

When it rained, the ground would get muddy, and that made the job especially difficult, because your feet would constantly get caught in the slop. The bus would come and pick everyone up at the end of the day—it could be as early as one in the afternoon or as late as six—and, man, that bus would reek. Everyone was tired and sweaty and hungry, and we'd sing songs on the way home just to take our minds off the stench.

All this, and for really lousy wages. I'd make about $350 a summer, which seemed like a lot of money back then. A couple of summers into high school, my friends and I realized that it was a lot more lucrative to do contract work directly for the farmers, because you could easily do an acre a day on your own, and you'd get about $100 an acre.

I didn't really need a whole lot of money, because my idea of fun wasn't all that sophisticated. A big Saturday night for me in high school was to get a bunch of friends together, blow about fifteen bucks on toilet paper at the supermarket, and then go toilet-paper the house of whichever of our friends couldn't go out that night. We'd toss the rolls up over tree branches, drape the bushes, and by the time we were done, the place was covered in streamers. It was cheap entertainment with a hint of danger. One time about seven of us piled into our buddy Mark's Datsun hatchback, and we drove off to TP our friend Maureen's house. But after we finished decorating her yard, we realized that we had left some fireworks on the lawn, and my best friend, Tom Petsche, volunteered to go back to retrieve them. So, of course, as soon as he picked them up, we started honking the horn, and Mark peeled out as if we were leaving Tom behind. Tom chased after the car, and we were looking back and taunting him, when all of a sudden I turned back to the front and screamed, "Tree!" We had driven onto a neighbor's yard, and about a half-second after I saw the tree, we drilled it at full speed. Nobody got hurt, but Tom had a few laughs at our expense that night.

Along with Tom, my best buddies in high school were Scott Mason, who used to torment me by blasting country music at every opportunity, and Dustin Hoffman—yes, that's his real name. Dustin goes by Dusty, but it didn't matter; we'd call him "Tootsie" and make every other acting reference you might imagine. The four of us were always hanging out at one another's houses, and we were all into sports. Tom and I were totally sports crazy, so we had an even stronger bond.

Largely because of sports, I got a lot of attention from girls, yet I really wasn't that interested. Maybe I was shy. Whatever the reason, I really didn't date many people. I went to a couple of proms, and I went out with a girl at another school for a little while, but I didn't have any legitimate relationships. You know how high school is—you talk to your friends, and they find out that so-and-so likes you, and then you hook up for two weeks and "go steady" and move on. I didn't get serious with anyone, and I didn't spend a lot of time worrying about it.

Honestly, sports was the most important thing in my life. That's all I did all day, every day, and it's all I ever thought about or wanted to do. Sports was my comfort zone, and away from the field or the court, I wasn't very outgoing or socially experienced. I probably didn't go on more than ten dates in high school, and chances are I was thinking about holding a basketball instead of stressing out about the possibility of a good-night kiss.

Some of the fondest memories I have are of the summer vacations my brothers and I took with my dad and Mimi up to Lake Vermilion in northern Minnesota. We'd spend two weeks of every summer at a resort up there with two other families that had kids

around our ages. Mostly I remember the outdoor activities, especially the waterskiing. During our teenage years the adults gave us
a boat with a little motor on it, and I was so fat that I couldn't even
ski behind the darn thing, so I always had to drive.

My true love was basketball. I'll never forget my first game-
winning shot, which came in the final game of my eighth grade
season for All Saints. My friend threw a full-court pass, and I went
up to catch it at the free throw line, turned around in midair, and
banked it in as the clock expired. As I got closer to high school, my
dad gave me the option of attending sports camps during the
summers, and I always thought football camp would be totally
boring, so I always chose basketball. I remember being named
MVP of a camp at the University of Iowa. At another camp, at the
University of Northern Iowa, two other campers and I beat a team
of college players in a game of three-on-three. Our opponents
included Kevin Boyle, who played at Iowa, and Terry Woods, an
Iowa State player, so we were pretty pumped. At the same camp, I
won a three-point shooting contest against Brad Sellers, an NBA
player who had gone to Wisconsin and Ohio State. For winning, I
got to keep his Chicago Bulls practice jersey. If only Michael
Jordan's had been included, too.

One great thing about high school basketball was our coach,
Dick Breitbach, who was a local legend. He was very hard on me
and big on discipline, but he was a great man who loved me like a
son and would do anything for me. He taught fundamentals, and if
you weren't fundamentally sound you wouldn't play for him.
Everything was about teamwork, and he taught you how to lead—
not by scoring a lot of points or being flashy but by doing the little
things it takes to help a team win. It was definitely tough love, and
in a lot of ways he and Coach Vermeil remind me of each other.

Coach Breitbach also was an assistant for our football team,
and I'll never forget this one time he blew up at me in front of
everyone. We had very few audibles in high school, but he had
told me that if I saw a certain look on defense, we would switch to
another play. So I saw the look and checked off, and my pass got

tipped at the line of scrimmage and was intercepted. I was still about ten steps from the sideline when he started chewing me out, and believe me, this guy could yell. Needless to say, that was the last audible he put in during my career. But the great thing was that five minutes after a blowup like that, all was forgiven and he loved you again.

Because of Coach Breitbach, I was able to join a traveling all-star team that went on a basketball tour of Europe the summer after my senior year of high school. We went to France, Germany, and the Netherlands, and other than griping about the food—McDonald's was our deliverance—we really had a blast. It was wild, because none of us had really been anywhere outside of Iowa, and here we were tripping around some of the coolest places on earth. We spent most of our time getting goofy in public and making spectacles of ourselves. We'd go to discos and take over the dance floor, grooving crazily to weird techno music we'd never heard. One time we went into a little bar in Amsterdam, and a bunch of guys from our group started dancing on tables.

I had never tried any form of alcohol, but I remember in Germany everyone kept saying, "You've got to try the beer because it's the best." I didn't really know what to compare it to, but I took a sip anyway, and I nearly spit it out on the spot. It was thick, black, and completely awful. However, not everyone in our group shared my opinion. That became obvious when people started showing up for the games with hangovers. A couple of times, some of our players were actually drunk when they took the floor.

When we were in Paris, I had a picture taken of me at the Eiffel Tower, and I blew it up and signed it to Coach Breitbach, thanking him for the opportunity and all he had done for me. I wish I could have helped reward him with a state championship, and our team was good enough to go all the way my senior year. But our hopes evaporated, partly because of me. In the first round of the state tournament, at Veterans Memorial Auditorium in Des Moines, we played a team from Pella that we thought was a joke. We determined this during pregame introductions. Everyone on the Pella team had a goofy nickname on the back of his warm-up jacket, and one guy, Jumping Joe, came out and did a flip when his name was announced.

We had a fifteen-point lead with about five minutes to go, and then Jumping Joe and his teammates started hitting everything. The worst part was that I went cold from the free throw line, which violated one of my biggest rules: never miss your second free throw. If you're any kind of a shooter, it's one thing to miss your first foul shot, but there's no excuse for bricking your second one because you should be able to correct what you did wrong the first time. (Don't worry, Shaq, I'm not talking about *you*.) But I was brutal in those final minutes against Pella, and I think I finished five for eleven from the foul line. We ended up losing in overtime, and if I hadn't been crying, I would've gotten to see Jumping Joe do a few more flips to celebrate as he left the floor.

That, sadly, was the last organized basketball game I'd ever play. I was a six-foot-two, 185-pound power forward—I led my district in rebounding as a junior and senior and ended up second on my school's all-time list—and I knew even before my senior year that college hoops would be a difficult transition. I wasn't tall enough to rebound with the big boys, yet I didn't have the quickness required for the guard position. Football, I figured, was my best chance to continue my athletic career. All I needed was someone who believed in me, and I looked to the most revered figure in Iowa to make my dream come true.

CHAPTER FOUR

DON'T LEAVE ME HANGING

The King of Iowa entered the room, and I froze with fear, mesmerized by his royal presence. The King—Hayden Fry, the University of Iowa's esteemed football coach—had summoned me to his castle, Kinnick Stadium, for an unofficial recruiting visit during my senior year of high school.

Hayden Fry!

He had sent a letter inviting me to a game—signed and all. When I opened it I was beyond excited. So on one resplendent Saturday morning in November of 1988 my mom and I, along with my best friend, Tom Petsche, made the half-hour drive to Iowa City and got to watch my beloved Hawkeyes defeat Northwestern. A school official greeted us, gave us a tour of the stadium complex, and even brought us onto the field to meet a few of the guys. When the game ended, the hosts took me and about a dozen other unofficial recruits into a waiting room near where the players dressed, and we waited expectantly for The King to arrive.

Then in he came, and a hush fell over the room. I held my breath—he was headed right toward me! I fantasized about what he might say: "So, Kurt, you're an All-State quarterback, and I love what you're doing at Regis High. I'd like to offer you a full scholarship and groom you to be the next Chuck Long. . . ."

42

The King got within a couple of feet of me, and I very nearly extended my hand. It's a good thing I didn't, or I would've been left hanging. Because Hayden Fry walked *right by me* as if I didn't exist and started schmoozing with some of the other recruits.

Man, I was crushed. The King had no clue who I was, and he never said a word to me. I went home bummed out but still hoping against hope that maybe I'd get another letter from him inviting me to come back for a legitimate visit.

As it turned out, my mailbox got less action than Cal Ripken's back-up. It was sort of harsh, because though I ended up being named All-State in both football and basketball, I felt incredibly small come recruiting time. My unexceptional size—six-foot-two, 185 pounds—and lack of speed hurt me in both sports, as did the fact that I came from a tiny school without much of a football tradition. Also, I was from Iowa. There's so much talent around the country, who looks at Iowa come recruiting time? You have to be really exceptional to get noticed, and my stats were just average: 1,600 passing yards and twelve touchdowns my senior year. These days, you hear about quarterbacks with 5,000 yards and thirty-five touchdowns in a season.

I was probably the best quarterback in the state of Iowa, but the Hawkeyes ended up signing a guy from Iowa City named Paul Burmeister who was taller and bigger than I was. The only other state school with a big-time program was Iowa State, and those guys didn't give me the time of day. Maybe it was because they ran a variation of the option at the time, and speed is not exactly my forte. If they watched film of me running, they probably said, "Why is this in slow motion? Wait, that *is* normal speed."

As my senior year wore on, it became apparent that I had two realistic options for continuing my athletic career: play football for a Division III school or play basketball for a Division II college. Obviously, my goal was Division I anything, but it just wasn't happening. The only football recruiting letters I got were from Division III schools, and I didn't even consider them. I figured I could take my chances and try to parlay a strong senior basketball season into a Division II opportunity in that sport, possibly a scholarship. My dad, by virtue of the divorce agreement, had agreed to pay for my college education, but I still wanted to get a scholarship, because it wasn't as if he had money to burn.

Late in the recruiting period, just about the time I had given up on a scholarship, I got a letter from Terry Allen, the coach at the University of Northern Iowa. No, it wasn't Division I, but it was the next best thing, Division I-AA. They wanted me to drive up to Cedar Falls for a visit and said the most they could give me was three-quarters of a scholarship, which sounded great to me. I knew I was going to take the offer, since it was the only decent one I had, but I waited until after the trip to accept it because I thought a weekend up there would be fun.

So Tom Petsche and I drove up to Cedar Falls, and once we rolled into town, it was like a whole new world—a champagne reception at the stadium, beautiful coeds on each arm, a BMW convertible with KURT as the license plate. . . . Yeah, right. Actually, our host was another old friend of ours, UNI running back Mike Schulte, so we just hooked up with him and said, "What next?"

There were no beautiful coeds waiting to show us a good time, but the guys on the team did try to give us an orientation into the party scene. They got me and Tom a couple of fake IDs and took us over to one of the bars by the school. Too bad they didn't know what a square I was. We lasted about ten minutes at the bar, and then we took off.

The whole UNI thing seemed like a great deal. Coach Allen told me that I probably would redshirt my first year, because they had two senior quarterbacks, but that I'd have a chance to compete for the starting job as a freshman the following season. I welcomed the redshirt year, which means sitting out the season without sacrificing a year of eligibility. It gave me a chance to adjust both to college life and to the next level of football. In high school, I basically just dropped back and threw to the open guy. Now I had to learn all the schemes and defensive coverages and fronts that I had never even paid a bit of attention to before.

In the meantime I had one more game to play. A few weeks before my freshman year began, I went to Sioux City to play in the Shrine Game, an all-star event featuring the top players in Iowa from the previous high school season. A man came and spoke to us before the game and stressed that we should start getting realistic about our football futures. "Don't get your hopes up," he told us. "Statistics show that 2 percent of you, or less, will even make it to an NFL training camp." Actually, for our specific group, it was higher than that. Along with yours truly, two other future NFL players were in attendance: Trev Alberts, who was the Indianapolis Colts' first round draft pick in 1994, and Adam Timmerman, who started at guard for the Rams during our Super Bowl season in '99. But the point was, even in the face of those daunting percentages, I never felt intimidated. Shortly after that speech, a family friend asked me, "What are you going to do when you're done with football?" I just stared back at her, blank faced, confused. *What do you mean? I'm going to be part of the 2 percent.*

Once I got to UNI, the first major decision I made was to pick a new uniform number. I had worn number 12 in high school, à la Roger Staubach, but that was taken, so I settled on 13. Later, as I got deeper into my faith, the number assumed added significance for me. It's my way of demystifying people's obsession with superstition, because in my view God is more powerful than luck or fate. Back then, though, I think I took 13 because it was the closest number to 12 and because a guy named Dan Marino was putting up some pretty nice numbers in the NFL with that jersey. If it was good enough for Dan, it darn sure was good enough for me.

I got to suit up for home games, which I thought was really cool, though I didn't go to any away games. I spent a bunch of time in the weight room, put on a few pounds, and got adjusted to school. My first semester didn't go that well academically—I had a 2.9 grade point average, the only time I didn't get above a 3.0 in college. I majored in communications and public relations, with a journalism minor. I still wasn't into the whole dating scene, but it was fun living in the dorms, and by the time my second year arrived I was raring to go.

The competition for the starting job came down to me and a sophomore named Jay Johnson, who was a year ahead of me and, to be fair, was better than I was at the time. He definitely understood the game more than I did, so I had no problem being the backup, except that I knew the math didn't work in my favor: if Jay stayed ahead of me his whole time in school, I could be on the bench until my senior year.

Then a few weeks into the season, Jay hurt his ankle, and it looked like he might miss our next game. We were going down to Stillwater, Oklahoma, to play Oklahoma State, a Division I school, and I thought, *This is it, my big chance; I'll go in, do well, and be the starter for four years.*

Jay was hurting badly, and I went out and had a great week of practice in his place. Then on Friday, the day before the game, he was gimping around before our walk-through and decided to give it a go. He ended up starting and playing the whole game. Jay was just okay, and we got killed.

That was the last whiff of opportunity I had that season, but then the next spring everything started to click. People always talk about the game slowing down for quarterbacks before they can become truly successful, and that was what happened to me during spring practice going into my sophomore season. I started to understand the game, and by the time fall rolled around, I thought I had overtaken Jay. I was a better passer than he was, and I think I caught up mentally and really became the superior quarterback.

On the last day of spring practice, they split the team into two squads and had the big public scrimmage, and I just tore it up. My team won easily, and people started saying, "Wow, this guy's pretty good." But Coach Allen stuck with Jay, and I guess to some degree I can understand why. Jay didn't lose many games during his career as a starter, and it's hard to pull your quarterback when you're winning. In my mind there were other reasons for the team's success: we had a great defense that would hold opponents to an average of about twelve points a game, and we had a couple of skill players on offense who would make enough plays for us to win. But the bottom line was that I stayed on the bench for three years, and after all that waiting I was getting mighty frustrated.

Sometime during my second season as Jay's backup, I remember standing in the locker room with Mike Schulte, my buddy from back home, and saying, "This is terrible. I'm never going to get a chance."

After that, Mike went and talked to one of the coaches and asked him what the deal was. That coach told him, "One of Kurt's biggest problems is that he's not a practice player. He steps it up for the games, but in practice he's not the same, so it's tough to get a read on him." I thought about it, and to an extent I agreed. I wasn't bad in practice, but I definitely elevated my performance when the chips were down. Always had, and still do; anyone on the Rams will tell you the same thing. When Mike told me what the coaches were thinking, I knew I had to meet this obstacle head-on and try to improve my practice performance, even though it went against my nature.

In the spring before my fourth season, I thought I outplayed Jay again. Even he thought so. One time we were talking, and he said something like, "You should probably be starting anyway." Granted, he wasn't going to go to the coach and volunteer to give up his job, but that's how clear it was that I deserved to be in there. It wasn't a personal thing—Jay and I had a good relationship, and it's not like the team was struggling with him in there. I don't even hold a grudge against Coach Allen, who's now the head man at Kansas. Still, it was tough to swallow.

After the Rams won the Super Bowl, Coach Allen called me and said, "Hey, I'm getting hammered by all these reporters who want to know why I didn't play you more in college." I laughed and said, "Good. They should give you a hard time." He knew I was joking. But, hey, I still wish he would've played me more.

So Jay went into yet another season as the starter, and I went into a deep funk. I think the coaches had realized that I had caught up with Jay, and Coach Allen tried to placate me by guaranteeing that I would play in the first game of the season. I wouldn't be the starter, but supposedly Jay and I would split time. I got all excited, thinking I'd have a chance to settle the issue on the field. But the game rolled by, and I didn't play at all. The same scenario unfolded for the second game: Coach Allen said he'd play me, and then changed his mind.

That's when I hit rock bottom. When Coach Allen didn't put me in, it made me feel like he and the other coaches had absolutely no confidence in me, that they didn't believe they could win with me in there. That hurt, a lot. There was no question in my mind that I was the better quarterback, and I finally had a long talk with my quarterbacks coach, Mike Smith. I said, "Coach, I can't do this. I can't sit behind him any longer." He sympathized, but it was Coach Allen's decision.

I didn't know what to do. I thought about quitting or bolting to another school. I even wanted to play basketball for Northern Iowa. Our hoops coaches talked to me about it, but the football coaches were opposed to the idea—I have no idea why, because they sure weren't getting much out of me. It ended up becoming a non-issue. Since our football team made the playoffs every year, the timing was always screwed up because it was too deep into basketball season for me to have a realistic chance of contributing.

For a while, transferring somewhere else for my final season of eligibility seemed like a viable option. I didn't have a plan or a destination in mind; the idea of leaving was sort of a spur-of-the-moment thing. I ran it by each of my parents, and though they hadn't been together for years, they responded as if they were living in the same house. Both said, "You're not a quitter. You made a commitment. Get your degree, because education is more important than football." My mom said it was the equivalent of a kid whining, "If I can't play, I'm gonna take my ball and go home." The more I thought about it, the more I agreed with her.

Around that time, I told Coach Smith I was thinking about leaving. He said, "You should just play this out and continue trying. We know you're good. Why go somewhere else where they don't know you?"

I actually went back to my dorm room and prayed about it, saying, *Okay, God, what should I do? Why am I not playing?*

I still went to mass from time to time during college. So it wasn't unusual for me to pray for God's help when I encountered some big problem or decision in my life. Prayer wasn't a daily habit like it is for me now, and I wasn't always sure God was answering me. But on this particular occasion I remember having a thought that seemed like an answer at the time. I wasn't nearly as strong in my faith back then, but the Lord kind of answered and said, *Hey, you know, there's a reason you're here. Stick it out—you're going to have one year to play. You get a free education. A lot of good things can happen because of this.*

Yet the rest of that season was exceptionally tough. I started to do crazy stuff, engaging in reckless behavior that could have jeopardized my career. Normally, during a football season, I wouldn't take chances with any other kind of physical activity. But I was so frustrated by then that I thought, *To heck with it.* One Thursday night two days before a game, when I played pickup basketball with a bunch of guys from my dorm floor, things got a little out of hand. I was being my usual hyperactive self on the basketball court, and I got elbowed right in the face and knocked out. When I came to, I was a mess. I'd sustained one of the worst concussions of my life. I was dizzy, throwing up, and for most of that night I was unable to sleep. I ended up going to the hospital to get checked out, but I never told the coaches about it, and I suited up that Saturday even though I still felt awful. Fortunately, I didn't play, because it might not have been a good idea.

Later that season we were killing Western Illinois, and the coaches decided they'd give me a chance to mop up and show what I could do. But, as fate would have it, I was sick as a dog that day, too. I must've had the flu, because I couldn't stop vomiting.

As one of the coaches came over to tell me I was going into the game, I was propped up against the side of the bench, unable even to stand. The coaches called instead for the third-stringer, Brett O'Donnell, and while I dry-heaved on the sidelines he threw his first touchdown pass.

A few weeks later we got our first big snowfall of the winter, and a bunch of people on my dorm floor decided to go outside and have a big Snow Bowl. Now, tackle football in tennis shoes on a frozen field isn't exactly the safest activity on campus. My friends didn't even ask if I wanted to play, because it was a couple of days before a game, but I went out and joined them anyway. "Are you sure?" they asked me. I knew it was stupid, but I didn't care. I wanted to play. I wanted to go out and have some *fun.*

I'll never forget that game, either. I was zinging the ball all over the place, catching passes, running through the snow, just like old times. It reminded me why I love football—and how much I was missing by not getting to play.

So Jay kept on winning and I kept on sitting. I felt I could do so much more to help us win, and a lot of my teammates agreed with me. Right before we played our first Division I-AA playoff game, from what I was later told, a bunch of our defensive players went to the captains, and eventually some of the coaches, and said, "We feel that if we're going to win the championship, Kurt needs to be our quarterback." Obviously, that made me feel good, but let's be real: what were the odds they'd make a change at that point in time?

Looking back, it was a blessing that I didn't leave, because things worked out for the best. The experience taught me a lesson about hanging tough, fighting through adversity, and waiting my turn.

For one thing, my lone year as a starter turned out to be pretty fruitful. I led our team into the Division I-AA playoffs and was the Gateway Conference's offensive player of the year. That wasn't enough to get me drafted by an NFL team, but it did win over a certain football luminary in a big way. After my senior season, I attended a couple of award banquets in various parts of the state, and who did I keep running into but Hayden Fry! The King not only knew who I was by then, he had nothing but good things to say about me. A couple of times he introduced me at these functions, telling everyone there how he wished he would've had me at Iowa, which was pretty funny given our history.

I never told him how badly I'd wanted to play for him or about the time he left me hanging. Down the road, he turned out to be a valuable resource. When I was playing for the Iowa Barnstormers of the Arena League, I'd call down to the Iowa football office to see if they could help set up my tryouts for various NFL teams. On several occasions, both Hayden and Chuck Long, who had returned to his alma mater to coach after his NFL career ended, were extremely helpful in that regard.

Now that I've done some big things in the NFL, Hayden *loves* to talk me up, and I get a kick out of it.

Besides, as much as it hurt at the time, I'm glad he blew me off that day in Iowa City. If I hadn't gone to UNI, I probably wouldn't have met the person most responsible for my success and my spiritual turnaround—not to mention the best little line dancer I've ever seen.

CHAPTER FIVE

FISHIN' IN THE DARK

During my gloomiest days of bench-sitting at UNI, if a prophet had told me that I'd eventually throw forty-one touchdown passes in an NFL season and be Super Bowl MVP, I wouldn't have been all that surprised. People might not have recognized my potential back then, but I've always had a ton of confidence in my abilities.

On the other hand, if that same seer had assured me I'd meet my future wife while doing the Barn Dance at a country music bar, I'd have laughed in the prophet's face.

Yeah, and Julia Roberts will marry Lyle Lovett.

Until my junior year of college, I absolutely detested country music. No, that's a bit of an understatement. Hearing a country tune, for me, was akin to ingesting year-old Limburger cheese. Here's how bad it was: given a choice between listening to country and hard rock, I'd have chosen hard rock—and I hate hard rock. Heck, I'd have probably slept on a bed of hard rocks before I danced to a country-and-western tune, let alone took lessons.

But there I was at Wild E. Coyote's, a bar a few miles away from the Northern Iowa campus in Cedar Falls, learning line dance steps so that I could work up the courage to get my groove on to the Nitty Gritty Dirt Band.

Let me backtrack a bit. The beginning of my fourth year of college—my junior year of football—was a real downer, because I was sitting on the bench behind Jay Johnson for the third consecutive season. This was the period when I was so fed up I was considering transferring to another school, and I wasn't the most uplifting person to hang out with. Some of my friends thought they could cheer me up by taking me out for a few beers, but since I had never been a drinker and liked going to bars about as much as I liked country music, it didn't sound all that promising. Still, I had just turned twenty-one and didn't want to be a total stick in the mud, so one night at the start of that school year I agreed to go along.

"Great," said my roommate Mike Hudnutt, an offensive lineman on our team. "We'll go to this country music spot away from campus."

"Whoa," I said, "you can forget that idea. That's the last place I want to be."

I told Hudnutt about how back in high school I used to ride around with my buddy Scott in his pickup truck, and he always tortured me by playing old-school country—the slow, yee-haw stuff. It was so depressing, I felt like sitting in bed all day with the lights off and the blinds closed. But Hudnutt had grown up on a farm and didn't want to hear my complaining. "Besides," he said, "we've got to get you into the new stuff. It's a lot better."

"I don't even own any cowboy boots," I protested. But Hudnutt and some of the other guys were persistent, and eventually they wore me down.

Sure enough, the first time I went with them to Wild E. Coyote's, I hated it. But Hudnutt and the guys kept dragging me out there, and I didn't resist, because it gave us a chance to get away from the campus scene. The club usually had an older crowd, which was nice, because around school I always had to talk about football and why I wasn't playing.

After a few visits, against my better judgment, I came to the realization that there was some country music I could tolerate. Mostly it was the "new country," the faster stuff, like Garth Brooks and Clint Black, which you could at least dance to, though I wasn't exactly cutting it up out there. I'd had a couple of girlfriends in college, but I still was relatively shy when it came to girls, especially on the dance floor.

Still, partly because we were football players, we got a decent amount of female attention, and there was one girl at the bar who I thought was pretty cute. It turned out she was dating somebody at the time, so I left it alone. At that point, I was beginning to tire of the scene.

Then one night I spotted this short, attractive woman who stopped me cold. She was wearing red boots, an eye-catching shirt, and a miniskirt, and even from afar you could tell she was the center of a lot of people's attention. I asked my friends about her, but nobody knew who she was, so I just sat back and eyeballed her for a while. Eventually, I saw her checking me out, too, but I didn't have the guts to approach her. She was always getting asked to dance and flashing her moves, while I was mostly hanging back and watching.

Yep, this was Brenda, and she seemed way out of my league. There were a lot of things I didn't know about her at the time—she was four years older than I was, had been in the marines, was going to nursing school and had two kids—but she sure looked good in that outfit. She was a little bit country, a little bit rock 'n' roll, and unlike me, she could do the two-step and all the other dances.

Once I noticed Brenda, I had a whole different attitude when it came to Wild E. Coyote's. All of a sudden the two best nights of the week were Wednesdays and Saturdays—the two big nights at the bar. Wednesday night was Ladies' Night, and on Saturdays after our games the place was packed. I couldn't wait for those nights, and now I was leading the charge to go out.

Soon I had another reason to be scared: even if I did get up the courage to ask her to dance, once we hit the floor I was guaranteed to be embarrassed. Luckily, they gave lessons at Coyote's on Monday nights, so a couple of times I showed up and at least learned some of the basics. What I didn't realize at the time was that Brenda was also taking lessons, at the Cattle Congress Grand

Ballroom across town. She was either a quick learner or a real natural because she looked so much at home on the dance floor I never would have guessed she was almost as much of a novice as I was.

Line dancing was a new craze back then, at least in Iowa. When a couple of friends at church signed up for lessons, Brenda's mom talked Brenda into going along, thinking it would be a good way to get her out of the house and give her a nice break. So after Brenda and her mom had taken a few lessons they started showing up at Coyote's with their friends to put what they'd learned into practice.

We met, appropriately, on the dance floor. I had worked up to the point where I would do some group dances, and there was one called the Barn Dance where the guys form a big circle and the girls form another one inside it, and you rotate around with different partners, whoever's in front of you. When Brenda and I paired up, we both started laughing, because we'd been building up to the moment for so long.

"It's about time," she said, and we started talking. I asked her if she wanted to dance later, and we ended up spending the rest of the night dancing and talking. During the last dance of the night, she dropped the bomb on me: "I want you to know I'm a divorced mother of two." I paused, not sure how to react.

"If I never hear from you again," she added, "I'll understand."

I don't know if I took that as a challenge, but I certainly wasn't scared away by the fact that she had two kids. True, it may not have been what I was expecting to hear, yet it's not like I was in a state of panic, because I really didn't know her yet. I had been watching her for so long that, if anything, I was intrigued by the whole thing. So the next morning I decided to get a closer look at Brenda Meoni and her two kids. I showed up at her house with a red rose in hand. I guess one of my friends must have known where she lived; I honestly don't even remember how I knew where to go, but there I was.

It's funny, looking back, how that must have seemed to her. Brenda was living with her parents at the time, and her mom had seen me frequently at Coyote's, where I guess my football buddies and I were usually surrounded by a lot of people. At one point, I later learned, she had told Brenda, "Look at all those women around him," and shaken her head.

Now, here I was, unannounced, doing my best Romeo. As soon as Brenda let me in, I saw Zachary, who was three at the time, cruising around on the living room floor. So I instantly went over and started playing with him, and after a while Brenda came over and said, "There are some things about him I want you to know."

That's when I learned the short version of the accident that had nearly killed Zachary when he was four months old. Later I heard every gory detail, and now seems like as good a time as any time to share the story.

Brenda was a Marine corporal specializing in intelligence and was stationed in Damneck, Virginia. One day she got a call from her husband, who told her something was wrong with the baby. When she got home, Zachary was in and out of consciousness, and at one point he stopped breathing and had to be revived on the way to the hospital. Nobody knew what happened—her husband said Zachary suddenly stopped breathing while taking a bath—and doctors ran every test imaginable but couldn't figure out why his head kept swelling. Finally, twenty-four hours after the incident, Brenda's husband confessed that he had accidentally dropped Zachary into the bathtub.

At that point, doctors told Brenda and her husband they doubted Zachary would make it. She remembers sitting in his room in intensive care, staring outside his hospital window at the highway below, and watching the cars zoom past. She says she felt like screaming, "Stop! Don't you people realize that while you're all rushing off somewhere, my child is dying?" She promised herself and God that when this ordeal was over she would always remember what that felt like, that she would make a conscious effort to appreciate the important things in life and not get bogged down in trivialities.

Brenda had a lot of conversations with God in that hospital

room because this medical crisis was also a real crisis of faith. She'd had what some people refer to as a "born again" experience when she was just twelve years old. She'd asked for forgiveness and invited Jesus into her heart. And she'd gotten so serious about her faith that she was actually teased and called "Jesus freak" at school. But she wouldn't let anything stop her from telling others about her Christian faith.

Friends and people at church were so impressed with her spiritual commitment that they assured her God would be able to use her in some very special way. Brenda remembers people praying over her at church and one woman telling her, "God has big plans in store for you!"

Brenda had believed that. And when she had graduated from high school, she'd decided that God's big plans for her included enlisting in the Marine Corps. She'd been lay reader for the base chapel services and continued to be outspoken about her faith. She'd fallen in love with another Marine and become convinced that God's plans for her included getting her boyfriend on the straight and narrow, marrying, and then seeing what great and exciting things were in store for the two of them after that. But she skipped step one, moved right on to step two, and then discovered the first great and exciting thing in store for her was getting pregnant three months after the wedding. Zack was born around the time of their one-year anniversary, and the accident came just four months later.

Suddenly, Brenda felt her life wasn't turning out so great. And the awesome, all-powerful God she'd believed in for years didn't seem to be healing Zachary. Brenda quoted Scripture promises. She prayed. And she believed God would perform a miracle.

For the next three days Zachary experienced hourly seizures that lasted several minutes each. The episodes got worse and worse, and eventually he was having grand mal seizures, where the whole body shakes violently. It didn't look good, and doctors said that even if he lived he wouldn't be able to have much of a life because half of his brain was damaged. They said his brain looked like Swiss cheese because of all the pockets of destruction. Doctors also knew he couldn't see because his retinas had hemorrhaged, though there was a chance the body would absorb the blood and he'd eventually be able to make out objects right in front of his face. That's exactly what ended up happening, thankfully, though it took a couple of years.

Brenda kept praying for a miracle, and in her mind nothing was happening. Eventually, doctors told her they couldn't understand why Zachary was staying alive and that since there was nothing more they could do for him, she might as well take him home. Three weeks later he got sick again and had to be readmitted for another several days. Brenda ended up getting an honorable discharge from the Marine Corps and returning to Iowa with her husband and one very needy baby. The three of them tried to start over again in Cedar Rapids.

Not surprisingly, the ordeal they'd been through put a real strain on their marriage. For a long time Brenda struggled with forgiving her husband for the role he'd played in Zachary's accident. She thought maybe having another child would rekindle their relationship and bring them closer together. So she got pregnant. Eight months later, when, she said, her husband started acting awkward and cold toward her, she pressed him to know what was wrong. After an hour of hemming and hawing he admitted he was attracted to another woman.

After everything else this seemed like more than she could take. And remembering what the Bible said about adultery being grounds for divorce, Brenda decided right then and there she didn't *have* to take this. She packed up, drove Zack to Cedar Falls, and moved in with her parents. Jesse was born a month later, and the month after that Brenda's divorce went through. She then enrolled in nursing school, figuring that would be the best way to care for Zachary, who continued to confound the doctors by making remarkable developmental progress.

So many things are difficult for Zachary, but he makes up for it in other ways. Best of all, he has a happy life, and he exudes pure, undiscriminating love toward those around him. That first day I met him, as we wrestled around on the carpet, he laughed and hugged me and smelled my hair, and a lifelong connection was born.

Thus, on my first visit to the home of my future wife, I gave more attention to her son than I did to her. At the time, I'm sure I was putting on a show for Brenda, convincing her what a good guy I was. But once I started playing with Zachary, I was hooked. Jesse, who was about nine months old at the time, didn't really take to me at first, but she was such a beautiful, sweet-natured child that she, too, captured my heart.

Part of it was that I've always loved children, and I'd always felt that I wanted to start having kids at a relatively young age, like my parents did with my brother and me. Even though I'd never been in a serious relationship, I remember thinking it would be great to start having kids in the next couple of years so I'd still be young enough to do a lot of activities with them, to be involved in sports and all. If I had found the right woman back then, I would've pushed to start a family right off the bat.

All this, of course, was premature. Not only was Brenda divorced, she wasn't really eligible, either. Early on, she told me she was dating a guy named Mark who lived in Des Moines, which is about a two-hour drive from Cedar Falls. I didn't know how serious they were, but on paper he had me beat in a lot of categories. He was a teacher; I had no job. He had a strong, supportive family that lived in Cedar Falls; my family lived an hour away. He promised Brenda stability; I told her I wanted to pursue my dream of playing pro football—not exactly what a divorced mother of two wants to hear. It also didn't help that Brenda hated football at the time.

Still, I hung in there because I could tell Brenda liked me, and it wasn't like there was any pressure to make a choice. All we were doing was showing up at the same establishment a couple of nights a week and dancing. Even after I showed up at her house after that first night we danced, I still didn't have her phone number. It was

Halloween, and as usual I showed up at Wild E. Coyote's on a Saturday night looking for Brenda. She wasn't there, and pretty soon I was a scary sight. I had a couple of drinks too many, which wasn't like me at all. And which probably explains the truly intelligent move I made next: I lifted my glass of vodka and lemonade off the table with my mouth, rolled my head back so I could drink it, then tried to put it back onto the table without any hands. It was a great trick, until I bungled the dismount and the glass smashed all over the place. Fortunately, I didn't swallow any glass, though I did get an 8.6 from the Russian judge.

The bouncers kicked me out of the bar, which was timely, because I was about to embark upon the first of many vomiting sessions. As I was being ushered out I spotted Brenda—wearing her marine fatigues as a Halloween costume—but she didn't notice me, which was probably just as well. We hadn't seen each other in a while, and she had read in the paper about how I had been too sick to play in the previous week's game—the one in which I was throwing up because of the flu and our third-string guy went in instead and threw his first career touchdown pass. So Brenda, trying to act like she was interested in football, spotted Hudnutt at the bar and said, "Are you Kurt Warner's roommate?" When he said yes, she asked, "How's he feeling? I heard he was sick." Well, Hudnutt assumed she was talking about my current state of inebriation, so he said, "He's not doing too well; he had to go home." They kept talking like that about my *illness,* with Brenda feeling all sorry for me and Hudnutt thinking I was a total knucklehead. Anyway, Brenda wrote down her phone number and asked him to give it to me, which was a significant step in our relationship.

When I think back to that period, I was a real Casanova. Another night, after I'd again had too much to drink, Brenda drove me home—and she had to pull over twice because I got sick. I was in bad shape, so she walked me up to my apartment and helped me into bed, at which point I threw up again. Sounds romantic, doesn't it?

To make matters worse, I had this dog named Buddy, a cocker spaniel that my previous girlfriend and Scott, the guy who used to torture me with country music back in Cedar Rapids, had given me for my birthday. Buddy loved me but took an instant disliking to Brenda. She was trying to put her student nursing acumen to use and take care of me, and the whole time Buddy sat there and growled at her, looking like he was ready to attack. That was the first battle of what turned out to be a four-year war, but that's another story.

Amazingly, despite the growling dog and my Technicolor yawns, Brenda stayed interested. She was still dating this guy Mark—he'd drive in on some of the weekends—but I didn't care. All I knew was that she kept showing up at the bar and hanging out with me, and that was the only thing that mattered from my perspective. After one night of dancing, we went outside to the parking lot and started kissing, so I knew I had a chance to win her over.

Looking back, I think the situation was probably ideal for allowing our relationship to flourish. First off, I lacked two things essential for dating—a car and money. Brenda didn't have much cash, either, and I'm not the kind of guy who would have let her pay for anything, anyway. So, other than maybe going to a movie once or twice, we basically just saw each other at the bar, and every so often I'd come over and play with the kids on the floor.

Because things were allowed to build gradually, every time I saw her I was excited. I'd show up at Wild E. Coyote's, and if she wasn't there I'd wait a couple minutes and bail. When she was there we always hung out, and we especially liked dancing to this song by the Nitty Gritty Dirt Band, "Fishin' in the Dark." It became *our song:* as soon as the first notes were played, people would look around and say, "Where're Kurt and Brenda?" and we'd be the first ones out on the floor.

The better I got to know Brenda, the more impressed I was. I liked her self-assured manner, her independence, and her strength of character. Most of all, I was struck by the force of her convictions and her willingness to stand up and fight for what she believes in rather than take the easy way out.

The ordeal with Zachary, and the divorce that followed, might have broken a weaker person. But Brenda had an incredible spirit and, it seemed to me at the time, a rather remarkable faith in God. After everything she'd been through, you would have expected her to have some serious doubts about God. And in her heart she was asking God a lot of "why" questions about all that had happened to her. On an emotional level she was still struggling to understand where those big plans were that everyone had always said God had in store for her. And yet, despite all her heartache, underneath the questions and the uncertainties there remained a solid core of bedrock beliefs to which she continued to cling. And Brenda wasn't shy about discussing and defending those beliefs, as I learned shortly after I met her.

By January, we had known each other for about three months, and the moment of truth had arrived: would she be my girlfriend, or would she get more serious with Mark? It had gotten uncomfortable, because Zachary was always calling me "Mark" by mistake, and he did the opposite with Mark on at least one occasion. I'm sure Mark wasn't too thrilled—I don't know if he even had a clue I existed before that—but when Brenda told me that Zack had called him "Kurt" by mistake, I was kind of honored.

On the couple of occasions when Brenda and I kissed outside Wild E. Coyote's, I would think, *She's leaning my way.* I was just hoping there was some way I could convince her to go against logic and be with me. Then, in January, Brenda had Jesse's first birthday party at her house and gave *me* one heck of a present: as the party was ending, Brenda got into her car and drove to Des Moines, and that night she broke up with Mark.

Now I had my first real girlfriend, and even though I didn't have a car or money and she lived with two young kids and her parents, I was loving life. It didn't take too long for me to get serious. One day that next summer I was lying on the floor with Zachary, playing that drawing game called MagnaDoodle. I drew a little flower on the screen and wrote "I love Momma" on Zachary's behalf and then underneath added, "I do, too." Zachary walked it over to Brenda, and I held my breath. The "I love you" was a big step, and I was obviously hoping Brenda would reciprocate. She erased my flower and wrote a message of her own on the screen then gave it to Zachary to bring back to me. My heart was pounding as I read her message: "I love my momma, too."

Ouch, babe.

It made sense, though, that Brenda wasn't yet ready to give her heart to me in that way, because her marriage had ended so badly. But I jumped in headfirst anyway. I'd write corny, gooey poems about Brenda and the kids and leave them on her pillow. A sample:

There is only one who has hold of my heart
She makes my life fun, she's my other part
Without her here where would I be?
I really don't know and I don't want to see
I hope you are with me through thick and through thin
Because in the end I'm sure that we'll win
Times are tough but it won't be long
'Til we're on top singing our favorite song
The song that has us growing old together
A song that makes us happy in any ol' weather
The song where we watch the kids grow up
When we see their dreams begin to erupt
Through these years our hands will continue to hold
Our passion still burning though facing the cold
I can't imagine singing without you
Or learning to love somebody new
So to me there is only one thing left to do
Something very special from me to you
A question to see if you will be mine?
I beg, pretty please, be my Valentine!

As you can see, Brenda had a pretty clear idea of where I stood. I'd romanticize our future together, asking, "Are you going to follow me when I go to the NFL?" I'm sure she was thinking, *Yeah, right,* but to her credit she never doubted me out loud.

I had gone home to Cedar Rapids during each of my three previous summers, picking up cash by renting out canoes and paddle boats at a park and every so often detasseling corn. Mostly because of Brenda, I decided to stay in Cedar Falls and work at a bank that summer before my fifth year at UNI. They loved me at the bank, partly because I was the only male teller in the state of Iowa and also because people knew I was going to be the quarterback the next fall. I had to shave every day, which was brutal because I hate razors. I had been trying to get by with a beard trimmer every few days, which is exactly what I do now—another fringe benefit of being an NFL player. To work at the bank, I also had to upgrade my wardrobe drastically, and I remember Brenda taking me to Target to get some dress shirts and ties. My math skills were pretty lousy—the balance in my teller's drawer was always off—but I had a lot of fun.

Football was around the corner, and I couldn't wait. Finally I'd get a chance to be The Man. I remember the previous season a hotshot high school receiver named Dedric Ward had come to campus on an official recruiting visit, and we'd been introduced at the gym. Instead of asking me about the school or the program, the first thing he'd said was, "Hey, are you any good? If I come here, are you gonna be able to get me the ball?" I just laughed and said, "Don't worry—I'll get you the ball." The guy hadn't even played a down, and that was the first thing he had to say? I will say this about Dedric, though: he backed it up. He was a quality receiver for us that next season, and he ended up making it to the NFL, with the New York Jets, a year before I did.

My first game as a starter was a disaster. I threw three interceptions, and we got beat by McNeese State. Then we went to play at Wyoming, a Division I-A school, a pretty huge game for us. I was playing well, and we were hanging right with them, but just before halftime I got thrown to the ground and ended up with a separated shoulder on my throwing arm. I had almost 200 passing yards at the time, and bam—that was the end of my day. It was only a slight separation, but it tightened up after we iced it down at halftime. So I watched my backup, Brett O'Donnell, come in and play pretty well. But Brett—we called him "O.D."—threw an interception late in the game and we lost 45–42. Now we were 0–2, I had a bum shoulder, and I was starting to wonder, *What have I done to deserve this?*

The nightmare continued the next week in our home game against Jacksonville State. The big scout in the Iowa area, a guy named Dan Shonka who worked for one of the scouting services used by pro teams, came to see the game. That was great except for one slight problem: I couldn't throw worth a darn. My shoulder was still bothering me, and I was just horrendous. I tried to throw a couple of corner routes, and they sailed about fifty feet in the air because I had no control. I was lobbing balls up and praying my receivers could run under them. Fortunately, the rest of the team played well, and we won the game 35–0, though I was 13 for 35 with three interceptions.

The next week my shoulder was feeling much better, and from that point on things started rolling. We won eight of our last nine games and finished first in the Gateway Conference, and I was voted the offensive player of the year. The only game we lost from then on was against Western Illinois; we scored a go-ahead touchdown with thirty-five seconds to go but got beat on a last-second field goal.

We opened the Division I-AA playoffs at Boston University, which was undefeated and ranked fourth in the country. We were beating them by two touchdowns late in the game when Dedric Ward broke free on a long route that would have given us a clinching touchdown. He was open at the five yard line, and, yes, I got him the ball—but he dropped it, right through his hands. Boston U ended up tying the game, and we went to overtime. We should have won, but our All-American kicker somehow missed an eighteen-yard field goal that would have ended it, and his attempt on our next possession was no good from thirty-two yards out. We stayed alive by blocking Boston U's field goal try, but as their kicker fell on the ball our All-American linebacker grabbed him by the face mask. They got a first down at our ten yard line and scored to win the game.

It was a crushing defeat, and I was crying my eyes out in the locker room, knowing I would never play another college game. In fact, I wasn't sure where my next game would be. I was hoping an NFL team would draft me, but I knew it would be an uphill battle. I stayed in shape during the spring, took a couple of graduate level classes, and worked in the public relations office of the UNI alumni association, still confident I'd have a future in football.

Either way, I was thrilled about my relationship with Brenda, but not everyone shared that sentiment. I'd get a lot of subtle comments from friends—*Do you really think this is going to last? Are you sure she's right for you?*—and some far more blunt opinions from my mom. She didn't like my getting serious with a woman who had so much baggage, and not only did she make her feelings known, she wasn't very nice to Brenda on a lot of occasions. I don't put too much weight in what others say, but it was especially difficult with my mom, and it stayed that way for several years.

Brenda was getting her share of questions, too. Her parents were obviously very protective of her, and the fact that she was living with them didn't help, because whenever I went over we all ended up being bunched together in such close quarters. One night Brenda and I were together on the living room couch, and let's just say we weren't fishin' in the dark. At an extremely inopportune time, her mom walked into the room. She gasped then went into the bathroom and slammed the door, and I was like Dennis Miller on *Saturday Night Live:* "That's the news and I am out of here."

CHAPTER SIX

LOST IN A SUPERMARKET

Now that I've won a Super Bowl, earned NFL MVP honors, and graced multiple covers of *Sports Illustrated,* some people wonder whether I'll get a big head and turn into yet another obnoxious sports star. You know, the guys who refer to themselves in the third person and react to mildly impressive feats as though they'd just proven the existence of alien life.

Don't worry, I don't think I'll become a jerk. Humility is only a flashback away, and one of my favorite reality checks is to remember the stretch I spent in Cedar Falls after my college career ended. During those fifteen months, I went from being a big man on campus to the guy who'd walk your groceries out to the car for you in the middle of the night. I also got brushed off by pro teams from Green Bay to Barcelona, lived in a basement, and ate meals purchased with food stamps.

Thankfully, Brenda and I stayed together, because it seemed like everyone else I encountered couldn't wait to reject me.

The succession of snubs began almost as soon as 1994 arrived. After my impressive senior season at UNI, I was hoping to catch the eye of an NFL team. There was a chance I'd get drafted, though the fact that I had been a starter for only one year of college wasn't helping. Also, I was coming from a Division I-AA program, so visibility was a problem.

The idea was to get invited to the NFL scouting combine, which is held each February in Indianapolis. The combine, essentially, is a giant meat market at which several hundred pro prospects are run through drills and subjected to various physical and mental evaluations. I signed with an agent, Jack Wirth, who told me it was his understanding I had been ranked somewhere between ninth and twelfth among draft-eligible quarterbacks. This was based on a consensus of scouts across the country who evaluated players throughout the season. Since twenty-four quarterbacks would be invited to the combine in Indianapolis, I liked my odds.

Physically, I thought I was good enough to play in the NFL. I just needed a break, and I hoped I'd get it in Indy. I was excited about the opportunity to display my skills and open some eyes. I started watching videotapes from previous combines, working on all the passing drills so I could be as impressive as possible.

Naturally, I got skipped over.

Now my only chance was that some NFL team would come to campus and run me through a private workout. And four of them did: over the next several weeks people from Green Bay, Cincinnati, Tampa Bay, and Atlanta arrived to watch me throw. Coaches from other teams came out to watch a couple of my teammates, and I ended up throwing some for them, too.

Still, as my college coaches had determined long before, I'm not a practice player. I needed a chance to show what I could do in a real game, under fire.

So with stars in my eyes and a bounce in my step, I boarded a plane for Mississippi and prepared to launch my pro career. I was headed to a poor man's Senior Bowl—a postcollegiate all-star game for fringe players like me hoping to sneak onto an NFL team's roster. I don't remember the actual name of the game, but that's probably just as well.

You could call it the Fiasco Bowl.

Just as the name suggests, this was the most disorganized

event in the history of football. It was a week-long affair that took place at Jackson State University, where Walter Payton, the NFL's all-time career rushing leader, had gone to school. Right away I could tell it was extremely low budget. I remember we had to take a long walk across an unused field just to get to practice, and nobody seemed to know what was going on once we got there.

As advertised, there were a lot of scouts watching—at least until game day, when they suddenly disappeared. That meant we had to impress the scouts during practice, which was unfortunate, because our practice sessions were a joke. All the coaches would do was hold up play cards and say, "Okay, let's run these." None of us really had any idea what the heck was going on, and it showed.

There were other problems as well. As players, we had to pay our own way to get down there, and the organizers were supposed to reimburse us. But when we showed up, it became clear there was no way that would happen. They told us our reimbursement checks would be tied to the size of the crowd, and judging from the operation a large haul from the gate was not likely. So now we were losing money and prestige in one fell swoop.

Sure enough, come game day there were more marching band members in the stands than there were spectators. Thankfully, only a couple of scouts stuck around for the game, because it was even worse than the practices. On the first play, the coaches called a pass, and I dropped back and got drilled by an untouched defensive end. My left tackle helped me up and said, "Uh, sorry. I didn't know if the play was a run or a pass."

At that point, I was just hoping to escape without getting injured. I made it through the game, and then a couple of the other guys and I decided to drive back to Iowa to save money, since it was coming out of our own pockets. One of them, Matt Eyde, who had been a backup quarterback at Iowa, ended up playing in the Arena League for a couple of years. I have no idea what happened to any of the other players who had the misfortune of playing in that so-called game.

In late April the NFL held its seven-round draft, and I knew there wasn't a very good chance I'd get picked. The first day, when the first two or three rounds are held, was a total write-off, but on day two I drove with Brenda to my mom's house in Cedar Rapids and turned on the TV, hoping somebody would pick me.

It was one of those nerve-racking days you always hear about from people in that position: a lot of pacing around, not much talking, anticipation every time the phone rings followed shortly by a letdown. My mom was at work, so it was just me and Brenda there, and every so often my agent would call. Most of the time the only sound in the house was my walking back and forth across the creaky wooden floors, which was sort of eerie.

The draft ended, and I still hadn't been picked. Now my best hope was to sign with someone as an undrafted free agent. A few minutes later my agent called again and gave me the lowdown: Tampa Bay, which had drafted Trent Dilfer with the sixth overall pick, was willing to sign me, as was Cincinnati, but there would be little or no signing bonus from either team. San Diego and Green Bay were each offering $5,000 to sign, and at the time, believe me, that was an extremely significant amount.

So it came down to Green Bay and San Diego, and this was the major difference: San Diego was inviting four other free-agent quarterbacks to camp, whereas I was the only quarterback in my position being brought in by Green Bay. The catch was, the other three quarterbacks on the Packers' roster were Brett Favre, Ty Detmer, and Mark Brunell, and their spots looked pretty set.

Looking back, you could make a case that San Diego was the better call. The Chargers ended up going to the Super Bowl that year with Stan Humphries, but he lasted only a couple of seasons after that, and they've been looking for a quarterback ever since. Meanwhile, Brett Favre went on to be a three-time league MVP, Mark Brunell became an All-Pro after getting traded to the Jacksonville Jaguars, and Ty Detmer, who had won the Heisman Trophy at BYU, has been a starter for Philadelphia and Cleveland.

Still, Green Bay seemed like the better opportunity at the

time, because you never know what's going to happen in training camp—someone might get hurt, or if the team likes you they can cut you from the active roster but bring you back as a member of the practice squad, which gives you a chance to stay with the program and develop as a player. The Chargers had so many people trying to claw their way onto the roster, including, of all people, Trent Green, who had been their third-stringer as a rookie the previous season and ended up getting cut that August. The deciding factor was that I'd at least get an opportunity to show what I could do with Green Bay, though it turns out I was mistaken.

Shortly after I signed, the team held a minicamp in Arizona, and right away I got a taste of the good life. When my plane landed at Sky Harbor Airport in Phoenix, I walked off the jetway and saw a man holding a sign that said, "Warner." He grabbed my luggage and led me to a waiting limousine. I tried to play it off, but this was the first time I'd ever been in a limo! By the end of the drive I couldn't resist turning on the TV and playing with all the buttons.

Once practice began, reality set in. I quickly got the unsettling feeling that I was in over my head. Mike Holmgren, the Packers' head coach, is one of the game's great offensive minds, and he ran a complex version of the West Coast Offense. It was a lot to try to master right off the bat, especially for a guy who had been a starter for only one year at a small college. So picking up the offense was difficult, and even though I was confident that my physical skills were impressive, I was kind of overwhelmed.

There's a story that has come out from that first minicamp about a moment when I supposedly was too scared to call a play. One of the coaches—probably Steve Mariucci, who was the quarterbacks coach and is now the head man at San Francisco—told me to go run a certain play during a drill, and I refused to enter the huddle because I wasn't sure how to execute it. I don't remember that having happened, but Brett and a couple other people have recounted the story, so it's probably true. I guess I was so nervous at that minicamp that I was afraid to make a fool of myself. What I do remember is that I flew home thinking, *Man, you've got a lot to learn.*

Nevertheless, life was looking up. I went out and bought the first vehicle I'd ever owned, a '93 GMC Jimmy two-door, using part of the signing bonus as a down payment. The car, of course, was green, for Green Bay. That May, when I finally went through commencement ceremonies at UNI, I had "Go Packers" written in masking tape on the top of my graduation cap.

In July I drove the Jimmy to Green Bay and reported to training camp. I'll never forget the first day I entered the locker room and saw what life in the big leagues was like. First I went in and got fitted for shoes, and they gave you as many pairs as you needed. That was a change; at UNI, you had to have a hole in the bottom of your shoes before they'd give you another pair. I'd hear guys on the Packers yell to the equipment manager, "Hey, I need some gloves," or, "Let me get one of those hats," and, presto, those items would appear instantaneously.

Of all the guys on the team, Reggie White, the Minister of Defense, was the player who awed me the most. The first time we met, we were standing side by side at urinals outside the locker room shower. I looked up and saw one of the great defensive linemen in NFL history, not to mention a strong Christian who has done so much to help disadvantaged children. I was so nervous I almost forgot to take care of business. The weird thing was, it seemed like every time I had to go to the bathroom, Reggie was right there standing next to me. Our bladders were synchronized exactly.

Once I went out to practice, the stands were packed with Packers backers. I figured the attendance would drop off after the first day, but if anything the crowds got bigger. You'd have people pressed up against the fence surrounding the practice field, and if you threw a nice pass in a drill there'd be a huge roar from the fans. I remember thinking, *Does anybody work around here?* because the place was always overflowing with adults on weekdays.

By now I had studied the offense and felt like I knew it pretty well. Physically, I felt I could hold my own with Brett and Mark and Ty, and I waited for my chance to prove it.

It never came. I didn't play in either of the first two exhibition games, and practice repetitions were extremely hard to come by. When it came to seven-on-seven drills, which are the best judge of a quarterback's skills, I got only fourteen reps in the five weeks I was there. Fourteen reps. I actually counted because I couldn't believe how little they were using me.

A couple of weeks into camp I was starting to get the picture: the question wasn't whether I'd be cut, it was when. And, more important, whether they would then sign me to the practice squad and keep me around for a year. Back then you got a couple of thousand dollars a week for being on the practice squad. More significant, it would have been good for my career to remain in that atmosphere.

During my time with Green Bay, I dealt mostly with Coach Mariucci, but every once in a while Coach Holmgren would come over and ask me how I was doing. I thought it was pretty cool that he acknowledged me because most of the time I was basically an invisible man during practice and meetings. So Coach Holmgren's small talk would give me a glimmer of hope, and other coaches and players were telling me that they thought I'd picked up the offense very quickly, and I felt good about that. It's just that I never got a chance to show anybody what I could really do.

I'd always assumed that once you got to the professional level, the best players were the ones who made the team and the guys who got cut simply weren't as good. But, as I came to find out, that wasn't necessarily the case. There were people who made the team simply based on physical potential, and others who sneaked onto the roster because of circumstance—say, a bunch of guys at their position got injured.

Obviously, I faced an uphill battle trying to beat out guys like Brett Favre, Mark Brunell, and Ty Detmer. But the weird thing was, I came away thinking that in terms of skill level I might've been the best all-around quarterback of the bunch. Each of them had strengths that I couldn't match: Mark could run like a deer, Brett had the strongest arm, and Ty was as smart as a coach. But when you put everything together, I felt my total package compared favorably with all of them.

Still, there was something about Brett that transcended all the physical skills you might measure. Even in that context, I could tell he just had a knack for being able to pull out a victory under rough circumstances. Something about him was special; no matter how bad things seemed, he could find a way to win. I remember telling friends of mine, "This guy's going to be one of the best quarterbacks in the league, you mark my words." They were, like, "Yeah right." Back then, Brett was known for being reckless and throwing too many interceptions. Three MVPs and two Super Bowls later, my friends knew exactly what I'd meant.

By the middle of August, I started flinching every time the phone rang in my dorm room at St. Norbert's College. I wasn't alone. Except for the guys whose jobs were safe, every one of us was dreading the phone call from "The Turk," the team official assigned to tell players they'd been released. Sure enough, just before our third exhibition game, one of the personnel guys called my dorm room and said, "Come downstairs, and bring your playbook." A couple minutes later I was officially released, and while the rest of the team went out to practice, I loaded up my stuff and cleaned out my locker.

I wrote a note to Coach Mariucci and the other three quarterbacks saying, "Thanks, it's been fun," and got ready to hit the road. One of the equipment guys asked, "Hey, don't you want to take your shoes?" I was blown away. For a second there, I was actually excited, thinking, *Yeah, I got cut, but at least I got these cool shoes for free.*

From what I understand, Coach Mariucci hadn't even been told that the team was releasing me, and it wasn't until he saw my empty locker that he learned the news. He called me a week later and said, "I didn't know anything about it. I wish I could've been the one to have told you." I was hoping he'd make it up to me by offering to sign me to the practice squad, but it didn't happen. Teams can have up to five practice squad players, but the Packers kept only three because of their salary cap situation, and I wasn't one of them.

Overall, I'd still say it was a positive experience. For one thing, the time with the team gave me confidence that from a physical standpoint I was good enough to compete at that level. Also, Mooch—that's Coach Mariucci's nickname—and the guys were an extremely close-knit group, and I loved being around them. They were all great people and had a lot of fun. Brett likes to tease everyone—he and the others would call me "Chachi," after the *Happy Days* character, because they thought I looked like him, and "Pop," as in Pop Warner—but it was all in good fun. Those guys actually still use those names: Coach Mariucci called me "Chachi" before we played the 49ers in early October, Ty called me "Pop" when we played Cleveland, and Mark called me "Pop" at the Pro Bowl.

I read a quote from Coach Mariucci recently that said I wasn't ready for the NFL back then. On one level, I understand his reasoning. At that point I had only one year of college experience, and I probably couldn't have stepped in and performed the way I ended up performing in 1999. I didn't know Green Bay's offense like the back of my hand, and I certainly experienced a lot over the next five years that helped prepare me for my chance with the Rams.

That said, my second reaction is this: of course he has to say I wasn't ready because they cut me, and now that decision doesn't look so good. It's easy to say I needed more seasoning, but how could anyone really have known when all I got was fourteen reps at practice? How can you tell what someone's capable of doing when he doesn't get an opportunity to show he's ready?

As I said, I love Coach Mariucci, so I'm not trying to take a shot at him. Besides, he's certainly not alone. After I started doing some good things with the Rams, a lot of former coaches and personnel men—like Terry Allen, my coach at Northern Iowa—were asked why I didn't get more of a chance to prove myself earlier in my career. I've heard all sorts of excuses, and some people have come out and admitted, "Well, maybe we should have played him more." It's frustrating when people judge you without ever giving you a chance to change their perceptions. If, at any level, I had gotten an opportunity to play but then performed unspectacularly, I could see that. But in college, for example, I'd go out and shine in our spring games yet still end up riding the bench. Things like that are really difficult.

I've given it a lot of thought, and I'm still not sure why coaches wouldn't just give me a chance. I don't know if there was some way I came across that caused them to say, "We can't trust this guy," or what, but it has been a common theme throughout my career. And while I confess it's a great feeling to go out there and prove people wrong, that's not what drives me to succeed. If I'm playing, say, the 49ers, I don't sit there thinking, *I've got to show Coach Mariucci he made a mistake,* because that's not me. All in all, I'm pretty happy with the way things worked out and where I am today.

Of course, back in August of 1994 I was pretty devastated. When the Packers cut me I suddenly had to confront my future, beginning with finding a place to live and figuring out a way to make my car payments. It was like, *Today is the first day of the rest of your life,* and I had no idea what the rest of my life would entail.

Giving up on football wasn't an option, so I tried to come up with a plan that would put me in the best position to make it back to the NFL. I wanted to stay involved with football, so I figured I'd go back to Northern Iowa and do the coaching thing as a volunteer graduate assistant. That would allow me to keep working out on campus, maybe throw a little, and watch some film. I know that might sound pretty pathetic, like I was this has-been who couldn't let go of his past glories and kept hanging out on campus. But I never felt that way, and I think people at UNI understood my situation and knew I still had a chance to do some things on the next level.

I had my immediate sights on the World League—now called NFL Europe—which serves as sort of a farm league for NFL teams while fanning pro football's popularity overseas. The World

League plays its games in the springtime, so its draft was in the fall. This time I was pretty optimistic. The Packers had written a letter of recommendation on my behalf, and my agent made it sound like it was pretty much of a lock that I'd get picked.

Nobody televises the World League draft, but I still waited by the phone on draft day—and again I got passed over. The Rhein Fire didn't want me, and neither did the Barcelona Dragons or the London Monarchs or anyone else. I was surprised and scared. Now I had to get a job, and fast.

First, I solved my housing dilemma by moving in with Brenda and the kids. It probably says something about where each of was spiritually at the time that neither Brenda nor I had any serious moral qualms about this. I think we both viewed it more as a matter of convenience than as an indication of a more serious commitment to our relationship.

Unfortunately, she didn't have her own place at the time, so "home" was the basement of her parents' house. Basically, it was just one medium-sized room, and a totally unfinished one at that. The floor was concrete, and it was really cold down there, especially in late fall and winter. We always had to wear sweats and socks, and if you spent any amount of time down there during the day you had to have a blanket wrapped around you. It was also really, really dark; we had a lamp or two, but that was the only light.

It was an old house, and every time anyone moved you could hear every squeaky footstep. When my girlfriend was the one moving around, earplugs were in order. I've always kidded Brenda, the former marine, that if she were an American Indian her name would be "Heavyfoot."

Brenda's mom had done a nice job of decorating, giving it that country look, but she could do only so much. She tried to cordon off a corner and make it a pseudo–living room area, and she brought down a nine-inch TV. The thing was, it was so cold down there that we'd always have to go upstairs to watch their TV if there was a show we wanted to see.

There were also spider webs everywhere, and you had to walk through the laundry room to get to the bathroom. Other than that, it was a pretty ideal spot.

Since none of us ever wanted to spend much time down in the basement, we tended to ignore what was going on down there. One morning I remember hearing Brenda scream, "Kurt!" and I ran down to see what the fuss was about. Zachary, who was about four years old at the time, had gotten hold of my beard trimmer and shaved his head. Well, he'd shaved *parts* of his head. There were a bunch of holes all over what had been his hair, and Brenda gave him a buzz cut—the style he favors to this day.

One of the reasons we rationalized living together was because Brenda's mom was about to have foot surgery, and that meant she wouldn't be able to walk for at least four weeks. Brenda was going to nursing school at Hawkeye Community College during the day, and her dad was working, so that meant somebody had to watch the kids in the mornings and afternoons. That somebody was me. This made my employment situation a bit tricky. I needed a job that would allow me to watch the kids all day, work out, and help with football practice in the late afternoons.

It didn't take a bachelor's degree for me to figure out what that meant: night shift.

I applied to some hotels in town, thinking I'd be pretty good as a night desk clerk, but nobody was hiring. Then I tried the Hy-Vee, which was a twenty-four-hour grocery store. That's when I got my infamous job stocking shelves and engaging in other glamorous tasks like bagging groceries and helping customers load them into their cars.

Talk about a humbling experience. That's just about as humbled as you can get, to go from being in an NFL camp, where you're treated like a king and have a contract for a couple hundred thousand dollars if you make the team, to stocking shelves for $5.50 an hour, which was minimum wage.

This was when I started picking up on the "He's a has-been" vibe.

It wasn't so much that people would come right out and insult me, but I could tell exactly what they were thinking. A lot of customers knew who I was, and sometimes they wouldn't do the greatest job of concealing their surprise. It'd be like, "Hey, Kurt. What are you *doing?*" Or, "I didn't know *you* worked here." I'm pretty sure it was innocent, that they weren't trying to make me feel bad, but it came off as, "What kind of loser goes from the NFL to stocking shelves?"

Then there were my friends, many of whom didn't help matters by dropping in to visit me at work. Again, they didn't overtly mock me—I think they realized that I was humbled enough already—but they had a little fun with the situation. We had this drive-up window, and sometimes I was the guy who had to push the groceries outside and load them into customers' cars. It was always a treat when you'd bring the groceries outside and someone you knew was waiting there with a grin.

Since this was in the middle of the night, we got our share of drunks, some of whom would come to the drive-up window and ask for kisses or silly things like that. One night some rowdy hecklers pulled up and started honking their horn like crazy, and when the drive-through worker sent me outside to deliver their groceries, I cringed and bit my lip. When I got outside it was even worse than I imagined. Brenda's friend Shawn was driving the car, and in the backseat were a pair of hecklers: Brenda and her friend Stacy. The two women were hooting and laughing, and I laughed along with them. But truth be known, it made me feel like an even bigger dork than usual.

Like I said, it was humbling. I had to wear this blue shirt with a name tag: "Hello, my name is Kurt." I had to sweep the floors, and if something broke I had to mop up the mess.

The work was pretty tedious. You'd start out the night by going to one of the aisles and pulling out the little shelves at the bottom of each food display. Little shelves? Allow me to explain. Most people don't even know these shelves exist; they're like minidrawers below the lowest shelf, and they're pretty well hidden.

I was shopping with Brenda one time a few years after my stint at Hy-Vee, and she was looking for some spice that she needed, but there weren't any more containers on the shelf. So she said, "Darn, they're all out," and I said, "Actually, they're not." Lo and behold, I pulled out that bottom shelf and found a bunch of extras. I thought I was pretty cool, but instead of being happy that I found the spice, Brenda was totally embarrassed that I knew about the secret stash.

Anyway, you'd start out the shift by trying to move as much of the stuff from the hidden shelves onto the regular shelves as you could. Then you'd bring out a bunch of random stuff from the back room on a big pallet, drop it into the middle of the aisle, and start grabbing boxes, cutting them open, and putting the items where they belonged. You'd finish the night by doing what we called "facing"—stacking everything two deep on each shelf and putting the excess back into the hidden shelves.

Other than, say, a broken-mayonnaise-jar disaster, the hardest thing for me was trying to stack small items with my large hands. I still get queasy at the thought of having to handle those tiny cans of mushrooms or the maraschino cherries. I'd try to stack those little cans, and I'd always end up knocking down the whole display and having to start over. I was much more comfortable with large cans of stewed tomatoes or the big, plastic juice jugs. But those mushrooms just killed me.

The experience wasn't all bad, though. I enjoyed my co-workers, and we had a lot of fun with the whole football thing. I certainly kept my arm in shape, because the managers were pretty loose. They probably felt sorry for me, being a frustrated quarterback and all, so they let us get away with quite a bit of simulated football activity.

We'd play catch with toilet paper rolls and marshmallows and gummy bears, and there was also this Nerf football display, so you can imagine what happened with those. When we weren't throwing passes to each other, we threw food *at* one another. Anything that came loose—candy, cookies, peanuts—was fair game, and you had to be on your toes. If you knew one of your co-workers was stocking in the next aisle, because you heard the cans moving or saw his head, you'd start lobbing things over the top. Or if you were really ambitious, you'd run around to the front of the aisle and drill the guy. You always had to clean up your mess afterward, so you had to pick your spots.

Breaks were also a lot of fun because we set up this makeshift goalpost in the back room, and we'd take turns booting field goals. I'm not sure how much of this was inspired by my presence and how much of it was just what those guys did to amuse themselves, but it sure kept things lively. The breaks were only fifteen minutes long, so mostly we'd use the time to shove some food into our mouths. We didn't so much decide what to eat as let things develop: whatever items broke open during our shift were fair game. Then again, come to think of it, we might *accidentally* drop something, or catch it on a sharp surface and tear it, if it looked appetizing enough.

Tragically, a lot of Oreo cookie packages and sugary cereal boxes fell by the wayside during my shifts.

I haven't talked to any of my co-workers lately; they're probably the only people from my past who haven't called me since I started playing for the Rams. Back then, they'd talk to me about football, asking me stuff like, "What are you going to do next? Where are you going to play?" I'd say, "I don't know. I'm hoping to get another NFL tryout." I'm sure some of those guys were thinking, *There's no way this guy's ever going back to the NFL.* You could hear the doubt in their voices or the way they'd always ask, "If you don't make it back, then what are you going to do?"

It's not like I can blame them for having doubts. I mean, really, who knew? I certainly wasn't looking down at those guys and their situations, either, because I was darn glad to get that $5.50 an hour. I remember being too embarrassed to tell my co-workers about the calls I'd gotten from the Arena Football League. There had been talk of a new team starting up in Iowa, and league officials had called me several times to see if I was interested. I'd blow them off and say, "I'll get back to you," because at that point I had no interest whatsoever. I had seen a couple of games on ESPN at, like, 2 A.M., and it looked sort of low budget and strange.

It was a crazy, crazy time for me, especially during that month when Brenda's mom was off her feet. First, there was the matter of sleep, or lack thereof. I'm not the world's greatest snoozer—even now, I spend a lot of wakeful hours in the middle of the night, especially during football season—but this was pretty extreme. I'd watch the kids until Brenda got home from school in the afternoon, then I'd go up to campus and sneak in a workout before practice. I'd get home just before dinner, and then I had to start work at the grocery store at about eight. My shift varied; sometimes I'd get off as early as three in the morning, sometimes not until seven, but either way I had to get up with the kids by seven-thirty or eight, so there wasn't much of a window there.

Even when good chunks of sleep were available, I sometimes chose to stay awake, because that was the only decent time I could spend with Brenda. The worst stretches, usually, were during those evening hours when I'd be drowsy and thinking, "I can't handle this." But then I'd go to work and get my motor running again, and I'd be fine—other than nodding off at the wheel on occasion. I also remember having to work the holidays; I went straight from Thanksgiving dinner to the Hy-Vee.

Brenda and I were hanging tough, yet there was a lot of stress, beginning with family politics. My relationship with Brenda's parents was pretty good by that time. They obviously loved their daughter and treated her like the twenty-five-year-old independent mother of two that she was. Any concerns they might have had about Brenda's and my living arrangement they kept to themselves. They seemed to like me and always treated me with respect. But the situation was still strained: we were totally cramped in that house, and of course I didn't feel comfortable asserting myself in that environment. It was tough because I had been relatively independent in college, and now I felt like I was tiptoeing around. I always felt a need to help out, and I never felt like I could really relax because it was their place, not mine.

Meanwhile, Brenda's relationship with my mom was just awful. I wanted so badly for the two of them to get to know each other because I was sure that once my mom saw what Brenda was all about, she'd love her almost as much as I did. Looking back, though, I think the problem was that my mom really didn't try to get to know her. I'd bring Brenda over to her house in Cedar Rapids, and my mom wouldn't ask her anything about herself or include her in conversations. Brenda would say, "Sue, this is a beautiful picture. Where did you get it?" And my mom would answer, "Well, I got it at the—Kurt, did you know that I got this picture at the so-and-so . . ." Then she'd be talking to me, and Brenda would be out of the conversation. Basically, my mom didn't go out of her way for Brenda at all, and when the kids would come over she didn't treat them badly or anything, but she never gave us the sense that it was okay to have them around.

It was extremely uncomfortable for me, because I was getting it from both sides, and I was the one who had everything to lose. My mom was so important to me, and now I had the two women I loved fighting each other. Even worse, at least during that stage, they were waging their battles through me instead of directly facing off with each other.

In one ear I'd have my mom saying, "I don't know if she's the right one for you." Then, the next minute, Brenda would pull me aside and say in my other ear, "I don't deserve to be treated like this; I'm never coming back to this house."

Sounds fun, doesn't it? If you've ever been in a situation like this, you know exactly how disconcerting it is to be caught in the crossfire.

After a while, I came to the realization that I believed in Brenda and what she was all about, and I was going to stand by her. If that meant having a tough relationship with my mom, so be it. I felt like

I had to make a choice, and I chose Brenda. So for a time we seldom went to see my mom.

We've all made a lot of progress since that time, and I hope the time will come when they each can appreciate the wonderful things I see and love about each of them. For so long my mom was such a big part of my life and my drive to succeed in sports. Now that I've reached the culmination I think it's hard for her to let go, to realize she's not the integral force in my life. That, of course, is a distinction that belongs to Brenda and our kids, as it should. The thing is, when our kids become adults, I think Brenda will have a similarly hard time letting go. She and my mom are alike in some ways. Both made enormous sacrifices to raise their families and forged incredibly strong bonds with their children, and neither one is shy about voicing her opinions.

I think part of the conflict back then was because my mom saw my relationship with Brenda as being undesirable for her son, given the divorce and kids. But eventually, once she saw how in love we were and how special our bond was, my mother was finally able to get over her protective instincts and start treating Brenda like a daughter. Early on, though, I wondered at times if they'd ever be able to get along.

To add to the family strain, Brenda and I had chronic money problems. She was living off student loans, and every so often over the next couple of years she'd get ambitious, find some Section 8 housing, and move into her own apartment with the kids. That would last maybe a few months, and then she'd realize she couldn't make ends meet and move back in with her parents. She also lived car to car: she'd buy a some old wreck for about $500, figuring that her dad was a decent enough handyman to keep it running for that semester or until she could get her next student loan. It was a crapshoot as to when it would break down, and it led to some embarrassing situations. This one time when I was still in college, I picked up another UNI player, Jeff Stovall, in Brenda's Nissan Sentra, and we drove to a school in nearby Waterloo to read books to some of the local children. On the way back we started driving up a somewhat steep hill, and the car began wheezing and losing power. If an ice cream truck had been on the same street, it would have blown by us. Eventually the car conked out, but we were at least able to turn it around and make it back to the school, albeit at a maximum speed of ten miles per hour.

A lot of people have a stigma about being on welfare or other government assistance, but I never did and never will. Brenda was eligible for food stamps back then, and it didn't bother me one bit. I didn't know how they worked. All I knew was you could use them to get food without having to spend any money and that I would eat some of that food, so I thought it was pretty cool. I know there were times it was a blow to Brenda's pride. She'd get up to the cash register with her groceries, and you could see people checking out what she was buying. Like, if she wanted to splurge and treat me or her parents with a steak, they might look down their noses or shake their heads. Or if she bought candy, the person at the register might give her a look. It was like she had to buy a bunch of ramen noodles—something really, really cheap like that—or she was being irresponsible.

Some people tend to romanticize the days when they didn't have much money, but, trust me, it wasn't that great in our case. We're not people who need a bunch of wealth to be happy. Still, it definitely helps when you're at least above the poverty line.

How romantic does this sound? At the height of our financial struggles, we drove around in this big, old green jalopy that doubled as a shelter for wayward mice. We know this because one time when we were vacuuming out the trunk a dead mouse nearly got sucked into the vacuum cleaner. Not only was the car filled with a pervasive dead animal smell, you could actually hear the little buggers running around inside the front paneling or wherever they hung out. We used to pound on the dashboard to scare them, and they'd be quiet for a while, though a few minutes later we'd detect them in a new location. This was a car, by the way, that died every time it made a left turn, so we had to come up with creative routes in which we went only straight or turned right.

Ah, there are so many warm and fuzzy memories. One time we moved from a low-income apartment to a rental house, and chose the coldest day of the year to do it. In the middle of a blizzard, with snow up to the tops of the tires, my car finally died—with the kids in the back and no phone in the new apartment. Eventually some friends who were helping us showed up and drove us over to pick up some more stuff. Not every day was as dark as that one, but there were plenty that came close.

I had to come up with a better plan. I had blown off all those overtures from the Arena League, thinking, *No way, that's a last resort.* As winter dragged on and the right-turn-only reality took its toll, I began to lose my bravado. The next time the Arena folks called, I wasn't so dismissive. It was March, and I had been working at the Hy-Vee for six months.

Last resort had become first resort.

CHAPTER SEVEN

BIG HEAD KURT

Back in the summer of 1994, when I got released by the Green Bay Packers, it seemed like the worst thing that ever happened to me. Looking back, however, I now realize something even more distasteful could have gone down.

What if the Packers *hadn't* released me and I had gone on to become a star? I shudder to think about what my life would be like now.

Very quickly I would have turned into a falling star, because five years before my 1999 season with the Rams I wasn't mentally, emotionally, or spiritually prepared to handle success. It would have been a nightmare, not just for me but for everyone around me. I know this because, on a smaller scale, my first taste of fame as a pro football player turned me into a guy who thought he was much too cool for school.

Once I got out of the grocery store and back on my feet, I ended up becoming a pretty good player for the Iowa Barnstormers of the Arena Football League. It may not sound like I hit the big time, but in Iowa that team was the closest thing people had to a major pro sports franchise. Around Des Moines, where the Barnstormers were based, I started getting a decent amount of attention. And, to be honest, I ate it up.

At that stage of my life I wanted to succeed, but for all the wrong reasons. I wanted to show everybody how great I was, and—I'll admit it—I liked the star treatment. As humbled as I had been by having to stock shelves for six months, it wasn't long before I started strutting around like God's gift to football—and I use that term intentionally, because I was as out of touch with the Lord as I've ever been.

I abandoned my values, surrendered all perspective, and in the process very nearly lost the people closest to my heart.

Before I tell you what a dufus I was, let me bring you up to speed. After months of blowing off the Arena Football people, I finally began embracing the possibility of playing for the Barnstormers, who were starting up as an expansion franchise in the spring of 1995.

In March, before I signed a contract or even agreed to play, some Barnstormers officials asked me and a bunch of the other prospective players to attend a little promotional shindig in Des Moines. The event took place on the same day that Brenda had to travel to Des Moines to take her nursing boards. That meant we got to make the two-hour drive together and stay two nights in a complimentary hotel room. That alone was worth the trip; up to that point, the best accommodations we'd ever enjoyed were of the Motel 6 variety. This was a Ramada Inn. We were living large.

The next day Brenda went off to take her exam, and I reported to Vet's Auditorium, our eventual home field. This was the same venue in which I had suffered that crushing defeat to Jumping Joe and his Pella High mates in the state basketball tournament six years earlier, and it required a whole new configuration for Arena ball, which featured a field fifty yards long, eighty-five feet wide, and bordered by four-foot-high sideline barriers made of high-density foam rubber. The only problem was, at the time of the event the setup was far from finished. There were no walls up, just two sets of bleachers that bordered a crude AstroTurf® field. But the Barnstormers had invited a bunch of sponsors down, so we had to put on a show, and the prospective players suited up and began staging a makeshift practice. Then they had us split into two groups and play a sort of ragtag exhibition game, which was a nice idea, except we weren't prepared for that kind of contact.

The harsh thing was, this guy named Jose Jefferson, a receiver that I had buddied up to that day and the night before, ended up tearing his Achilles tendon during the exhibition.

Brenda had already finished her boards and had shown up to watch the proceedings. When Jose went down, there were no doctors around and she went running over to tend to his injury. At that point I was thinking, *She'd better pass her boards because otherwise I can see the malpractice lawsuit.*

Jose was a track guy, and there's no guarantee that he would have made the team, but getting an injury in that context was just brutal. Though the guy tried to rehab the injury and hung around the team for the next year, he never played football again.

Shortly after that the Barnstormers offered me a contract. By then I had gotten rid of my agent, so I did the deal on my own. There wasn't much room for negotiation; they had a standard base salary for everyone and a formula for extra cash payoffs based on performance incentives. For example, you might get $100 extra for every touchdown or a $200 bonus for a 300-yard passing game. It made for some interesting moments during games that were otherwise decided; a lot of players got pretty good at doing math in their heads. I was getting a little more than $1,000 a game, and, believe me, I wasn't complaining, because it sure beat stocking shelves for minimum wage.

The team also paid for an apartment in Des Moines, which I shared with another player, kicker Aaron Price. But when Aaron got cut his replacement, Mike Black, became my new roommate. Right away it was clear we had a Felix Unger–Oscar Madison thing going. Mike was the neat freak, à la Felix: his clothes were on hangers that were spaced an inch apart, and his shoes were stacked to perfection. My clothes were from Target, but he was a total pretty boy: he had all these silk shirts he would dry-clean after each wearing, and he was obsessive about making his skin as bronze as David Hasselhoff's, even if that meant going to a tanning salon. You can imagine how much he loved it when Brenda would come down with her two young kids and lay the place to waste.

Worst of all, the guy was a serial dust buster. Every morning at seven o'clock sharp, Mike took out a vacuum cleaner and started attacking the carpet. He apparently wasn't bothered by the fact that I was trying to sleep. He'd just go right on vacuuming while I buried my face in the pillow. The great thing was, we ended up becoming good friends in spite of ourselves. Just like Oscar and Felix, I guess.

Brenda passed her boards and landed a nursing job at a long-term care center in Cedar Falls, which meant she could afford to get her own place. But now that I was in Des Moines, we were mostly restricted to seeing each other on weekends, usually at my place. Right before Brenda was about to visit for the first time, before I had a roommate, I freaked out because the furniture in my apartment was absolutely disgusting. The team had been given a bunch of stuff from a Holiday Inn that had flooded, and even by my low standards it was unsuitable. So I told one of the Barn-stormers' officials, "You've got to get me some better furniture; there's no way I'm having my girlfriend and her kids see this garbage."

The team agreed, but it took a few days, so the first time Brenda and the kids showed up the apartment was absolutely bare. I remember that for the first meal we had there together we spread a blanket on the floor and sat around and ate off it. When it was time for bed, we spread out on the same floor and covered ourselves with the same blanket. We were thinking, *What in the heck have we gotten ourselves into?*

Soon my employers were looking at me and wondering the same thing.

There were two exhibition games before the start of the regular season, and our coach, John Gregory, named me the starting quarterback. I was a little nervous because the Arena game was so much different from what I'd been used to my whole life. There are only eight players on each team, you pass on almost every play, and the dimensions of the field are small. Plus, the padded walls are part of the field, and everything happens so fast. It's like watching football on one of those old, sped-up newsreel clips. You don't have much time to go through your progressions or dance around in the pocket. You just drop back, make a quick decision, and get rid of the ball.

In theory, I knew I could do well in such an environment, because accuracy and staying cool under pressure are two of my strong points. But when we traveled to St. Louis, of all places, for the first exhibition game, I had no idea what awaited me.

The Kiel Center was a house of horrors, and I was just horrendous. The speed of the game totally overwhelmed me, and I abandoned my fundamentals and froze up like a fifteen-year-old on a date with Ashley Judd. My receivers would break their routes, and I'd be back in the pocket, waiting to figure out where to throw it. I remember coming off the field at one point thinking, *I'm terrible. Just awful. There's no way I can do this.* In practice things hadn't seemed that fast, but now I had serious doubts about whether I could handle the speed of the game.

It turns out I wasn't alone. I didn't know it at the time, but I read something this year that suggested there was talk in the front office about cutting me because I just looked so lost out there. Who would think they'd consider cutting their starting quarterback instead of just demoting him? That seems a little drastic, but I guess I was that lousy.

We had this star receiver named Willis Jacox who was real close to Coach Gregory because Willis had played for him up in Canada. From what I heard long after the fact, Willis, who was an older guy, went into Coach Gregory's office and said, "This guy's no good. We've got to get somebody else in there." I guess Coach Gregory ended up telling him he wanted to give me a little bit more time, which was great, because I certainly wasn't the only one stinking it up.

At that early stage our whole team was awful. We had been practicing together only a couple of weeks, and those practices had been shoddy. We held them outside, on grass instead of AstroTurf®, with waist-high hay bales bordering the field to simulate the retaining wall. So guys would go out for passes, make tough sideline catches, and then flip headfirst over the hay bales. The whole thing was just goofy.

Our second exhibition game was in Hartford, Connecticut, and while I wasn't great, I definitely showed some improvement. I actually did a couple of good things out there that caught the coach's eye, and I was able to keep my job for the season opener, which was in Milwaukee against the Mustangs. When I took the field for the first time that night, it was like somebody flipped a switch and turned on the lights. All of a sudden I wasn't freaked out by the speed, and I understood our scheme enough to get the ball to the right people. We ended up winning, 69–61, and I was named the MVP of the game.

After that, things started rolling for me and the team. I adjusted to the initial shock, and from then on it seemed like football, rather than some alien activity. We ended up with a 7–5 record, which was good enough to get into the playoffs. No one gave us much of a shot because we were playing the Arizona Rattlers, who were the defending champions, at their place in Phoenix. But we hung tough, and with time running out we were down 52–49 and had the ball on their thirty yard line. I dropped back to pass, was flushed out of the pocket, bought some time, and threw a high pass to the back corner of the end zone. Tony Young, a seldom-used receiver, had slipped free, and he made the winning catch with no time remaining. There was a loud gasp, and then the crowd was silent—just stunned. It was just an awesome, awesome moment, one of those euphoric scenarios you always fantasize about that end up being even better in real life. At that point it was quite possibly the highlight of my football career.

That got us into the semifinals against Orlando, a team that had lost to Arizona in the previous year's Arena Bowl and had the best player in the league in Barry Wagner. We got to play that one at our stadium, and by that time the Barnstormers had become a pretty big deal around town. It was one of those back-and-forth battles, and at the end of the game we were down by seven and moving in for the tying touchdown. I drove us down to the one yard line, and we were out of time-outs with the clock ticking down. Coach Gregory was yelling at me from the sidelines, trying to get me to run a pitchout to our running back, hoping we would catch them off guard. I wanted to pass because an incompletion would kill the clock and give us another chance, but I went with the coach's call, and our running back got stopped short of the goal line to end the game.

As disappointing as that defeat was, I was in a great space—at least on the surface. Arena ball had worked out, and now, in my little world, I was being treated like a star. When I walked into a restaurant or bar, I could see people noticing who I was and getting all excited, and it made me feel good to get that kind of attention.

I had been brought up to be a good person who treats others well and doesn't get caught up in money or other superficial things. But during that first season, as I sowed my professional oats and tasted a glimpse of postcollegiate glory, those beliefs started slipping. I don't know if my arrogance was obvious on the outside, but I remember what was going on inside my mind, and I was thinking, *This is pretty cool.* But really, it wasn't. I was playing football for the fame, not for the love of the sport.

Because I was now looking at life in a more selfish way, I started doing uncharacteristic things. I would go out and drink semiregularly, with my teammates or even by myself. There are a lot of moments I wish I could take back, because when I think about them now it embarrasses me. I wasn't very mature, in a lot of ways.

It's possible that I'm being hard on myself, and I don't want you to get the wrong idea. I may have been a little cocky on the inside, but I don't remember big-timing people or talking down to them. I don't recall treating other people like I was a somebody and they were nobodies. It was more the way I felt inside, and, trust me, I was extremely unclear on the concept.

It was during this period that I made what might have been the biggest mistake of my life. I broke up with Brenda because—and

I'm ashamed to admit this—I was caught up in myself and my success and I was thinking the grass was going to be greener on the other side.

Translation: I thought I could put my newfound popularity to good use and become a babe magnet, I guess.

Thankfully, we stayed broken up for only a couple of weeks, and she was receptive when I came crawling back.. That was yet another instance in which Brenda showed tremendous faith in me, and at a point when I didn't necessarily deserve it.

Why did I break up with Brenda? Well, she was two hours away in Cedar Falls, and I was thinking, *I'm pretty cool, and she doesn't understand my reality. She's far away, we don't ever see each other, we're having problems communicating, and it's almost like we have two separate lives. Maybe I can test the waters and do better.*

I was making money and getting attention, and I believed I could probably get any girl I wanted. Meanwhile, Brenda and I had been doing our share of fighting, and one of our running arguments centered on religion. Looking back, I think she was recognizing some of the things that were going on with me, that I was getting caught up in the world and losing my grip on what was important. And despite the questions she was still wrestling with, she remained convinced that a more personal relationship with God was what I needed. She would often implore me to take my faith to the next level, but I didn't want to hear it. I thought she was just trying to control me, and I wanted to be free.

So one day while Brenda was in the middle of her shift as a nurse at the Cedar Falls Lutheran Home, I called her up and said, "It's over." The next day, I showed up at her front door in Cedar Falls and, ever the romantic, pulled out a cashier's check for $1,500 and gave it to her. I said, "I want you to put this in a savings account for the kids, because I want them to have something for the future." Brenda was furious. She kept saying, "You're paying me off? You're giving me a check, and that makes everything okay?" She ended up spending that money on food and clothes and bills, because funds were scarce and she didn't have the luxury of putting it away.

I drove off singing "I'm as free as a bird now . . . ," certain that good times lay ahead. I went on a couple of dates and tried to put Brenda out of my mind, even though I missed her and the kids. Brenda, to her credit, kept calling me through that period, saying, "I love you. I know God wants us to be together." Remember, this is a woman who made a difficult but firm decision to split from her first husband the moment she learned of his interest in another woman and never looked back. Thankfully, she didn't write me off just as abruptly. She kept believing in our connection, and she didn't even tell the kids we had broken up. In her heart she thought there was a chance I'd come back to her, and I'm extremely grateful that she kept the faith.

After a couple of weeks the notion of being the big stud around Des Moines didn't seem so appealing anymore. I'd go to a bar for a few minutes, get a little bit of adulation, and then go home alone. Everything felt hollow. I missed Brenda. I missed Zack and Jesse. I missed the old me.

I knew what I had to do. I called Brenda and said, "Listen, I've given it a lot of thought, and now I realize that you're the one I want."

"Well," she said, "it's about time."

We got back together, but that didn't solve all of my problems. We still had our share of fights, and I still wasn't the type of person I wanted to be. And though I couldn't see it then, my priorities were still a little out of whack.

It took a little while longer before I was ready to make the most important transformation of my life. Within a few months, God used Brenda to break through the walls of my heart and help us both take our faith to an entirely new realm.

But, we wouldn't get there without facing the biggest test of all.

CHAPTER EIGHT

BLOWN AWAY

If you ever find yourself trapped in an elevator with me or anyone in my family, and the subject turns to movies, here's a friendly piece of advice: don't bring up *Twister,* the disaster flick starring Helen Hunt and Bill Paxton that hit the big screen a few years back.

Less than a week before that film opened—on Sunday, April 14, 1996—Brenda's parents, Larry and Jenny Carney, were killed by a freak tornado that blew their newly constructed home in Mountain View, Arkansas, to smithereens. Obviously, it was an extremely difficult ordeal, especially for Brenda and the kids. To make matters worse, it seemed like every time we turned on the TV, a trailer for *Twister* would appear on the screen. The kids would burst into tears, reliving the horror time and time again, and we'd turn it off as fast as humanly possible.

To this day Zachary is scared to death of storms. Anytime he's awakened by heavy wind or rain or thunder, he runs into our bedroom and ends up sleeping with us. It makes sense. People have tried to tell him that he has no reason to be scared of storms, but in his mind a storm was what took his grandparents. It didn't help that the immediate aftermath of their death coincided with a major motion picture about tornadoes.

We just couldn't get away from that movie. The hype was everywhere, and that's all anybody wanted to talk about with Brenda: "Hey, have you seen *Twister?*"

"Uh, no. My parents were just killed by a tornado."

How's that for a conversation killer?

It is said that the Lord works in mysterious ways, and never was that more true than during the time of that tragedy. It took place at a time when I was feeling closer to God than I ever had before. Yet because of her heartache, Brenda, who for so long had tried to persuade me to see the light, was again in the process of asking a lot of tough questions about her faith.

Before I talk about the accident, it's important to give you an idea of my mind-set at that time. Brenda and I had gotten back together, and over the course of that next year—from the latter part of my first season with the Barnstormers through that off-season and into the beginning of my second Arena League campaign—some significant spiritual battles and changes had taken place in my life.

Some of those battles involved Brenda. She is someone who usually thinks of a spiritual rebirth as an epiphany because one Sunday night when she was twelve years old, Brenda was at church when they showed a movie, *Distant Thunder,* about what the Bible says will happen at the end of times. In an emotional reaction to the message of that film, she practically ran down to the altar of the church to pray and cry and ask forgiveness. That was the moment she first asked Jesus into her heart. She said she felt cleansed. She knew something very definite and real had happened, that her life was somehow different and would never be the same again. In her words, "I was saved that night."

I've heard some people refer to such an experience as "finding religion." I had never thought I particularly needed an experience like that because I'd always had my religion. That's where Brenda's thinking and mine collided head-on. She kept arguing that a truly meaningful faith was much more than a religion, it's a relationship. "It's a personal relationship you have with God," she'd say. "And to have that, you've first got to ask Jesus into your life."

The hard thing about Brenda is that she's not subtle about her views, and to her it was imperative that I be saved. So whenever the subject of religious beliefs came up—at least every Sunday morning, when we had to decide whether we'd go to her church or mine or separately to our respective churches—she always spoke and acted as if she were right and I were wrong. That made me extremely defensive. Sometimes I'd get mad and tell her, "My faith *is* personal. It's just between me and God and is no one else's business. My spiritual beliefs are not something I need to talk about with anyone."

But that was another point of contention, because Brenda would pull out her Bible and show me verses like Mark 16:15–16, where Jesus instructed his followers to tell others about him. I didn't know how to argue with Brenda when she started quoting the Bible like that, but I do remember thinking, *No way I'll ever do that!*

Brenda insisted that telling others what you believed was an essential part of being a Christian—the implication again being that I wasn't one.

I took real offense to that because I still believed what I'd always believed: that being a Christian meant being a good person and doing your best to follow the Ten Commandments and always trying to do the right thing. Like Jesus did. Like God expects. And if you work at it hard enough and are indeed a good person, when you die you get to go to heaven and are saved from eternal damnation.

Oh, boy. That was a whole other issue with Brenda. "You aren't saved because of the good things you do!" she argued. "No one can ever be good enough to earn salvation. We all sin. We all fail to measure up to Jesus' perfect standard. So the only way to be 'saved' is through God's grace." She said it was a gift. But you just had to ask for it like she had first done when she was a kid. She told me that was the only way anyone ever got to heaven, and then she quoted more Bible verses to back up her argument.

Now, she was saying I wouldn't be going to heaven unless I changed my thinking. And, that really bugged me.

I had seriously undermined my position during that first season with the Barnstormers, when I acted like such a jerk and broke up with Brenda. Blinded by my first professional success and the glare of the limelight, I'd temporarily discarded many of the values I claimed to have believed in all my life. I'd messed up big time and, in the process, almost lost the most important people in my life. So I had to admit, to myself anyway, that down deep I wasn't such a good person at all. Maybe I could benefit from the kind of help Brenda claimed that God gives to people who have a personal relationship with him.

Another thing that happened during my time in Des Moines—and this proved important—was that Brenda was not alone in her beliefs. During my first season with the Iowa Barnstormers, I had become friendly with one of my teammates, Dave Bush, who had beliefs similar to Brenda's. He started a Bible study during the second part of that season with a pastor, Pat Sokoll, and I began attending it regularly. When the season ended another Christian, Matt Eller, signed with the team and got heavily involved with the group.

At that point I was getting nearly identical messages from two unrelated factions: Brenda in Cedar Falls and my Bible study partners in Des Moines. They were my strength in Des Moines while Brenda wasn't around, and it's like I was getting educated from both sides. I had been feeling a void in my life when I got caught up in the fame and broke up with Brenda, and now I was starting to get a clear picture of what I lacked. I certainly didn't have the sense of hope and peace and assurance that Brenda and my Christian friends had in their faith.

There was no single, magic moment where I shed my skin and emerged anew. Instead, it was a gradual feeling that probably evolved over the course of about ten months. I finally reached the point where I knew what I needed to do. I probably asked Jesus into my heart three or four times, because I didn't really know when my official salvation would occur. It's like I wasn't sure which one was going to take. I'd pray and ask God to forgive me for all the times and ways I'd messed up in my life. I'd tell him I wanted him to come into my heart, and I'd promise to live for him. And each time I prayed like that, I would wonder, *Am I doing this right? Am I saying the right things?*

I didn't tell Brenda or my Bible study buddies about these prayers. Pride was probably part of the reason. But the bigger consideration was that I didn't feel any big, emotional experience like Brenda had described. There was no overnight metamorphosis. In fact, it wasn't until Brenda's parents were killed that I finally realized for certain that something had begun to take place in my heart and life. You would think that would have been the lowest point imaginable, yet I actually got closer to God and to Brenda than I ever had before. I had this new sense of peace within me through the whole experience that actually enabled *me* to give *her* spiritual strength and guidance.

The night before Brenda's parents were killed, we had our first preseason game in Moline, Illinois, against the Albany Firebirds. Brenda's sister, Kim, and her husband, John, live nearby in Eldridge, Iowa, so we all got together that night and spent some quality time. The next day I went back to Des Moines, and Brenda and the kids went home to Cedar Falls. Her dad had recently retired after thirty years of working for John Deere in Iowa, and he and her mom had just moved into their dream home alongside the White River in Arkansas, which had been completed only the week before.

This was the same night that Brenda's dad celebrated his fifty-fourth birthday. I had planned to wish him happy birthday by phone, but I got distracted by our game and decided to put off the call. It was a decision I would later regret and still do.

Brenda called her dad on Sunday afternoon. He asked Brenda how the weather was in Iowa, and she said, "It's cold; I hate Iowa." Her dad replied, "Well, move down here. All we have are tornado warnings." He told Brenda that he and her mother were going to their new church that night to get baptized and that they would call back after that.

At 10 P.M. Brenda got a call from her sister, and Brenda said, "Kim, hurry up. Mom calls me at ten every Sunday night, right after the Sunday night movie." There was a short pause, and then Kim said, "Honey, Mom and Dad were killed two hours ago in a tornado."

It seemed so senseless and random: because Brenda's mom had a headache, she and her husband had decided to skip the baptism and stay home. There was a tornado warning—very common in those parts—but, in a rather freak occurrence, two twisters converged right at the spot where Brenda's parents lived. Their church was totally unscathed, so had they gone as planned, they would have been fine. But their house was blown to bits; there literally was nothing left but dirt and scattered debris. The tornadoes also blew through a couple of neighboring houses and an RV park across the road, killing five others, and cut a seven-mile swath through the area.

The devastation was unbelievable. People were recovering things that belonged to the Carneys ten miles away from where their house had been. Ten miles—think about that. Somebody found one of her father's suits, still covered with the plastic from the cleaners, lying in a far-off ditch, as if a person had gently placed it there. One of the eeriest moments took place after their funeral, when we were leaving to go back to Iowa. We stopped at a gas station about a half mile away from their house, and when Brenda went inside to pay for the gas, she saw her school portrait from the seventh grade in an unbroken frame standing atop the counter. She said, "That's me," and the lady behind the counter said, "Oh, honey, somebody found this a couple of miles away, but we didn't know who it belonged to, so we thought we'd put it here and see if somebody recognized it."

When Brenda got that wrenching phone call from her sister, she hung up immediately and called me in Des Moines. I was in bed and sort of nodding off, and all she said was, "Mom and Dad were killed in a tornado. I need you." Click. I was in a state of shock. I tried to call her back a couple of times, but the phone was busy. So I quickly got dressed and went downstairs, and I informed my roommates what had happened and said, "Tell the coach I won't be there for practice."

Then I was in my car, speeding down the dark highway, praying that it was all a big mistake. So much was racing through my mind.

I was thinking, *Maybe it's not real. Maybe she had a nightmare, woke up and called me, then the phone got disconnected and she fell back asleep. I'll get there and it'll all be a big nothing, and I'm going to be a little annoyed and very relieved.*

I didn't have a cell phone, so I couldn't call, and I didn't want to take the time to pull over and use a pay phone. It's normally a two-hour drive, and I probably got there in an hour and fifteen minutes. As soon as I walked up to Brenda's front door, I knew that it hadn't been a dream. A bunch of her relatives were there grieving, and I just hugged her and tried not to show the depth of my sadness, because I knew her pain was so much greater.

Throughout the next few days, I don't remember really sitting Brenda down or trying to find the right words to soothe her. I just felt that God put me there to be a shoulder for her to cry on, to be a rock, and I tried to play my role. I never got emotional or showed my pain to her because I didn't want to burden her with that. I figured I would grieve on my own. Instead, I concentrated on helping out with the kids—explaining the situation to them and answering their questions because Brenda was usually too upset to have those conversations. I wanted to let her mourn on her terms. I'd hold her, listen to her, and let her vent her frustrations without injecting my own feelings or opinions. Brenda actually got mad that I wasn't showing more overt grief, but I just felt it was more important to stay cool and collected.

I suddenly felt so in tune with God that I was ready to quote scripture, to tell her God this and God that and remind her that "God causes all things to work together for good to those who love God, to those who are called according to his purpose" (Romans 8:28, NASB). That's what I was thinking and praying about, but I held my tongue, because I knew she'd tell me I was an idiot and that I didn't know how it felt. There was nothing I could do to make the situation any better, so I didn't pretend that I knew something she didn't.

I let her cry on my shoulder and say what she wanted to say. This was interesting, because she was saying some pretty strong things. Here I was all warm and fuzzy about my newfound faith, and she was saying things like, "This isn't fair. How could this happen? How could this most powerful God, who I believe could stop the world if he wanted to, allow this tornado to hit them?"

She was hurting and angry. Some well-meaning Christians in her life would say to her, "Well, they're in God's hands now. At least they went together. God called them up." That was not what she wanted to hear. She'd thank them and bite her lip, and later she'd fly off the handle to me, saying, "Why would God call them up? He didn't need them. *I* need them." She would say that she was mad at God, that she couldn't believe he had saddled her with this burden after all the trauma surrounding Zachary's accident. She'd even say to me, "It's not fair that it happened to me—you have three parents and now I have none." For whatever reason, I had enough inner peace and understanding that I knew it was better not to respond, that she needed time to work through it on her own.

The immediate aftermath of the tragedy was as trying as you would expect. The next morning, a Monday, I drove Brenda and the kids about an hour south to some random rest stop on the side of the highway, where we had arranged to meet John and Kim and their daughters, Alexandria and Victoria. Brenda and our kids joined the others in Kim and John's van, and they all drove straight to Arkansas, while I went back to practice in Des Moines. I arrived before any of my teammates, and as soon as guys began walking into the locker room, I just lost it. It's like I was determined not to break down in front of Brenda, but as soon as I got away I felt the magnitude of the loss. I was just bawling, and guys were coming over and hugging me because they had all heard the news by that point. Nobody really knows what to say in that situation, but my teammates were very supportive.

Brenda and her sister had to identify the bodies on Tuesday, and I flew down and joined them that evening. The next morning was the memorial service, and it's weird how you act sometimes in surreal situations like that. We were all dressed up for the service, but first Brenda took me by her parents' property so I could see the devastation for myself. It was a stunning sight to behold, and for whatever reason I began searching the area for belongings of theirs, like a detective looking for clues. I just wanted to find something to help Brenda hold on to her parents—not necessarily to bring closure to the situation, but at least to find an item that meant something to Brenda and her sister.

There was a creek adjacent to their land, and I saw a piece of paper on the other side of the stream that seemed like it might be important. So I jumped across the creek, getting myself all muddy in the process, and retrieved it. Now Brenda was upset. I was a mess, and my trip over the creek ended up making us late to the memorial service. But I felt somewhat vindicated because the piece of paper turned out to be some insurance document—one that notified us about a policy entitling Brenda and her sister to extra money they otherwise might not have known existed.

Two other bizarre things happened that day. After the service, the four of us—Kim and John and Brenda and I—decided to take the Carneys' ashes to the river near their house. When we were in the church parking lot, getting ready to drive over to the river, Brenda turned to me and blurted out, "You know, Kurt, if you don't marry me, it's going to be really stupid that you were here." None of us could believe she said that. I told her, "Don't worry about it." But she repeated, "I'm just telling you that it's really stupid that you're coming with me to do this if you're not going to marry me."

We got to the riverbank, and it was time to scatter the ashes. Brenda and Kim each had a box, and Brenda cleanly emptied hers into the breeze. We watched the ashes as they peacefully wafted onto the rushing water. Then we looked over at Kim, who isn't very athletic, and she was having a far more difficult time executing the task. She was shaking the box to try to get the ashes out, and this big billow of dust formed and blew them right back at her. The ashes were going up her nose and into her mouth, and she was gagging and coughing up a storm. Brenda and Kim couldn't help it; they just burst into laughter. I guess it was just their way of dealing with the drama.

I thought it was sort of funny, but I felt a little weird about having too much fun in that situation. And John, Kim's husband, didn't find it humorous—at all. He didn't say a word as he drove us back in his van, while Brenda and Kim had the giggles like a pair of schoolgirls. Every so often Kim would find more ashes on her face or hair and wipe them away, and the two of them would start up again. Long after the fact, Brenda and Kim joked that "the two Catholic boys"—John, like me, was raised Catholic—couldn't handle that kind of humor.

The marriage comment, however, was no joke. Brenda's words might have caught me a little off guard, but I understood her point: it was time to put up or shut up, and I was definitely leaning toward the former. The upshot of her parents' death was that she and I became closer than ever before. One of the first things I said to her was, "We belong together. You need to move down to Des Moines and be with me now." The tragedy taught me how precious life is and allowed me to see how quickly you can lose somebody. It's too bad it took such a tumultuous event to make me understand that, but after that everything changed. All my interactions with people close to me became something to cherish, because those people might be taken from me at any time. Suddenly, when I thought about Brenda, there was an incredible urgency that we be together as much as possible. In light of her parents' loss, I said, "Come live with me; let's not waste any more time apart."

Brenda had a job at the Cedar Falls Lutheran Home, and they gave her three weeks off to grieve. After that she decided to quit, because she couldn't stand working around so many dying people in the wake of her parents' tragedy. That meant I had three new roommates, and I was becoming convinced that the arrangement should be permanent.

First there was the matter of getting through the football season, and early on that seemed like a daunting task. The next Saturday morning, after we had returned home from Arkansas, Brenda and her sister had another memorial service in Cedar Falls for all the friends and relatives in Iowa. That night we had our second exhibition game—fortunately, it was at home—and I went straight from the service to the stadium. I had a big game, earning MVP honors and a game ball. After each of my first two touchdown passes, I asked to keep the footballs—the only time I've ever done so in that context on any level, even the NFL. I later had each ball engraved with the message "In loving memory of Mom and Dad," and I presented one to Brenda and another to Kim that next Christmas.

Unfortunately, my hot streak ended once the real games began. Of all the statistical plateaus I've been able to achieve, my most remarkable numerical stretch may have taken place in the first four games of that '96 season: I threw eleven interceptions during that span, and in Arena ball, where you pretty much have to score on almost every possession, that's just outrageous. Early on, I had more interceptions than I did touchdowns, and that's unheard of in the Arena League. Somehow, we managed to win two of those four games, but I was definitely struggling.

Obviously, I was dealing with some heavy stuff off the field, but nobody outside the team knew that, and the fans certainly had no clue. Some Arena fans aren't the most sophisticated folks on earth, partly because they tend to have foam on the brain. Beer flowed freely at our games, and we had a lot of drunks in the crowd. When things were going well, that was awesome. The fans in the front row were so close to the players, and they'd lean over the railing and ask us if we wanted a beer.

On the other hand, when you were on the road—or, at home, when things were going poorly—it could get pretty gruesome. Getting beer thrown on you was just part of Arena football. Fans would yell and scream the most obscene things, right in your face, and you just had to try to take it for what it was.

Brenda, as you might imagine, wasn't as willing to let the comments roll off her. Every time she went to one of our away games, she'd be up there screaming her lungs out for me and the Barnstormers, and the people around her would start in with their heckling. She'd give it right back to them, of course. They'd call her every name in the book, and I do mean all of them.

One time, in Orlando, Brenda got into it with a Predators fan who looked like he just rolled out of a belching academy for Hell's Angels rejects. He was saying, "If Warner was any good, he'd be in the NFL. I'm probably as good as him." Always the shrinking violet, Brenda shot back with, "Hmmm, let me see: a guy with a cutoff Harley Davidson T-shirt and a ponytail, or Kurt Warner? I don't know; you decide." It degenerated from there, until he said, "How many thousand people in the stands, and I get planted next to an Iowa . . ." I can't even finish the sentence. Let's just say he called Brenda the worst thing you can call a woman. He was one classy dude.

During the period when I was struggling after Brenda's parents' death, the home fans got pretty abusive. Brenda always took the kids with her to the home games, and everyone was yelling, "Warner sucks. Get him out of here. Go back to the cornfield." The kids were crying. They were having a tough enough time as it was, and they didn't understand why people were being so mean. Brenda asked the people around her to cool it, saying, "Do you mind? These are his children." One of the hecklers shot back, "Well, he sucks. I can't help it if he sucks."

The crazy thing was, despite all the adversity I was dealing with on and off the field, I felt this incredible, inner spiritual sense of well-being. I remember getting a call from my mom around that time. She knew things were going badly for me on the football field, and she asked, "What's wrong? What's the problem? Is your head screwed on right?" I had never had a spell like that in football, and obviously the loss of Brenda's parents was very painful. Yet I remember telling my mom, "I've never been happier." My life was finally aimed in the direction it needed to be, and my faith was as strong as it had ever been; I believed God had a plan for me. I loved Brenda more than I ever had, and now she and the kids and I were all together in Des Moines.

It was weird: other than the fact that her parents were killed and I was playing terribly, everything was great. I knew what I wanted—Brenda, the kids, and a new relationship with God—and even though I still loved football and had a passion for it, the game suddenly didn't seem so all-important. I told my mom, "I don't know what's going on with my game. Things just aren't going my way right now, and I'm struggling. But so what?" It wasn't bothering me like it would have in the past.

The point was, I could finally see the big picture, and everything in my life was good other than those two things. And, I couldn't explain why either had happened. I think a lot of times we want to explain everything. We want an answer, even when there isn't one. I realized that I didn't know why I wasn't playing well, and it didn't matter. I knew I just needed to trust God with that and everything else in my life, and I didn't allow it to get to me.

Sure enough, shortly after that horrific four-game streak, my game came around. The next week we went down to Memphis to play the Pharaohs, and I stunk it up again. So Coach Gregory yanked me and put in my backup, Ron Lopez, and he didn't play very well, either. With a couple of minutes left in the game, Coach Gregory put me back in, and I responded by driving us to a touchdown. Our defense held, and I drove us down again. On the last play I scrambled out of the pocket, avoided the rush, and threw a ten-yard touchdown pass to Chris Spencer to win the game with no time remaining. Brenda's maternal grandmother, whom we call "Chach," had driven down from Arkansas, and she told me afterward that she nearly had a heart attack because of that play.

The day after the game, Coach Gregory sat me and Ron Lopez down and tried to assess the situation. He asked me what I thought was going on, what the problem was. I said, "I don't know. I can't really pinpoint what's wrong. I still feel like I can lead the team and that we can be successful." I really felt I wasn't necessarily the only reason we were struggling. Willis Jacox, our best receiver and our top player from the year before, had held out in a contract dispute, and he was just getting back into playing shape. Consequently, there was a lot of shuffling: we had some new guys on the team and others who had switched positions, so continuity was a real problem.

I remember Lopez trying to beg for the job, saying, "Hey, just give me another chance. I know I can do it." He hadn't played very well when he got the opportunity, but he thought he could be the guy. I just sat back and said, "Hey, it's up to you, Coach. I still feel I can lead us and that we can win."

Coach Gregory stuck with me, and we went on to win our last nine games. We finished with a 12–2 record, the best in Arena League history at the time. After my embarrassing start to the season, I went on a rampage, throwing forty-seven touchdowns against just four interceptions the rest of the way. I was named first-team All-Arena League, and we stayed hot through the playoffs and ended up in the Arena Bowl, battling the Tampa Bay Storm for the championship at The Barn—our home turf.

It was a great game, lots of action back and forth, and with a couple of minutes left we got the ball trailing 42–38. With about a minute to go I threw what I thought was the go-ahead touchdown pass, but the officials ruled that our receiver was down at the one yard line. So we had first and goal to go for the championship. Twice we ran. Twice we passed. But, amazingly, we couldn't get in. It came down to a fourth and goal, and my pass was incomplete.

For the second year in a row, my title dreams were squashed a yard from the end zone. That's why in the Super Bowl, when Mike Jones nailed Tennessee's Kevin Dyson at the one and we rushed onto the field to celebrate, I really felt for the Titans—for a couple of seconds, at least—because I knew how tough it was to come so close to victory in a huge game.

So, although the '96 season ended on a sour note, my life was on a major upswing. I remember thanking the Lord for my good fortune and making a request: *No matter what situation you put me in, please just give me a job and allow me to take care of my family.*

I didn't care if I had to work until I was ninety; as long as I could provide for my family, I would feel exceptionally blessed.

I had resisted Arena ball at the start, and there were times early on when it seemed so low budget. But now I was making pretty good money—thanks to all the incentive clauses, I was pushing up against $60,000 a year—and I earned extra cash over the off-season, working with kids at the Riverfront YMCA in Des Moines, which I loved. There was no other job I could envision getting at twenty-four that would pay me that kind of money, and I was having a blast doing it. It was probably the most fun I've ever had playing football, because it was so high scoring and pass oriented, and I could just sit back there and throw. Plus, in my heart, I knew my dream of making it to the highest level of pro football was still alive.

Five months after being confronted with the sudden death of Brenda's parents, we had managed to regroup and forge ahead toward a bright future. For the first time, I felt like my heart was at peace and my life was in order. Almost.

Now, there was just the matter of making it all official. It was a huge step for me to take, and I was determined to do it with flair.

CHAPTER NINE

FAMILY MATTERS

I love to throw the deep ball, to air it out and take over a game with one grandiose gesture, and off the football field I'm the exact same way. On September 18, 1996, when I asked Brenda for her hand in marriage, I was determined to make a bigger splash than Rush Limbaugh doing a cannonball off a high-dive.

If you think about it, our engagement could have been totally anticlimactic. She had been married once before, we'd been together for nearly four years, and we lived with each other for much of that time. What's more, we had already gone ring shopping together, and Brenda was gently probing me about when I was going to propose.

To sweep her off her feet, I knew I'd have to be creative. I had already purchased a ring, paying it off over a three-month period that summer, and now I was hiding it in the back of my sock drawer. Brenda never looked there, at least to my knowledge, though I wouldn't have put it past her. Even after I'd bought the ring and was plotting my strategy, we had a couple of animated conversations about when I was going to purchase it. There was no way I was going to let on that it was already in my possession.

To have any semblance of surprise, I needed a diversion. When we purchased our first house together in Des Moines, I knew my chance had arrived. I timed the proposal to coincide with the closing of the sale, because that would give us an excuse to celebrate.

First I placed a courtesy call to Chach, Brenda's maternal grandmother, to ask for Brenda's hand in marriage. Chach gave me her blessing, and I begged her to keep it a secret for the next couple of days. The only other people who knew were our friends Mike and Mary Pat Schulte, whom I needed to help execute my elaborate plan. And it was elaborate. I still can't believe all the planning that went into it. I made a long to-do list that served as my guide. For sentimental purposes, I still keep that old, weathered checklist in my wallet.

The setup began with a celebration dinner. We started off at the new house, which had just been constructed and was totally empty. I had brought over nice outfits for Brenda and the kids, and we all got dressed up and waited for our wheels. Up pulled a limo I had rented to whisk us off to a fancy dinner at a restaurant called Christopher's. Brenda and I had been in limousines a few times before, when I had done various TV shows or appearances, but this was the first time we went out and got one for ourselves, so it was very exciting.

Brenda, I knew, would be suspicious, and I could tell she was anticipating a proposal as we arrived at the restaurant. We ordered appetizers, which was a big deal for us. When we were growing up, on the rare occasions either of us would go out to eat with our respective families, we pretty much had to limit ourselves to main courses. Tonight it was no-holds-barred. Then, as a further luxury, we ordered dessert. Brenda got this goofy smile on her face because she thought the ring was coming then.

But dessert came and went, and by the time we got back into the limo, her smile had turned to a deflated pout. She stayed silent while I talked to the kids on the ride home. When we arrived back to the house, I got out of the limo to pay the driver, and she blew right past me and opened the front door.

Showtime.

The first thing Brenda noticed was the pile of rose petals at her feet. Mike and Mary Pat had sprinkled them through the house in a path leading to the backyard, and Brenda's first reaction was,

"Oh, my gosh, Kurt, somebody broke in!" Then she realized that most burglars don't leave a trail of flowers for their victims to follow. The path of petals was marked on each side by candles that Mike and Mary Pat had lit awhile earlier. So Brenda followed the trail through a hallway and out to the back door, which opened up onto a large patio area.

Now she didn't know what to think. I followed her outside and got ready to swarm into action. There was a bottle of champagne—and a bottle of Sprite for the kids—on top of an outdoor table, along with four glasses. Then, underneath one of the chairs, I had some other supplies stashed. I reached down to turn on our old, bulky boom box, and voilà: our old song from Wild E. Coyote's, the Nitty Gritty Dirt Band's "Fishin' in the Dark," began blasting through the backyard. There was also a single red rose, with the engagement ring hidden inside.

After I reached down to play the tape, I grabbed the rose with one hand, and with the other I flipped a small light switch. There was a big, wooden privacy fence in the back of the yard, and I had gotten Mike and Mary Pat to position several rows of Christmas lights to form the words, "Will You Marry Me?" When I flipped the switch the sign lit up, and since I was already leaning over to grab the ring, I stayed on one knee, pulled out the ring, and popped the question to Brenda.

A few seconds later I popped the question again, this time to the kids. That was sort of weird, because Jesse, who was only four at the time, was convinced that I was going to marry *her.* She and Brenda would have arguments in which Jesse would say, "Mama, I'm the one he loves. He's going to buy the ring for *me.* " So I really wanted to make sure she understood what I was doing and that she wouldn't be upset.

Thankfully, she wasn't. She and Zack yelled "Daddy!" and we all gave one another a big group hug. Then we danced to the song, and since the house was totally empty—no phone, no lightbulbs, no furniture—we piled into my Blazer and drove off to call my parents and Brenda's sister and brother-in-law. We pulled into a little strip mall in a Des Moines suburb and used a drive-up pay phone, since we were hardly part of the cellular revolution.

Things had gotten a lot better between my mom and Brenda by that point. They had aired out their feelings on a couple of occasions and were working hard on getting along. So my mom was excited, and Gene and Mimi were fired up as well. Then the four of us drove back to the new house and slept there together on the living room floor with two pillows and the emergency blanket from the back of my pickup truck—a night I'll never forget.

The future had never looked so bright and exciting. But then, for the past several months, I'd been looking at life in a new way. I think Brenda had begun noticing a change in me even before her parents' deaths. Afterward, I know she did.

The time soon came when I told her about praying to accept Christ, how I hadn't been sure I'd done it right but that I knew something definitely had happened in my heart. I was convinced of this because of the new sense of peace and inner strength I'd experienced during that stressful time. I told Brenda I definitely wanted to start living my life for God. She was thrilled for me. And so were Pat Sokoll, my pastor in Des Moines, and Matt Eller and Dave Bush, my teammates and Bible study buddies. I began to talk with them about the implications this could have on my life and on some of my lifestyle choices.

I was struck by the strong conviction that as a Christian I needed to be especially concerned about the example I set for others (which I took to mean everyone from fellow Christians to nonbelievers, whose perceptions of Jesus were limited to what they saw in me, to young people who might look to me as a role model). That's when I told Brenda, "I think I need to stop drinking." It wasn't an especially tough decision for me to make. Except for a couple of fairly short periods in my life, I'd never been much of a drinker. I didn't like it all that much. And I especially didn't like what drinking did to me. When I'd drink I remember thinking, *This is not who I really am. Or who I want to be.*

Brenda raised another topic she thought ought to concern me

My first helmet: Kurtis Eugene Warner, 1971

Looking cool: On Lake Vermilion in northern Minnesota, age 9

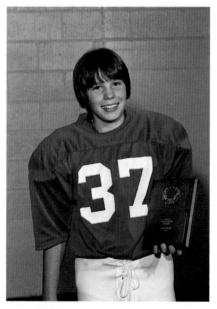

Call me "Pop" Warner: My first football team, All Saints, in the Catholic Parish Football League, 1983

One rebounds, the other passes: I was a two-sport athlete at Regis High School

Crossing one end zone: Graduation from Regis, 1989

Quarterback for University of Northern Iowa:
Note the clean uniform—I was still only a backup

A big catch on Lake Vermilion with my friend Steve Zier

*Two of my biggest fans: Celebrating a Panther victory with
my brother Matt and my dad, Gene*

Way above par for the course:
Brenda and I pretending to be golfers

Cutting it up at Wild E. Coyote's

Hanging with Buddy

The best catch of my life: Brenda and I on our wedding day, October 1997

Hey, go deep: The bridesmaid can't cover you!

In the huddle: Zack, Kade, and me

Three things that are more important than football:
Jesse, Kade, and Zack

*Even Kade's two favorite guys with
beards couldn't make him laugh*

The home team: Jesse, Me, Zack, Brenda, Kade

just as much or more: my language, mostly on the field. When ESPN broadcast Arena League games, they miked the quarterbacks. And there I'd be in living color, cursing up a storm. "If you really intend to be a man of God, it needs to be in all areas," Brenda told me.

"But that kind of talk is just part of football," I told her. I had about as much chance of swaying her with that logic as I did of beating Deion Sanders in a hundred-yard dash.

There was one other area of our lifestyle that we'd both successfully ignored for a long time. And now, shortly after we got engaged, Brenda and I made a mutual decision that dramatically altered our day-to-day lives. I don't even remember how the subject came up or who raised it, but we quickly determined that it was a good idea to stop having sex until our wedding day. Since we didn't get married until the following October, this was quite a test.

As Brenda and I began to consider the option of refraining from premarital sex, we discussed our thoughts with the people in my Bible study group and their wives, and I think they were touched by the commitment we made. We told them that this was an area we were challenged in and that we wanted to make a testimony to the Lord by taking this step.

Looking back, I think it might have been a lot easier to keep that vow if we had opted for a shorter engagement or if we hadn't kept living together. Part of our motivation was what the Bible says about avoiding the appearance of wrong so as not to cause others to stumble by following your example. I now realize it would have been a clearer example of our new convictions if we had gotten married sooner or I had moved out. But our decision seemed like a pretty significant step at the time, when we were admittedly not as conscious of the ramifications of others' perceptions as we are today.

I've heard that the Reverend Billy Graham, whom I admire deeply and was blessed enough to meet at a ministry he gave in St. Louis during the '99 season, will not allow himself to be seen alone in public with his own daughter, because he doesn't want anyone to get the mistaken impression that he's running around with a woman other than his wife. That's the point I'd like to get to, a level of awareness from which I consider the larger ramifications of everything I do and live not just for myself but for the Lord and for the potential impact I can have upon the Christian community.

To me, an important ramification of our vow was that we were becoming conscious of our role as Christians and potential leaders in that community. I felt God had a plan for me. Perhaps it was to spend my whole career with the Barnstormers influencing people in Iowa, though I hoped it would be even more substantial. We wanted to prepare ourselves for the big things God had in store for us, and the sex embargo was part of that.

Our only "permissible" form of affection was what Brenda calls "grandma kisses"; anything more than that, and it could mean trouble, and fast. Were we perfect angels? Of course not.

Today Brenda and I tell young people that if we had life to live over again, we'd do things differently. We very much wish we'd waited, and that we could have given each other the very special gift of virginity on our wedding night. But we know if that had been the case we wouldn't have Zack or Jesse, and neither of us can imagine life without them. Which says to us that God is so great that he can bring real blessing and good out of any situation.

Perhaps that old axiom about refraining from sex before competition has some validity, because I went out and played my pants off during my third and final Arena League season. Even though I broke the thumb on my throwing hand ten games into the season, I played through the pain and led us to an 11–3 record. Once again I was voted first-team All-Arena League, and we made it to the Arena Bowl.

That fulfilling third season with the Barnstormers almost didn't happen. Right before the season began I had gotten a call from the Amsterdam Admirals of the World League asking me to come over and play because they were having some problems with their quarterbacks. For so long I had pushed to play over in Europe because I thought it would be the best path to the NFL. But now it didn't feel right. I had already gone through preseason with the Barnstormers, who had given me a pretty decent contract, and we had just bought the house and were getting settled. Meanwhile, it was halfway through the World League season, which was only ten games, and there was no guarantee I'd be starting right away. Even if I did, I'd have to learn a whole new offense, and who knows if NFL teams would even notice I was out there. I prayed about it and came to the conclusion that I should stay with the Barnstormers.

It was the right call, because I had really come to enjoy the Arena League. Sure, it had its cheesy elements, some of which improved over time. For example, we went from practicing on an outdoor field lined with hay bales as makeshift walls during our first training camp to staging our preseason workouts in an indoor soccer facility—with hard, unforgiving walls. At the outdoor field our kickers had to use a pair of telephone poles, without a crossbar between them, to simulate goalposts, which apparently had been too much of a luxury for the Barnstormers to afford.

The league was cut-rate in other ways as well. If you wanted a Barnstormers T-shirt, they made you pay for it out of your own pocket. When we first started up, we had practice pants that were hand-me-downs from Iowa State and Drake. So we practiced with different-colored pants, none of which fit particularly well. The helmets didn't fit, either; they'd just buy a bunch of helmets in generic sizes, and you had to squeeze into whichever one they gave you. Pads were also a problem. Instead of quarterback pads or other specific styles, you just grabbed whatever was there. Also, we had to pay for tickets to our games, and they always put Brenda and the kids up in the nosebleeds.

Our team owner, Jim Foster, was the guy who created the whole Arena football concept, and he fashioned himself as a sort of P. T. Barnum. So he made sure the Barnstormers lived up to their name, and there were gimmicks galore. He'd give people nicknames to try to sell T-shirts, and he made the whole scene a big show.

That's how I came to be called "Houdini," a nickname that surprised my teammates as much as it did me. Foster gave it to me, I guess, because I was good at avoiding the pass rush, getting people to miss, and making plays afterward. You know, my escapability. Get it? It was even more ridiculous when you consider my dubious foot speed. To put it kindly, I'm slower than a 1985 desktop computer. My teammates teased me mercilessly, though they knew they could land a nickname, too, at any time. Just ask Larry "The Enforcer" Blue or Carlos "The Assassin" James.

Man, was it corny. Once, on an off day, they made us go out to a farm for some promotional event. Every player got to pick his own baby pig, and you could either slaughter it or have it be raised. Brenda and I lost track of ours. Oh well, there went that season's big perk. Another time, after a game in St. Louis, we had to rush back for a mandatory appearance at The Pork Expo in Des Moines.

It seemed like there was always some kind of promotional gimmick that took place at the games, and there was often an embarrassing glitch that killed the moment. Before one game at Vet's Auditorium, they hung a banner to commemorate our first-place finish from the previous regular season. While it was being raised to the rafters, one of the cables detached and the banner rolled sideways and went limp. That was nothing, however, compared to what happened before a game in Minneapolis. All these stuntmen were being whisked back and forth above the field, and one of them got stuck in mid-flight. The poor guy had to stay up there while they figured out a way to rescue him, and the start of the game was delayed by half an hour.

Our owner was incredible, too. The team flew commercially, and he was the only guy in the whole organization who sat in first class. He'd try to convince us that he got bumped up—yeah, right. He'd make his wife and kids sit in the back with the rest of us, and he'd be up front buffing his face with hot towels.

It was always a treat come contract time, because instead of having Foster or a front-office guy handle the negotiations, he delegated those duties to the head coach. A lot of us didn't have agents, so we'd have to go into Coach Gregory's office and try to hash out a deal before every season. It was rough. Coach Gregory would be downplaying our accomplishments, which is always nice. Then you'd get into an argument, which also was a killer, because how could you expect him not to carry that onto the field?

Money issues were a huge distraction then, and they're still plaguing the league today. As a team leader, I was always telling the guys, "Don't worry about the money; let's go out there and win this game, and that stuff will take care of itself." But the truth was, it was a major concern. We were trying to get some better rights for the players, things like year-round health benefits and a 401(k) plan, but it was a struggle. Just before this most recent Arena League season, the owners locked out the players and announced they were canceling the 2000 season because of a dispute over many of the same issues. They ended up forging a temporary agreement, which was good, because otherwise a great opportunity would have been wasted. The Arena League has been riding high lately; the NFL secured an option to purchase a 49 percent interest, and my success with the Rams generated a ton of positive publicity and paved the way, I hope, for other players to get noticed by NFL scouts. Canceling the season would have been the worst thing possible, because it would have destroyed all that momentum.

When I started having success in the NFL I became sort of a poster child for the Arena League, and I was happy to be in that position. Arena football is a great game, and there are other guys who can catapult to the NFL now that people are looking at it more seriously. I think there are others like me out there, guys who could thrive in the NFL if only they were given a chance. But it's a tough assumption to make, because you don't know how anybody is going to adjust to changes until he's thrust into that situation.

There are guys as talented as I am, possibly more talented, playing in the Arena League and in other lower-profile leagues. But I think the key is that if you get an opportunity, you have to be able to adjust quickly enough that you don't lose your window. You've got to be able to enter whatever game, whatever situation you might be thrust into, and produce at an early enough stage for people to say, "Hey, this guy's got something." Some guys might be able to develop into productive players given a season or two, but realistically, NFL teams won't wait around for that to happen. Because I was able to make quick transitions to various professional levels—the Arena League, NFL Europe, and my first training camp with the Rams—it gave me a chance to enter the 1999 season as a backup. And when Trent Green went down, another successful adjustment on the fly paved the way for all the good things that have happened since.

Once it became clear that I could survive and thrive as an NFL quarterback, the speculation began: who is this guy, where did he come from, and what's his secret? One of the leading theories is that my time in the Arena League was ideal preparation for the quick reads and sharp passes I ended up having to make in Mike Martz's offense. While that wasn't the only reason for my success, I definitely believe Arena ball helped me. First, because of the speed of the game, I had to develop a very quick release and learn to make instant decisions. I think the biggest problem players have going from one level to the next—and this is especially true for quarterbacks—is adjusting to the speed of the game. Once I got accustomed to the speed of the Arena League, everything else began to seem slow by comparison. When I finally went to NFL Europe in '98, everything felt like it was happening in slow motion, and it seemed like I could stand back there forever.

Second, I credit my experience in the Arena League with improving my accuracy. The windows for completions were so small, and they closed so quickly, that you had to be very precise with your throws. This was especially true when you got down near the goal line, with the shortened end zones (eight yards instead of ten) and tight quarters. Often when a quarterback faces a heavy rush, his accuracy goes out the window. But I was under the gun on every play, so I had to learn to deal with it.

Third, and most important, Arena football allowed me to play rather than sit and watch. If I had made it in Green Bay and backed up Brett Favre for four years, I don't think I would have developed nearly as much as I did with the Barnstormers. All those pressure-packed situations, all those games that came down to the wire, helped me improve as a football player. That's how you learn the game and fine-tune your skills; you can do only so much in practice. Think about it this way. When I joined the Rams, I had probably played in more games over the previous few years than anyone in that locker room. I'd been in tense, championship games and faced every type of situation you can imagine, and that's why I was so prepared when my opportunity finally came.

Skeptics say, "Yeah, well, they were minor league games." I'm not saying the NFL doesn't have better, faster, stronger players, but at some point, football is football. Whatever the venue, whatever the rules, it comes down to reading, reacting, and making plays, often while being stalked by people trying to knock you into never-never land. It doesn't have to be any more complicated than that.

Besides, there are some NFL players who might not be able to make it in the Arena League. If you're good enough, I believe you can succeed at any level of football, but there's no doubt that the Arena League favors certain styles. A quarterback like Dan Marino, who has a quick release, would fit in better in the Arena League than someone with slower reactions, a windup delivery, or a penchant for scrambling. Also, while there are many standout NFL receivers who succeed by running great routes and finding seams in zone coverages, it takes a great one-on-one player to be a successful Arena League wideout, because you basically get man-to-man coverage all the time. And NFL cornerbacks who thrive on bump-and-run technique might struggle, because in Arena games receivers are allowed to get running starts after going in motion.

The truth is, I was content playing Arena football. If a better opportunity hadn't come along, they would've had to throw me out of the league to get rid of me. If I had ended up spending my entire career in that league, I could have lived with it and been happy. There's a quarterback I met playing Arena ball named Ben Bennett. He was a hot prospect coming out of Duke and had a cup of coffee in the NFL, but he ended up playing Arena ball, and by the time his career ended he held most of the league passing records and was the quintessential big fish in a small pond. Believe me, I would have been content being another Ben Bennett.

Someday, I dreamed, I might be able to earn a six-figure salary with the Barnstormers. In the meantime I loved playing, and I was able to take care of my family. I now had faith that the Lord would carry me through, and if this was as good as it was going to get, football-wise, so be it. It was just another test of my faith, and I decided to make the most of it, rather than moping about the opportunities I wasn't getting. I give Brenda a lot of credit, because she never put any pressure on me to make a change. She never said, "You've got to do something else with your life. What are you doing? When are you going to get a real job?"

The experience taught me a lot about patience and allowing things to develop in their own time rather than at the pace we feel is appropriate. Your situation might seem bleak, but often you look back and realize it was part of a larger plan. I believe that the Lord has a plan for each of us that's better than anything we can imagine—even if that plan isn't obvious to us at every stage.

I also loved the fact that during the off-season I was able to get paid for doing something worthwhile. During the summer after my first season, Larry "The Enforcer" Blue and I founded a youth alliance program that allowed us to give back to the community. It was cosponsored by the Barnstormers and the Des Moines YMCA. Larry and I, along with other teammates, would go out to schools and work with at-risk kids. We'd do everything from helping them with their homework to providing counseling sessions. We also did recess programs where we set up games and other physical activities and tried to get them involved. Basically, we tried to be mentors to them in whatever capacity we could. This was the first time I began to formulate ideas about sharing my views with others and preaching the gospel.

Most of all, when I think back to the Arena days, I remember how much fun I had on a daily basis. I liked my teammates, and my coaches—all of whom I think were over sixty—were fun-loving and hilarious good ol' boys with horrible tempers. When they got mad, they'd just fly off the handle, and there were times I did my share of instigating.

This one defensive assistant we had, Art Haege, used to be particularly fun to tease. During our special teams practices I'd try to come as close to hitting him with a football as I could. I'd be about thirty yards away and see him walking down the sideline, and I'd try to bounce a throw off the turf so it would whiz right past him. He'd whirl around to see where it came from, and I'd put my hands in my pockets and look away. A couple of times I actually nailed him, but he had fun with it. He was a total riot, a great guy who had a story for everything.

My head coach, John Gregory, was a good guy as well, but I came to find out later that he did some things that may have hampered my career. Though I was happy playing with the Barnstormers, I continued to pursue the possibility of reaching the next level. One of my college coaches, Dick Moseley, knew some coaches over in the World League, so I'd ask him to put in a good word. With the help of a local TV station, WHO, I put together a bunch of highlight tapes that I sent out to various NFL teams. When universities in Iowa would have their tryout days for seniors, I'd show up and work out for the pro scouts and coaches as well. Those guys would always humor me by taking my highlight tapes, but I doubt any of the tapes ever reached a VCR.

Also, I'd always ask Coach Gregory to see what he could do about getting me a shot in Europe, or possibly in Canada, where he had coached in the past. He'd tell me he was being my advocate, but later other people came to me and said that he actually had been doing the opposite: telling those teams that he didn't think I was ready. Maybe that's what he really believed, but I also think he might have been dogging me because the Barnstormers were having a lot of success with me in the lineup. Either way, I have no hard feelings, because he was a great coach to play for and did a lot to further my development as a quarterback.

During my three seasons with the Barnstormers, I threw for 183 touchdowns and 10,164 yards. Ten games into that last season, I hit my right thumb on a helmet and broke it, but I kept on playing. I'd tape it up so it wouldn't bend much, and that limited my strength and ability to grip the ball. But I felt like I could get away with it in Arena ball because the dimensions are such that you don't have to use all your arm strength on many of the throws. It wasn't like it is on a big field, where I often have to grip it and rip it.

It was painful, but it worked, and we finished with an 11–3 record. For the second consecutive year we made it to the Arena Bowl, and this time we flat-out got beat by Arizona. I had a few nice moments, but I also threw two interceptions, and we lost 55–33.

And that was that. I didn't know it at the time, but that was the last game I'd ever play for the Barnstormers. Over the next few months a lot of exciting things started happening. At season's end Brenda and I were heavily into planning our wedding, which took place a couple of months later. During that hectic period the Chicago Bears called and offered me a tryout, which we scheduled for immediately after our honeymoon.

Everything was coming together so wonderfully. I was about to have it all—the house, the future, the wife, the kids, the dog. . . . Well, actually, the canine front wasn't so cheery. Remember Buddy, the cocker spaniel a girlfriend had given to me in college? My mom had taken the dog when I left to go to Green Bay, but when Brenda and the kids moved down to Des Moines and we got our own place, Buddy was part of the package. That was fine by me, but Brenda wasn't thrilled because that dog still hated her. She'd try to hand me the phone, and Buddy would bite her. One time he also bit Chach, her grandmother, when she was visiting from Arkansas.

Brenda and I had a running argument about whether I should get rid of the dog. She'd tell me, "If he turned on me, he could easily turn on the kids. All it will take is one time, and then how will you feel?" I felt like she was trying to put a guilt trip on me so that I'd get rid of the dog. I held firm until one night when Brenda got the flu and Buddy stayed up on the bed with her. She told me to come up and get the dog, and when I moved to take him off the bed he gave me a really nasty growl. This was the first time he had ever growled at me, and all of a sudden I could see his dark side. I went down to the bottom of the steps and called for him, and he stood at the top of the stairwell barking and going nuts at me. I walked upstairs and reached up to get him, and he tried to attack me, and that was it. The next day I had him put to sleep. When I got home Brenda said, "Great, Kurt. He bit me and bit me and bit me, and he lived. But he turned on you once, and now he's dead."

She was right. I was guilty as charged. But I figured once I lost control of him, he could turn on the kids. And I didn't want to give him away to another family that might have to deal with his temper.

We got married on October 11, 1997, at St. John American Lutheran Church in Cedar Falls, the same place we'd had the memorial service for Brenda's parents. It was a big production, with video cameras, microphones, and more than 250 guests. Before the ceremony, my mom asked me if I was nervous. "I'm used to 12,000 people," I said, referring to a typical Arena League crowd. "I can handle 250." My brother, Matt Warner, was the best man, and Matt Post, Tom Petsche, Dusty Hoffman, and Scott Mason were my groomsmen. Jesse and Zack were dressed as the miniature bride and groom. Since Brenda and I wanted to see them walk down the aisle, we had them go last, after Brenda. She was a bit choked up when she walked down the aisle alone, because she obviously missed her dad at that point.

Brenda's parents, we believe, were with us in spirit that day. Their impact was definitely felt, because we used part of their life insurance premium to pay for the reception, not to mention the down payment on our house.

It was a sweet, emotional ceremony, until the very end. Brenda and I kissed and turned to face our guests, and then the pastor said, "Let me present to you Mr. and Mrs. Meoni." It was like that scene from *Four Weddings and a Funeral,* only worse: Meoni, of course, was Brenda's name from her first marriage.

Zachary and Jesse still went by the name Meoni and in fact still had a relationship with their father, who lived in Iowa with his new wife and visited with them regularly. Brenda's divorce agreement stated that the visits had to take place in her home, so he and his wife would come to our house every two weeks. Still, at that point, I considered Zack and Jesse to be my kids. I had helped to raise them, and they were starting to call me "Daddy" much of the time.

The kids and Brenda had a surprise for me at the reception that ranked as one of the most emotional moments of my life. After the toasts were completed, Jesse, who was nearly six at the time, took the microphone and said, "Daddy, may I have this dance?" Jesse was dressed just like Brenda, with the white dress and long, white gloves and everything, and she looked absolutely beautiful. We danced to Bob Carlisle's "Butterfly Kisses," and there wasn't a dry eye in the house. Then it was Zack's turn. While I sat in a chair in the middle of the dance floor, he stood in front of me with a micro-phone, and did a word-for-word rendition of Tracy Byrd's "Thanks to the Keeper of the Stars."

The thought of losing the kids was inconceivable to me. Before we got married, when Brenda and I would fight or contemplate breaking up, I would tell her, "If we split, I get the kids." And the thing was, I meant it. Even though I knew it would take the most stunning legal outcome since the O. J. trial for that to happen, I still told her, "I'll fight for them."

Now, even after our marriage, I felt insecure. If something were to happen to Brenda, I still stood to lose the kids. Brenda and I talked about it, and shortly after we were married she called up her ex-husband and asked to meet him in a restaurant. When they sat down, she asked if he would consider allowing me to adopt the kids. She said, "You've made mistakes that affected all of us.

That's not for me to judge, but what I want you to know is that Kurt loves those kids, and now with my mom and dad gone I want to know that if something were to happen to me, they'd be with the person who raised them up." She gave him her word that he could still be part of the kids' lives and visit them as much as he had in the past. I give him credit, because he knew that legally he wouldn't have any visitation rights whatsoever once he gave them up for adoption. But he trusted Brenda and agreed to the adoption, and, at least from our vantage point, things seem to have worked out well. Visits obviously became less frequent once we moved out of state, but there have been times when we've been back in Iowa and have dropped off the kids at his house, and he and his wife have come to St. Louis as well.

Two months later I officially became a father. It was an extremely powerful moment for me. This was the final piece of the puzzle, and all of a sudden I felt an incredible sense of security, knowing that there was no way I would lose the kids. They changed their last names to Warner. Our family was now complete.

Finally, I had the stability I'd long craved. It didn't last long. Before winter was out, our family would experience a major life event, a daunting medical diagnosis and my relocation to another continent.

CHAPTER TEN

SIN CITY

The ferryboat cruised merrily across the Noordzeekanaal, and I had a picture-perfect view of Amsterdam, the next stop on my NFL-or-bust tour. It was a lovely March afternoon, and two of my new Amsterdam Admirals teammates and I set out to explore our temporary home. Once off the boat, we took a few steps into the city and were promptly treated to some Dutch hospitality.

"Pssst. You're Americans, right? You want to score some killer stuff?"

If I hadn't been so unnerved I would have laughed out loud. Drugs? Me? You'd have better luck selling hair gel to Michael Jordan.

It was like, *Well, Kurt, you're not in Iowa anymore.*

The four-month stint I spent in Euro–Sin City during the spring of '98 was full of shady encounters like that one. All you need to know is that to get from my apartment to the church where I worshiped frequently during my brief NFL Europe career, I had to walk straight through the infamous red-light district. There were hash bars and strip clubs galore, unclothed women in the windows, and others at the front door trying to drag you inside to see the show. I'd always smile politely and say, "Nope, I'm going to church." I may have been the least adventurous guy in the city, but I ultimately experienced an ample share of ecstasy.

There are many reasons I'm glad I was sent off to Amsterdam before I landed in St. Louis. The experience allowed me to prove

128

myself on an NFL-sized field and join the Rams with a little bit of credibility, but that pales in comparison with what my stay overseas did for me personally. Living away from my family, in a city where temptations were great and there was sin all around me, I reaffirmed my faith and grew even stronger in my spiritual commitment. I also led a Bible study for several of my teammates, and I believe God's grace allowed me to be a rock for those guys. Looking back, I view my time in Amsterdam as having been a time of preparation—for the NFL and for the bigger things the Lord had planned for me in the future.

First and foremost, I had to get my house in order. By marrying Brenda and establishing the type of family that is consistent with my beliefs, I grew as a Christian and as a man. What if I had become an MVP and Super Bowl champion before then, when Brenda and I were living together out of wedlock? What kind of message would that have sent? Also, if I had hit it big a couple of years earlier, would I have been bold enough then to speak openly about my faith?

Right after I signed with St. Louis in December of '97—I'll get to that story shortly—I had an interesting conversation with Pat Sokoll, the pastor in Des Moines who led the Barnstormers' Bible study group. Things had been working out very well for me, especially after I got married, and he pointed out that the timing might not have been coincidental. He said, "The Lord's plan might have been that you had to wait for your big opportunity, because your whole life wasn't in line with what he wanted for you." It made sense.

When I had that conversation with Pat, it was the first time I really started to understand how what I do influences other people. It wasn't just about getting my ducks in a row or asking, "What do I have to do to get in tune with God?" It was bigger than that. Before I went to Amsterdam, I had been totally consumed with my own journey. Now, as I moved outside of my comfort zone, I began to understand that to live one's life for God you have to become less self-centered. It's sort of like the process you go through when you have kids, when your love surpasses your selfishness and helps you focus on the needs of someone else. Only for me it was even more dramatic.

Another great thing that happened in Amsterdam was that, for the first time, I lost my safety net. As I evolved as a Christian and became stronger and stronger in my faith, I always had people to lean on—Brenda, obviously, as well as Pat Sokoll and my two Barnstormers teammates, Dave Bush and Matt Eller. Now, for the first time, it was just me. Only I didn't feel alone, because I felt God's presence in my life more clearly than ever before. To me, that's what the Amsterdam experience was all about—learning to trust God to provide whatever I needed spiritually to handle any given situation. If I could be away from my family and survive Sin City amid all the temptations and pressures, if I could be my closest to Jesus in that difficult situation, then I could trust him to use any situation to help my faith grow stronger.

I was still taking baby steps with this faith stuff. But the people around me were pushing me to start walking on my own. People evidently noticed, because our coach, Al Lugenbill, asked me to lead the team prayer every week, and some of my teammates tried to emulate the example I was setting. For the first time in my spiritual life I was a leader, not a follower.

My road to that landmark, as usual, had its share of twists, turns, and speed bumps. And pests, one of which attacked me on our honeymoon in Jamaica (another place, incidentally, where I disappointed many a drug dealer).

A month before our wedding, in September of '97, the Chicago Bears had called and tried to set up a tryout. They had heard about me from their vice president of player personnel, Mark Hatley, who was friends with Tim Marcum, the coach of the Tampa Bay Storm, one of our Arena League rivals. I thought that was pretty funny: John Gregory, my own coach, was telling teams in other leagues that I wasn't ready for the next level, because he apparently didn't want to lose me. And Tim Marcum, who wasn't even my coach, ended up putting in a good word, probably because he wanted me out of the Arena League.

I had been without an agent for several years, so I dealt directly with the Bears' pro personnel director, Rick Spielman. He called three or four times trying to set up workouts, but the only option ended up being right before the wedding, so we just put it off until after the honeymoon. Once I was in Jamaica I got a message that the Bears wanted me to fly out to Chicago on a Tuesday, the day after we were due back. Man, was I excited! Finally, more than three years after the Packers cut me, I was going to get another look from an NFL team.

Brenda and I stayed at a resort in Ocho Rios, and I tried to relax, which for me is a relative term. Brenda would lie out on the beach or out by the pool, but I'm not very good at sitting around doing nothing, so I'd sign up for every competition they had at the resort: basketball, football, even lawn bowling. When I wasn't competing, I was usually off working out. Don't get the idea that it was totally unromantic, though: Brenda and I participated as a team in all the nightly events, and we placed second in the dance competition. We were more in love than ever before and reveling in our new commitment.

Then, on the second-to-last night, my throwing elbow swelled up to the size of a baseball. I went to a nurse who told me I had been bitten by something, probably a centipede or a scorpion. I'm thinking, *You've got to be kidding me. My one big chance, and now this.* I was in agony: I couldn't bend the arm, I had a fever, and I was extremely nauseated.

When I got home the elbow was still swollen. I was trying to hold off to see if it might heal because I was dreading having to call Rick Spielman. Finally, I called and told him the story. I said, "I'm really sorry; I'm not just trying to put off the workout. I really, really want to do this when my arm heals." I guarantee he was thinking, *Give me a break. We're giving this guy an opportunity to get back in the league, he puts us off once, and now he's coming up with all these crazy stories. Just tell us the truth—you're not ready to work out yet, or you don't really want to work out at all, or whatever—instead of giving us these lame excuses. We don't need the hassle, because there are a million Kurt Warners out there.*

What Rick actually said to me was, "Okay, we'll be in touch." He wasn't; that was the last time he called. I assume the Bears just figured, "This guy had his chance and we've got to move on."

It took a month before my arm fully healed, after I went to a doctor and got some antibiotics. I had blown my big chance; now it was time for Plan B. Al Lugenbill, the coach of the Admirals who had tried to get me to come over the previous spring, had never lost interest in me. He stayed in touch throughout the '97 Arena League season, and he kept ringing me over the next several months. I was intrigued by the prospect of playing overseas, but my situation with the Barnstormers was so good—the money was better than it was with NFL Europe, and now my family was settled in Des Moines—that I wasn't sure it was worth the risk. I felt I needed some security, so I told Coach Lugenbill, "I don't want to just drop everything and hope an NFL team notices me. If an NFL team will work me out and sign me, then allocate me to NFL Europe, I'll go."

He told me he knew of several teams that were interested in finding a quarterback and he would try to get one to give me a shot. The story I've heard is that he then contacted twelve NFL teams and told them my situation, asking, "Would you be willing to give him a workout?" My understanding is that eleven of them—all but the Rams—turned him down.

A few days later, in December of 1997, I was on a flight for St. Louis, totally jacked up for my big opportunity. So what happened? I went out and had the worst workout of my life.

I was awful. Just abysmal. The thumb I had broken in my final season of Arena ball hadn't quite healed yet, but I had assumed it wouldn't be a problem. Bad assumption: I had trouble gripping the ball, and I couldn't hit the broad side of a barn. Accuracy has always been my strong suit, the thing I felt could set me apart, and now I was totally erratic. I did some good things in terms of footwork, and my arm strength was relatively impressive. But I've always thought that if you're not accurate, you can't be any good. I figured I was done.

Coach Vermeil wasn't at the workout, and neither was Jerry Rhome, the Rams' offensive coordinator at the time. Instead, I was throwing for Charley Armey, the vice president of player personnel, John Becker, the director of college scouting, and Mike White, the quarterbacks coach. One of the receivers was Roell Preston, who ended up becoming a Pro Bowl kick returner for the Packers. I felt really frustrated after the workout. I remember telling John Becker, "Look, that's just not me out there. I'd love to come back again after my thumb heals and show you what I can really do." He told me, "Hey, if it was up to me, I'd sign you today. But the final decision is Coach Vermeil's to make." John said he would rate my arm strength very high compared to that of the other guys in the league. I was hoping he was sincere, but I figured he just said that to everybody, because the notion of signing someone with no accuracy seemed pretty far-fetched. Besides, I had been given so many snow jobs in the past, you'd have thought I drove a plow for a living.

I went back home and told Brenda, "Nothing's going to come out of this." My mom called, and I told her the same thing. I wasn't being a pessimist, just a realist. A few days later, the phone rang again. It was Al Lugenbill, saying he'd just heard from the Rams that they wanted to sign me. I did a double take. In the back of my mind I thought, *Maybe they're just doing this as a favor to Coach Lugenbill, because I really stunk out there.* At that point, I didn't care.

For the first time in several years I needed an agent. Mark Bartelstein had been recommended by Matt Eller. I called to explore the possibility and left Mark a voice mail. He called me back an hour later, and in that time he had managed to find out everything about my career, which impressed me. Neither of us had any idea how much business we'd end up doing together down the road, but, as I like to say, it was part of a larger plan.

I signed the contract—no signing bonus, no guaranteed money—on December 23. *Not a bad Christmas present,* I thought.

The best part about going to Amsterdam, in my mind, would be that I'd have a chance to show the Rams I wasn't so lousy. The bad part was that I'd have to be away from my new bride and our kids.

It was quite an emotional time. In January, I got a New Year's gift that topped the one I got for Christmas. Brenda was working as a nurse at an OB/GYN office in Des Moines. One night she came home and, while sitting across from me at the kitchen table, started telling me about a patient who had come in that day. She gave me this whole spiel about how this woman had been trying to have a baby, and her husband was going to be leaving the country soon, and it turns out she was pregnant. I wasn't really listening, but at one point I looked up and Brenda had this funny grin on her face. "It was me," she said. I was ecstatic—the Lord had blessed us with another child. We called my parents immediately and told them the good news. I was high on life—until I lay down to say my prayers that night and it hit me that I'd be leaving soon.

I can't emphasize how strong and supportive Brenda was during that time. She had every reason to be anxious about her predicament—being left at home, pregnant, with two kids to take care of and a husband off playing football on another continent, in the land of sin to boot. We discussed the situation and prayed about it. Long before, we had come to believe that if I was going to get another opportunity to make it to the NFL, it would come from NFL Europe. We decided we were willing to make at least one more sacrifice to see if we could cash in on this break—to see if this was what the Lord wanted.

The more we talked about it, the more we felt the Lord was directing me over there. Everything pointed that direction, from the tryout with Chicago falling through to signing with the Rams. Even though the separation wasn't going to be easy, especially for Brenda, we felt that this was what he wanted us to do, and we had to be faithful to that.

Months later, I found out that the burden Brenda was shouldering was far greater than I had imagined. Right after I left for Amsterdam, Brenda went in for a Pap smear, and it came back positive, meaning there were cancerous cells. They told her, "There's nothing we can do right now, and the irregular cells are slow growing. So we'll continue to monitor you, and you'll probably have to go through the pregnancy. Assuming all goes well, we'll wait until after you deliver the baby to see how many more cancerous cells we find." She decided not to tell me because she thought I didn't need that additional pressure. At the time, she didn't even know if she'd be able to have the baby; if things changed quickly, there was a chance they would recommend an abortion. If she were able to deliver the baby, it was also possible she'd have to have a hysterectomy shortly thereafter.

That was a lot for Brenda to deal with on her own, but, of course, she wasn't alone. Once again, her faith in God, along with some wonderful Christian friends, carried her through. When she finally broke down and told the people in our couples' Bible study group about the test results, they started praying for her. And when they met the following week, they'd collected enough money to purchase plane tickets so Brenda could fly over with the kids to visit and tell me the bad news face-to-face. I was shocked and scared, but I prayed for her health and hoped for a miracle. You can believe what you want to believe, but this is what we believe: God came through with the miracle. The following September Brenda delivered a healthy baby boy—whom we named Kade—and shortly thereafter doctors removed a piece of Brenda's cervix to determine the extent of the cancer. The biopsy came back normal: no cancer, totally healthy. The doctors told us that sometimes during pregnancy Pap smears yield inaccurate results. Our explanation is that Brenda was healed by the Lord.

From a football perspective, my time with the Admirals was a healthy experience. We had a three-week training camp in Atlanta— at the Falcons' facility, which is the same place the Rams ended up practicing before the Super Bowl nearly two years later. And, like our Super Bowl week there, the weather was lousy: it was cold, snowy, and miserable. I'd never been through two-a-days when it was freezing outside, but hey, I'm from Iowa, so I dealt with it.

There was only one other quarterback on the roster, a guy named Jake Delhomme, who was property of the New Orleans Saints. Jake was a good player but wasn't quite at my level in terms of experience, and I had pretty much been told it was my job to lose. I outplayed him early on, but later in the camp Jake came on and I started to struggle a bit. Our offensive coordinator, Joe Clark, sat us down and said, "Kurt, you haven't been playing quite as well as you did early on, and Jake, you've been playing better. But I'm going to start Kurt because of his experience."

Then it was on to Amsterdam. As taken aback as I was by the drug dealer who greeted me when I got off the ferry, it wasn't like I was totally clueless. I had been to Amsterdam before, when I toured with that all-star basketball team after my senior year of high school, so I pretty much knew what to expect. I'd checked out the red-light district and other parts of that culture.

This time, while there were obvious temptations, I honestly wasn't interested. I buried myself in two works of literature: our playbook and the Bible, not necessarily in that order.

For our first game we traveled to Germany to play the Rhein Fire, and though I did pretty well, we had a bunch of turnovers and ended up losing. We bounced back by beating the Scottish Claymores, and then I had a breakout game in a victory over the Barcelona Dragons: more than 300 passing yards in the first half and five touchdowns overall.

At that point I felt in command of my game. After the Arena League, everything seemed slow, like I had time to recite a psalm or two before I hit the open man. The only setbacks I had were physical. My throwing elbow got banged up, and I had to take a couple of cortisone shots to get me through the season. Also, at one point I tore some rib cartilage—the same injury that ended up bothering me in the Super Bowl—and, after warming up for the next week's game, sat out because Coach Lugenbill didn't feel I was ready. That was a drag because it happened to be a week Brenda and the kids were visiting. We lost the game, and I came back to play the next week.

When the year ended, we had won seven of my nine starts and finished with a 7–3 record, good enough to tie two other teams for first place. But instead of having playoffs over there, they take the top two teams and put them into the World Bowl, and we came up short on the tiebreaker and didn't qualify. It was the first time since my junior year of high school that I didn't have the chance to play at least one postseason game, and that was rough.

Despite missing the one game, I managed to lead the league in passing yards (2,101), attempts (326), completions (165), and touchdowns (15). I was proud of that, but I still felt frustrated about the season. Our offense had been tearing up the league early on, and then Coach Lugenbill—as head coaches are prone to do—put the clamps on us. We had been turning the ball over, and our defense was pretty good, so he just shut us down. Everything became quick drops and quick throws, like he was saying, "Okay, you guys have made too many mistakes. Just go out there and don't screw it up, and we'll be fine. We don't need you to score a lot of points. Our defense will keep it close, and you guys can win it for us at the end."

Man, that was maddening. It was completely opposite of the mentality I've always had—to be aggressive and to keep attacking. Now I felt tied down. The first time Coach Lugenbill got conservative, sure enough, we kept the game close and won it at the end. That was all the reinforcement he needed, and we ended up scoring in the final two minutes to win three of our last four games. Still, obviously, it wasn't enough to win it all.

Most important, I played well enough to get the Rams' attention. I got a few calls from St. Louis, and at one point Charley Armey came over and took me and Tom Nütten, another player on the Rams' roster, out to dinner. Charley's a great guy—his brother, Dick, is the House Majority Leader—and, along with Mike White, is a big reason I got the opportunity I did in St. Louis. He was probably the biggest advocate I had in terms of my making it onto the Rams' final roster that next fall. He went to one of our Admirals games and was really excited about what I did. Then at dinner

Charley told me, based on what he had seen in that game and at one of our practices, "You're doing some things better than any of the guys we've got back in St. Louis." That was high praise, and it gave my confidence a huge boost.

Still, as I said before, my football development took a backseat to my personal growth. I lived in a little dorm room with a teammate named Todd Doxzon, who was a brand-new Christian, and I was able to do some of the things for him that Matt Eller and Dave Bush had done for me back with the Barnstormers. I tried to guide him, to serve as a positive example, and to hold him accountable for his views and actions.

At the time, Todd was what I call a baby Christian. He very much wanted to live for the Lord, even though he wasn't sure of all that entailed. He was as confused about his faith as I had been a couple of years earlier. I was hardly a biblical scholar; Brenda, for example, could always quote Scripture pretty extensively, while I still have a long way to go in that regard. Still, even as early as my time with the Admirals, I knew what I believed and I knew what I'd found in the Bible that had applied to my experience, so I tried to share that as best I could.

I was leading our Bible study once a week. I'd make sure Todd was there with me, and we would pray together. Again, I believe the Lord used that experience to stretch and prepare me to become the witness he wanted me to be in the future. God placed me in an unfamiliar and uncomfortable atmosphere, and I had to find a way to get it done through him. It was all part of my evolution as a Christian, and the fact that I was out of my circle of comfort accelerated the process.

Other than the joy I received from my faith and the success I found on the field, I didn't have a whole lot of fun over in Amsterdam. Even meals were a nightmare. It's no coincidence that I lost a ton of weight during those four months. The team provided food for us at our dorms, but it was awful. We had cold cuts every day, and one night we had these ribs that were so tiny they looked like cat ribs. They served patties they called "hamburgers"

that were more like glorified meat loaf, and there were other con-
coctions that looked even more mysterious. Most notably, these
big pots of mush were always on display. I'm serious, it was mush.
There was green mush and brown mush, and they'd have a sign
over the serving tray that said either "Pork" or "No pork." That
was it—no further explanation required, apparently. Tom Nütten,
who grew up in Germany, ate the mush all the time and tried to get
me to join him. But I was never brave enough to try it.

When I went out it was usually to go to church, and because I
had to walk straight through the heart of the red-light district,
that was always an adventure. I was perpetually trying to convince some of my teammates to go with me. I never forced it on
anybody, but I wanted to be a constant reminder of God's presence and to hold people accountable for their faith. Some of the
guys were trying to fight the good fight, and I hoped to be a steady
presence for them—as they were for me—in the face of all that
temptation.

Every so often I'd be walking through the red-light district and
would run into some of my teammates. I don't know what they
were doing there, but since I never saw them at the church I
attended, I'm pretty sure their journeys had more to do with spirits than with spirituality. The next day in practice I'd always get
teased: "Hey, Kurt, I saw you in the red-light district last night.
What's up with that?"

Was I ever tempted? Realistically, no. I had no desire to watch a
bunch of naked women dance around or anything like that. But we
all have human impulses that test us on a daily basis, and my eyes
wandered every once in a while when I'd pass by the women in
the windows. Sex was just everywhere you went.

There are always times in life when you notice someone attractive, when things pop into your head. But the first step in dealing
with that, in my mind, is to be conscious of it. I've told Brenda
many times that I have no desire whatsoever to be with another
woman. That said, I believe part of the fight against temptation is
to avoid it whenever possible. Don't put yourself in a situation

where you know you could be tempted, where you know you might fall prey to weakness. Don't go hang out in a bar if you don't want that sort of thing flashed in front of your face. And, certainly, don't move to Amsterdam.

Another key, for me, is to have people around you that hold you accountable—other friends who will lift you up in times of weakness. It's like strength in numbers. When everywhere you go you're surrounded by believers, when you have friends who share the same convictions you do, it's so much easier to stay in line. If you're out there on an island and none of your friends share your standards, it's tough to avoid slipping, because you constantly have to go against the norm. I didn't have that support network in Amsterdam, so I tried to be a positive example for Todd and some of my other teammates because I knew it would make things easier for them.

By the time I returned from Europe, for the first time in my life I felt truly ready to lead—not only as a quarterback, but also as a husband, father, and perhaps even a man of faith. Now, in a very short period, I had to find a way to prove all that to the Rams.

CHAPTER ELEVEN

LIFE ON THE BUBBLE

I walked into the weight room on a late-August morning, and Will Furrer, my main competition for the St. Louis Rams' third-string quarterback job, acted like he had just been sprayed by a skunk. A few weeks earlier the two of us had been chummy as could be, but now Will pretended I didn't exist and stormed out of the room.

Cutdown day can be a jarring and vicious experience for pro football players, and the deterioration of my relationship with Will was an example of the brutality that ensues when jobs and careers are on the line. When I returned from Amsterdam and reported to the Rams in June of '98, Will really extended himself toward me. He was probably the guy who helped me most in terms of learning the offense, and one night during the first mini-camp he and his wife found a baby-sitter for Brenda and me so the four of us could go to dinner. We had a really nice time, and it seemed like a friendship was being forged.

At that point Will had every reason to feel secure. After all, the Rams' offensive coordinator, Jerry Rhome, was his biggest fan. Will and Jerry had been together as player and assistant coach on two previous teams, the Houston Oilers and Arizona Cardinals, and they seemed to be locked in football matrimony. Tony Banks was our young starter, and Steve Bono had been signed as a veteran backup, leaving Will and me to battle it out for the third and final roster spot. It was a competition that literally went down to

141

the last minute, and as soon as it became clear I had a chance to win it, our relationship completely changed.

As training camp progressed, Will became less and less friendly. He felt he was the odd man out and that he wasn't getting a fair shake, and he grew increasingly distant. When I saw him that morning in the weight room, he must have already gotten the bad news, and I guess he held it against me that I beat him out. He was saying good-bye to a couple of other players, but as soon as I entered he blew out of the room without even looking in my direction. I haven't seen or heard from the guy since.

Believe me, I know what it's like to suffer that kind of disappointment, and there were plenty of times when I felt I didn't get a fair shake. That kind of situation is so stressful, and this was just another instance when that stress took its toll on a relationship.

Making the team was a triumph for me, especially given the unsettling way my time with the team began. I flew home to Des Moines from Amsterdam in mid-June and two days later I had to go to St. Louis for a full-squad minicamp. Brenda and the kids came with me and we celebrated her thirtieth birthday. Not only was I exhausted, my throwing elbow was still bothering me from the NFL Europe season. When I tried to perform in the minicamp, it was clear that something was wrong. I did some nice things in the camp—Coach Vermeil says he remembers me throwing this crisp, fifteen-yard touchdown pass to the left corner of the end zone during a red-zone drill, which convinced him I was the real deal—but the elbow was really inflamed, and the pain was becoming unbearable. The doctors checked it out and discovered that I had partially torn ligaments in the elbow, which meant I had to go back to Iowa and rehab it for the next month before reporting to training camp.

The Rams hold their summer camp on the campus of Western Illinois University, in a town called Macomb. Suddenly I was away from my family again and left to face a major challenge alone. At that first minicamp, the only guy on the Rams I'd even heard of was Craig "Ironhead" Heyward, the burly running back who'd been featured in a Zest soap commercial. He turned out to be hilarious, a guy who was always joking around, even when we were on the field and everyone else was all serious. But I really didn't know any of my teammates going into training camp, and I had no idea whether I'd still be on the roster when the team broke camp and returned to St. Louis. Barring injury, I figured my only chance to make the team was to beat out Will, and that would be tough given his relationship with Jerry Rhome. Will was a good quarterback, and because he had been there the previous year he knew the offense and was familiar with the system.

To overcome all that, I knew I'd have to make the most of my limited opportunities to shine. It wasn't quite as bad as it was with the Packers in '94, when I got only fourteen significant practice reps in five weeks, but every play I had was precious. Tony got about half of the reps, and the three of us—Steve, Will, and I—split the other half. That meant I was getting roughly 17 percent of the plays, but at least it was the same amount as the other backups. Steve seemed likely to make the team, given his experience, though I suppose it was possible Will and I both could have been good enough to change the coaches' thinking.

As camp went on I thought I was doing well, but it was tough to tell: in our first preseason game, against the Denver Broncos at the Trans World Dome in St. Louis, I got in for one drive and completed all four of the passes I threw, moving us from our twenty to the Broncos' twenty. Then I got sacked and fumbled the ball away, and that was it—I never got back onto the field during the exhibition season.

It was hard to know what the rationale for that was. Will was definitely Jerry's guy, but I think Jerry also saw that I had talent and could do some good things. He gave me positive feedback a couple of times, but I still think he wanted Will there. It was diffi-cult because I just never knew what kind of internal politics were shaking out behind the scenes, and I didn't feel like the coaches had enough information on me to make a final decision.

Much later, I heard from somebody that it was a very, very close call between Will and me. From what I was told, it wasn't decided until well into the night before the final roster-cutdown deadline. This was after we had broken camp, and all the coaches were gathered in a conference room at Rams Park in St. Louis. Jerry spoke up for Will, and Mike White supported me. Coach Vermeil was really torn; his sentiments were split right down the middle. Finally, Dick went around and polled the defensive coaches—essentially, a straw vote—as to which of us they thought was the more impressive quarterback.

The next day when I saw Will storm out of the weight room, I had a pretty good idea what the outcome was. A few minutes later I officially found out that I had, indeed, made the team. I was pumped up beyond belief. Finally, I had made it to the bigs, and I had no intention of stopping there.

Later that afternoon Coach Vermeil stopped me in the hallway and congratulated me. We hadn't talked much in training camp, though he had said some nice things about me in the press. Now, for the first time, we had a substantial conversation, and I'll never forget what he said: "There's something special about you. You're going to make a difference here next year." Not *this* year, but *next* year. Looking back, I think it's eerie—it was almost like a prophecy. After we won the Super Bowl, Dick and his wife, Carol, had Brenda and me over for dinner, and I asked him if he remembered that conversation. He didn't, but it's a moment I'll never forget. It set the stage for the close relationship we developed over the next two seasons, a bond that transcended the typical player-coach interaction.

Shortly after talking to Coach Vermeil, I called Brenda to tell her the good news. She was like, "Great . . . now *help!*" This was on a Tuesday, and she had three days to get all our stuff packed up and move it down to St. Louis with the kids. They arrived on Friday, and we spent Saturday and Sunday moving into an apartment in Creve Coeur. Brenda had to get the kids ready to attend their new school in St. Louis by the next Tuesday—in Zachary's case, that meant ensuring that his special needs would be met, which is not a simple process—and it was exceptionally hot and humid outside. Oh, and Brenda was eight months pregnant, and she had to find a new obstetrician immediately. Other than that, it was a piece of cake.

Every morning I'd get to work and tell myself, *This is the good life*. Rams Park is a lovely facility, far more modern than the Packers' building, and the whole setup was so cool. They had a big weight room with all the workout equipment you'd ever need, not to mention a hot tub and a sauna. The locker room was spacious, and each player's locker area was large and spiffy. Shortly after I made the team, I went to grab something from my locker and was amazed to see a plaque bearing a photo of me above the stall, as well as a "Warner" nameplate.

This was a far cry from the Arena League. The Barnstormers' facility was inside Vet's Auditorium, and we were packed in like sardines. The locker room was tiny, and we used it for meetings and film watching as well, because there were no other available options. The Rams, meanwhile, had about twelve meeting rooms and two large conference rooms for additional film watching. Life in the NFL was as plush as I'd always imagined it would be, and I remember thinking, *This is what football* should *be like.*

Once we settled into the season, life with the Rams was . . . well, to be honest, it was sort of boring. Other than attending meetings and running the scout team in practice, there isn't a whole lot for a third-string quarterback to do. I did have one essential job: Breakfast duty. The deal was that first-year guys had to bring breakfast for their position-mates on Fridays, and that was the chore I worried about more than any other during the '98 season. It wasn't as easy as it sounds, because the two guys ahead of me had very different tastes: Tony liked McDonald's and other junk food, which was fine by me, but Bones, as we called Steve Bono, preferred fancy muffins and other gourmet stuff. I guess he got spoiled during his time with the San Francisco 49ers or something; it was pretty funny. Anyway, Fridays were probably more stressful than Sundays during my first year, because I didn't have much chance of getting into a game once the regular season began.

The highlight of my season, by far, came on Tuesday, September 29. Brenda was thirty-nine weeks pregnant, so the doctor had decided to induce labor. Conveniently, we scheduled it for my off day. I really wasn't prepared for the impact; I don't think anyone really can be until he or she experiences it. Brenda and my parents were really worried about me because I have a tendency to get queasy at the sight of blood. Even if Brenda's watching one of those medical shows on TV, I cringe and have to turn away.

But once I entered the delivery room, all that disappeared. It's cool how that happens. When it's your own flesh and blood, and you're witnessing a miracle, getting grossed out is the furthest thing from your mind. It was such an awesome experience. Brenda had learned that she was having a boy early on, but I had asked her to keep it a secret for my benefit. Amazingly, she did. I had sort of sensed it would be a boy, but obviously there was no confirmation until he entered the world. I cut the cord and got to hold him right away, and it was just magical.

The magnitude of the process overwhelmed me. There Kade was, screaming and yelling and wearing this little blue hat, and I'm thinking, *This little man is going to be a huge part of my life.* I couldn't believe how incredible the whole process is. To see what the woman has to go through before and during childbirth, and then to see it come to fruition, was just mind-boggling. Sometimes I walk outside and am blown away by the majesty of the scenery, and this was the same way—a reminder of how awesome God is. And in June of 2000, we learned that God had blessed us with a new child on the way.

Helping care for Kade during the early months of his life totally changed my perspective on parenthood. I'd met Jesse when she was nine months old, and Zack was only three. Before Kade was born I never thought I had missed anything. I had two kids, a great relationship, and all the love you could imagine. But if there's one thing I could go back and change in my life, it would be to have been there somehow from the beginning for my other two children. It's such a great bonding time, and so many special moments take place—rocking them to sleep at night or giving them a bottle or hearing their first words or seeing them walk for the first time. I have so much love for Zack and Jesse, it seems inconceivable to me that I wasn't there from day one.

The buzz from Kade's birth stayed with me throughout the season. I'd show up for work every day with a huge smile on my face, which made me a distinct minority at Rams Park. We had a fairly talented team, but we were losing, and the atmosphere was downright dismal. No, that's an understatement. Entering Rams Park was as chilling as a trip to Jurassic Park.

Coach Vermeil ran a strict operation and worked us extremely hard, and most of the players blamed his approach—and him—for everything bad that happened. There was even talk in the locker room of a player revolt, though I don't know how serious that actually was.

It was a difficult situation for me, because I had a much different perspective than the average player. I was so ecstatic to be in the NFL, finally; the last thing I was going to do was complain about the working conditions. Yet from the start of training camp that's all anyone around me seemed to talk about: "Practices are too long.... He's killing us.... We don't have any legs left.... That's why we fold at the end of games."

Obviously, for a quarterback, practices weren't as strenuous and tough as they were for other players. Our days were long, but it was more of a mental strain. In truth, I enjoyed the long practices, because it meant there were more repetitions to go around—and, by extension, more chances for me to prove myself. Besides, I'd rather work my butt off in the NFL than have a breezy Arena League workout any day.

Still, I couldn't believe how much complaining and moaning was going on around me. It created this mental lag that, in my mind, we never really overcame. The negativity kept snowballing into the season to the point where it was almost like we were defeated before we even took the field. It was a self-perpetuating process: we were losing, and everybody was trying to find a reason for it.

Instead of coming together as a unit, everybody was pointing fingers, and it was like, "Us Against the Coaches." It was different from anything I'd ever been a part of, and it created an incredible amount of tension. The players wanted some relief, and the coaches weren't about to change, so it was a constant issue.

In the second game of the season we staged an epic battle with the Minnesota Vikings and had a chance to force overtime at the end of the game. Down 38–31, we ran a play from the Minnesota nine yard line, and Tony Banks pulled down the ball and lunged for the end zone. He got stopped a yard short, and time ran out. The defeat had huge ramifications. Minnesota went on to finish 15–1, tying the second-best regular season record in league history, and made it to the NFC Championship game. We wheezed to a 4–12 mark, our ninth consecutive losing season. We showed some promise, beating three playoff teams from the AFC East (the New York Jets, New England Patriots, and Buffalo Bills). But we went 0–8 against teams in our division and conducted ourselves like losers.

Players seemed to believe that every time we took the field, we were going to lose. If we played well and won, that was great, but the expectation was that something would go wrong. That Minnesota game was especially brutal, because it fed into the mentality that we had stamina problems and would fall off at the end of games. Consequently, we had a built-in excuse for every defeat. Our division rivals, the 49ers, took the field with a winning attitude: *We know we're going to win.* For us, it was more like, *We might have a chance if the coaches would ease up a little.*

I'd been around sports long enough to know that we weren't going to win many games with that attitude. Sure, the practices were long and hard, but you can do one of two things—complain and stress out about it all the time or just deal with it and play. We did the former. There was a barrage of finger pointing, and people were always pointing their fingers everywhere but at themselves. This is the worst thing that can happen to a team dynamic. If I'd been in a basketball game with a bunch of teammates who moaned like that, I either would've walked off the court or gotten in their faces. Yet because I was a third-string quarterback clinging to a job, I wasn't in a position to do much of anything with the Rams. Had it been my place, I would've confronted some guys and said, "Come on, this is ridiculous. We're never going to win if we don't cut out all this crap and start playing football."

Instead I sat back and watched the disaster unfold. There were several players-only meetings, and guys would take turns standing up and complaining about how bad things were. After a couple of those meetings, Coach Vermeil was summoned to listen to some of the complaints, and he'd be up there in front of the whole team trying to defend his stance. He made it sound like things would change, but then practices stayed pretty much the same, and that alienated him from the players even more. There was discussion about a player mutiny; some guys were saying we should make a stand by not showing up to practice.

I'm glad that never happened, because I would have been in quite a quandary. Given my position, I had no intention of not showing up for practice. I was against it in principle, and it wouldn't have been the smartest career move. But I'm also a team player, and if everybody thought that was the best thing and the issue was voted on, I would have been hesitant to break ranks.

Life wasn't all doom and gloom. I had a lot of fun with my fellow quarterbacks, and Tony Banks and I developed a really good relationship. He was probably my best friend on the team that year, a really laid-back guy, and we had a healthy competition between us. There's a basketball hoop at Rams Park, and I used to beat him regularly in H-O-R-S-E. But, to my credit, I was never stupid enough to play him in a one-on-one, because that man has some serious skills.

Tony and I have similar senses of humor—very dry, with a penchant for friendly jabs. He'd come off the field after throwing an interception, and I'd say, "Hey, Tony, we're in blue this week." Or I'd make fun of his doo-rag. He was a guy that played better when he was relaxed and having fun out there, so I always tried to loosen him up, even in tense game situations. To his credit, he could dish it out pretty well. I'd throw an interception in practice, and I'd inevitably hear a crack like, "Kurt, aren't you supposed to complete more passes to our team than theirs?"

As our team's struggles continued, and media criticism intensified, I thought Tony was getting a bit of a bum rap around St. Louis. He's a good quarterback, and there were a lot of other reasons we were losing, starting with the negative attitude in the locker room. Yet he was getting most of the blame, which was unfair. I remember discussing this with Ernie Conwell, the tight end who later became a good friend of mine. Ernie was telling me how good he thought Tony was, and I agreed. "You know," I said, "I'd like a chance to get out there and play, because I think I could do what Tony's doing—and more." I think that surprised Ernie because he didn't realize I had that kind of confidence. It wasn't a rip on Tony, just a faith in my own abilities that most of my teammates hadn't yet seen. So much focus had been on Tony during our struggles, and I just felt that he was in a rut. He was pressing and trying to make plays all by himself, and he needed a new start.

The only chance I had to make a positive impression was in practice, when I'd run the scout team offense—a group of backups that impersonates the upcoming week's opponents—against our first-team defense. So I'd be Steve Young or Vinny Testaverde or Doug Flutie, and I took my role-playing very seriously. I approached every practice as if it were my tryout against our defense, and I wanted to tear it apart. I tried to complete every pass, even though our defenders usually knew exactly what was coming. I didn't care if it hurt their confidence going into that week's game; this was my audition for the future.

Most of the time I have to say that our scout team fared pretty well. In fact, at the end of the year the coaches voted me the winner of the Defensive Service Award, which goes to the scout team player who best prepared the defense for games. I got a nice plaque, and they put up a poster in the hallway outside the locker room with photos of all the award winners. The funny thing was, the poster was still up there the whole next season, when I had moved on to bigger and better things. At one point late in the '99 season Dexter McCleon, one of our cornerbacks, came up to me and said, "Kurt, I believe you're the first person ever to go from scout team player of the year to NFL MVP in one season." That cracked me up.

At the time, though, the service award was no laughing matter, given my utter anonymity. How anonymous was I? Well, at one point I got a call from a woman who works in the Chicago office of my agents, Bartelstein & Associates, passing along a sports-radio request. Some station wanted me to come on a show to discuss the 1983 Sugar Bowl. Hmmm, I thought. The '83 Sugar Bowl . . . I remember it well. I was eleven at the time, and I watched it at my dad's house. "I'd be happy to go on," I told her, "but there's just one problem."

"What's that?" she asked.

"I'm the wrong Kurt Warner." Obviously, they wanted *Curt* Warner, Penn State's star running back from that era who went on to become an outstanding player the Seattle Seahawks before his career was cut short by injury. It was a flattering comparison, but it happened all the time.

I was worse than a no-name; I was a wrong-name.

There were other inglorious moments. It was an unofficial policy that when a new player joined the Rams, Coach Vermeil and his wife, Carol, would have that player and his wife over for dinner at some point during the season. But for some reason Brenda and I never got invited. Even though I'm sure it wasn't intentional, it still made us feel sort of small.

No matter. After three years in the Arena League I was used to getting slighted. I remember back in the summer of 1997 when Mark Brunell, my teammate during my stint with the Packers three years earlier, went down with a serious knee injury while playing quarterback for the Jacksonville Jaguars in a preseason game. It looked like it might be pretty bad at the time, so I bought him a card and wrote, "Mark, I don't know if you remember me, but we were on the Packers together in '94. I just want you to know that I'm thinking of you and you're in my prayers." I sent it off to the Jaguars, and a few weeks later I got a letter in return—from the president of Mark's fan club, with a generic greeting: "Dear Mr. Warner . . . Thanks for your support." I'm sure Mark never even saw the card I wrote, but the point is, the people who went through his mail had absolutely no idea who I was.

Obviously, I was very thankful to have finally reached the NFL. And on the day before Thanksgiving I learned of another gift for which to be grateful. A bunch of the veterans were talking in the locker room about the complimentary turkeys the folks at Honeybaked Hams were giving out to Rams players. So, thinking it was a cool NFL perk, I stopped over after practice to pick up my free bird. When I arrived they told me that the only condition was that I participate in a promotional pitch. So out came a video camera, and I had to say, "This is Kurt Warner from the St. Louis Rams, wishing you a Happy Thanksgiving. Gobble, gobble."

After I finished I waited around for my turkey. Finally they broke the news: no free turkey. It was just a practical joke. I tried to play it off like I knew the whole time. "I actually came here to buy a ham," I fibbed. Then they told me how much the ham cost, and it was too expensive, so I went home empty-handed and ham-fisted.

I had fallen prey to the oldest NFL prank known to man, and if you think about it, I was a perfect mark. Having come from the Arena League, where we were ecstatic to get a free bottle of Gatorade, I *really* wanted that turkey. The next day at Rams Park, during our full-squad meeting, they rolled all the videos of the rookies and first-year players who had been duped, and the veterans sat there howling. They had an especially good time making fun of me. Many of them said that at twenty-seven I was the oldest person ever to fall for the gag.

I took the ribbing well; it meant I was starting to fit in. Gradually, my temperament and work habits at practice had made a positive impression. D'Marco Farr, who became a standout defensive tackle despite having been a late-round draft choice, used to say encour-

aging things to me all the time: "I've got your back. I believe in you.
I just want to see you get a chance." Frank Gansz, our very vocal
special teams coach—he would stride around practice with an old-
fashioned megaphone, barking out slogans and commands—used
to say, "There's *my* quarterback," when I'd walk past him. He'd tell
me, "You've got something special. I want to see you get a chance
because I feel you could lead us to a championship." John Bunting,
the linebackers coach, was also in my corner, as was my position
coach, Mike White. Actually, Mike's wife, Marilyn, was my biggest
supporter. Like Brenda, she's not shy about giving her opinions,
and from what I heard she was lobbying Mike pretty heavily on my
behalf. At one point Coach Vermeil came up to me and said,
"There's only one way to judge a quarterback, and that's based on
how he throws the ball. You can't throw it much better than you're
throwing it, so just keep it up."

Jerry Rhome, to his credit, didn't hold it against me that he had
lost the power struggle to keep Will Furrer. Over time our relationship grew. During games he would relay the calls to me on the
sideline via my headset, and I'd send the plays in to Tony, so Jerry
got a sense of my calm under fire. One time a little ruckus broke
out in practice—a bunch of people were getting irate, and everyone was yelling and screaming and pushing—and he sidled up to
me and said, "I'll tell you the two people here who can handle
pressure the best: you and me."

Late in the year, when we were out of the playoff picture, Tony
Banks got injured and Steve Bono became the starter. So I was the
second-string quarterback for our next-to-last game, at Carolina,
and the coaches told me they wanted to get me at least a little bit
of action. It made sense to give me a look because Steve obviously
was toward the back end of his career and wasn't going to be the
quarterback of the future. But the game was close—we lost,
20–13—and I ended up not playing.

As we headed into the last game, against the 49ers in San
Francisco, there was a lot of talk around the facility that I should
get the starting nod. I know this because a bunch of guys were

coming up to me and saying as much. Joe Phillips, a veteran defensive lineman who had come over from Kansas City the previous year, said, "I'd love to see you get your opportunity," as did Todd Lyght, our longtime left cornerback. I like to think it was because they were impressed with what I'd done against them in practice. Todd used to think I was cheating back there in the pocket because, knowing it was against the rules for anyone to lay a hand on me, I'd take my time getting rid of the ball. "If that was in a game," he'd grouse, "he would've gotten smacked. This guy can't have all day to throw the (bleep) ball." Then, a few weeks after I became the starter in '99, Todd said, "Damn, you really *can* hold onto the ball that long and get away with it. My bad."

Jerry Rhome actually suggested that I start against the 49ers, but Coach Vermeil decided to stick with Steve. His reasoning was that to start the third-stringer would send a message to our other players that we were giving up on winning the game. The 49ers had beaten us a sickening sixteen times in a row, and Dick wanted our team to treat the matchup with the proper degree of importance.

You hate to hope your team will get blown out, but in the back of my mind I knew that was the only way I'd see any action against the 49ers. Sure enough, defeat number seventeen was in the books by the fourth quarter, and with 3:38 remaining I made my NFL debut. The way it happened was crazy, because I didn't even know I was going in. I had my headset on and was ready to send in a play for Steve, and as the 49ers were kicking off I heard Coach Vermeil ask over the headset, "Kurt, you want to go in?" I was like, "Well, sure I do." I don't even think I had time to throw a single warm-up pass.

The next thing I knew I was out there. Obviously, the conditions weren't ideal—the 49ers' defenders knew we had to pass, giving them the freedom to tee off on me and gamble on coverages. I was on the field for two drives, completing 4 of 11 passes for thirty-nine yards. I made a few good throws and some that weren't so good, and even though my statistics weren't impressive, the experience gave me confidence. I felt comfortable in the pocket. I was making my reads, and the speed didn't overwhelm me. In the end I was able to say to myself, *This is no big deal; it's another football game.* That paid dividends the next August when I was thrust into action in far more pressure-filled circumstances. In football, as in faith, little things can sometimes pay huge dividends down the road.

So that was it for my rookie year: eleven passes, and have a nice off-season. I was disappointed I hadn't gotten to play more in the latter part of the year, but as I look back, it's probably better that I didn't. Maybe it wasn't the right situation. Perhaps it would have hurt my career, because it would have been tough for anyone to thrive under those circumstances. We weren't playing well. The attitude of the team was terrible. I didn't know the offense as well. I hadn't had very many reps. And we didn't have Marshall Faulk or a healthy Isaac Bruce.

As always, I point things back to the Lord and his plan for me. As I assess the situation now, it just wasn't my time. Maybe there was a reason I wasn't supposed to play, because if I had gone in and not performed well the Rams' attitude toward me going into '99 might have been a lot different. The next August, when Trent Green got hurt, I might not have been in position to pounce on the opportunity. When I did get that chance I thought of a line from the Old Testament, what Mordecai said to Queen Esther when she had to save the Jews: "You have been brought into the kingdom for a time such as this."

As the '98 season ended I prayed that the Lord would put me in a position to help rescue our franchise. The waiting was the hardest part.

CHAPTER TWELVE
WHIPPING BOY

Brenda and I sat down to dinner with our hosts, Trent and Julie Green, and about two seconds into the meal, my ever-subtle wife decided to confront the issue that had dominated our summer. In the Rams' quarterbacking pantheon, Trent was the golden boy and I was the whipping boy. Whereas Trent could do no wrong in the eyes of Mike Martz, our new offensive coordinator, I couldn't buy a break.

Halfway through the 1999 exhibition season, a few days removed from the end of a hot, muggy, demoralizing training camp, I had reached my boiling point—and Brenda was right there with me.

"You do realize," she said to Trent, "that you and Kurt are being treated a lot differently by Mike Martz? The two of you can make the same mistake, but Mike doesn't yell at you."

There was an awkward pause, and then Trent and Julie started laughing. So did everyone else at the table—rookie quarterbacks Joe Germaine and Gus Ornstein and our quarterbacks coach, John Ramsdell, and his wife, Brenda, "Heck, yeah, I realize it," Trent told Brenda. "Remember, I was with Mike for two years in Washington. Trust me, this is nothing. At least Mike doesn't get *too* personal. With Norv Turner it was *so* much worse. Every other word was a swear word."

Trent and Julie started reminiscing about the '97 season, when Martz became Norv Turner's quarterbacks coach in Washington and Trent was the third-stringer. Back then, apparently, Trent was the one who just couldn't do anything right. "But we're past all that now," Julie said. "Now it's your turn."

The Greens were sitting pretty at that point, and they deserved to be. They're two of the nicest people you could ever imagine. Trent had been an unlikely success story the previous season, replacing Gus Frerotte in Washington and putting up some impressive numbers. After Coach Vermeil hired Mike Martz to replace Jerry Rhome as our offensive coordinator, Mike lobbied hard to sign Trent as a free agent. In February Trent, who grew up in St. Louis, returned home to sign a four-year, $16.5 million contract. Tony Banks and Steve Bono, our top two quarterbacks from the previous season, were ushered out the door.

For the first time Trent was The Man, and he was living up to the burden. He had a great grasp of Mike's complicated offense, and he took charge from the start, performing impressively in practices and in our first two preseason games. All of a sudden our offense looked shockingly explosive. Isaac Bruce was healthy after two seasons of being dogged by hamstring problems, and Torry Holt, our top draft pick, gave us another deep threat at the receiver position. A predraft trade with the Indianapolis Colts had scored us a Pro Bowl halfback, Marshall Faulk, whose amazing versatility was the key to the scheme. Other skill players like number three receiver Az-Zahir Hakim and multipurpose back Robert Holcombe had loads of potential. And the line looked strong: we'd spent big free-agent money on Adam Timmerman, a standout guard from the Packers, and our highly touted left tackle, Orlando Pace, was starting to show why he was the first player picked in the '97 draft.

With Trent getting the ball to the right people, we seemed capable of great things, maybe even a playoff berth. Meanwhile, despite a mere eleven passes' worth of NFL experience, I had defied the odds and emerged as the number two quarterback.

There was a lot to celebrate that night at the Greens' house. He and I had a wonderful meal together, beaming about our good fortune and the promise of even better things to come.

The next night Trent took a shot to the knee that would change all our lives. In an instant, he was prone on the Trans World Dome turf, writhing in pain. As my emotionally devastated teammates and coaches looked on in horror, I stood there feeling empathy for Trent and uncertainty about my own situation. I wondered whether I'd finally get my chance or if I was just being set up for another fall.

In that tenuous moment I reflected back on all the ambiguity of the previous eight months, beginning with the immediate aftermath of the '98 season finale. I was back at the facility a few days later, working out every morning in the weight room. Partly, that was because I didn't feel I had earned any time off, having played only three minutes and thirty-eight seconds of one game. I wanted to get right back in and start preparing for '99, and the first step was to shed a few pounds. Most people assume you're in great shape by the end of a football season, but actually the big cardiovascular workouts take place in training camp and begin tapering off at the end of it. By the end of the year I feel fat and flabby.

There was another reason I was so religious about my workout schedule: money. We got workout bonuses of seventy dollars per day, and Brenda and I needed that cash. To paraphrase a popular rap lyric, when you're an obscure player with a family and limited job security, "it's all about the Washingtons, baby." It might seem ridiculous, given the exorbitant salaries throughout professional sports, but there are plenty of guys like me who aren't necessarily living large. If I made the team I was due to make $250,000, the NFL minimum for second-year players, though I didn't even have a signed contract at the time. With three kids and a bunch of outstanding bills, including Brenda's student loans from nursing school, I couldn't afford to be lazy.

Money was especially tight because we were in the process of buying our house in Creve Coeur, a St. Louis suburb. House hunting is stressful as it is, but it's especially tough when you don't have a ton of assurances about how long you'll be able to stay in the area. Our apartment complex was crowded and raccoon infested, and we felt like we needed to move somewhere bigger. We still had our home in Iowa so were paying that mortgage in addition to our rent. We weren't used to all those bills. I remember trying to get my taxes in as quickly as I could, because we were going to be living off that refund. Until then the workout-bonus money, and the cash flow it provided, was saving us.

It was decision time. We did a lot of praying about what to do because so much was up in the air. If they kept Tony Banks around, they'd probably want a backup with some experience who they felt could step in and play. I didn't love my chances of being that guy, which meant I might be staring at a second season as the third-stringer. Also, if they were to draft a quarterback, I might not make the team at all.

I went in to talk to Coach Vermeil at one point and asked him, "What's the deal? I believe I can be a backup. I want an opportunity to prove it." He told me, "I don't know exactly what route we're going to go yet, but worst-case scenario, I see you being the number three guy again. Possibly number two, but at least number three." That wasn't exactly what I wanted to hear, but it did give me a little more confidence that I'd be around for another year.

Brenda and I prayed about it, and we decided to take a leap of faith. We went out and found a house above our means that was being built in a modest development. As the house was going up we had to make every decision about the interior, and money was a constant worry. The builders would put something in front of us that would mean a higher price tag, and we'd try to cut corners. Like, they'd want to put a light in every bedroom upstairs, and we'd say, "We'll just put a lamp in there instead." We chose siding instead of brick for the front of the house. We wanted to have a nice, big house for the family, and we could live without the extras.

After we picked out the house, the only way we could get the money for the down payment was to sell our house in Des Moines. At the last minute, after a lot of praying, we accepted a bid that did the trick.

At about that point another obstacle cropped up: Coach Vermeil called me in and told me that I was one of the five players he was exposing for the upcoming expansion draft. The draft was a way for the new incarnation of the Cleveland Browns to stock their roster as they prepared to reenter the league in '99, and every NFL team had to put five players into a pool of potential draftees. The choice for our fifth unprotected player had come down to me and Tony Horne, a young receiver and special teamer with a lot of promise, and I was the lucky guy.

Coach Vermeil said, "We're doing this because we don't think there's any way Cleveland will pick you." Everyone expected the Browns to take a quarterback with the first overall pick in the regular draft—they ended up selecting Tim Couch—and it made sense that they'd go out and get a veteran to hold down the fort until the kid was ready. (They did a few months later, acquiring Ty Detmer, my old buddy from the Green Bay days.) I was an unknown quantity, and the Browns hadn't even bothered to work me out when I was desperately trying to find a team to sign me and allocate me to NFL Europe. It seemed like a safe bet that I wouldn't get picked.

Still, I was a little disappointed. I thought I had proven something the previous season, that the Rams knew enough about me already. I didn't want to have to go to another team and start all over. It would have been especially tough in Cleveland, because if they indeed picked a quarterback first in the regular draft, I'd have to compete against all that money and expectation. I had to hope that Coach Vermeil was right when he said, "We think there's only a slight chance they'll pick you. You're a Ram. This is no lack of respect for you."

Then, about a week and a half before the draft, I found out that the Browns had hired John Hufnagel as their quarterbacks coach. Uh-oh. Hufnagel had been the head coach of the New Jersey Red Dogs, one of my old rivals from the Arena League. All of a sudden I wasn't a nobody to the Browns anymore. I told this to some of the Rams' coaches, and they got a little nervous, too. A couple of our coaches came and asked me about the guy and how well he knew me, which actually made me feel a little bit better about my status with the Rams. At least they seemed concerned about the possibility of losing me.

Brenda and I were in the process of finalizing our deal to buy the house, but the deadline for closing was right before the expansion draft, so we asked for and received a week's extension. I watched bits and pieces of the draft—it wasn't exactly must-see TV—and once the Browns selected another young quarterback, Scott Milanovich of Tampa Bay, I was pretty relieved. I still had to sweat it out to the final pick, and then, finally, I could look ahead to another summer with the Rams.

Things were happening quickly. Mike Martz was hired, and John Ramsdell was named the new quarterbacks coach, with Mike White switching over to assistant head coach, which basically meant he was Coach Vermeil's right-hand man. Trent got signed and Tony was released, leaving me, I hoped, a clear path at the number two job. But in April the team drafted Joe Germaine, a quarterback from Ohio State, in the fourth round. Shortly thereafter word leaked that the Rams were having conversations with Jeff Hostetler, a former starter with the Giants and Raiders who had been out of football the previous year. Both Mike Martz and Mike White had coached Jeff in the past, and I knew the team wouldn't bring him in to be anything less than second-string.

There were quotes from Coach Vermeil saying that even if Hostetler didn't sign, they might look to bring in a veteran backup. A short time later I heard Paul Justin, another ex–Arena League guy who had been with several NFL teams, had been at our facility for a look. I was frustrated because I could easily turn into the odd man out. It was hard not to take it personally. I didn't care if they wanted to bring in someone to compete with me, as long as the competition would be legitimate. The previous summer I thought I had competed well, but it didn't matter because Tony's and Steve Bono's spots were set in stone. This time I told Coach Vermeil, "I don't care if you bring somebody in, just give me a chance to beat him out."

We had been searching for a house of worship in the St. Louis area, and in January of '99 we began attending Sunday services at the St. Louis Family Church. It felt very comfortable there, and Brenda requested a meeting with the pastor, Jeff Perry, to get to know him better. Normally, Pastor Jeff didn't schedule such meetings, and this was one of the rare occasions when Brenda tried to throw her weight around by using the fact that we were with the Rams. Jeff wasn't much of a football fan, and he had no idea who the heck I was, but Brenda's pitch worked on the secretary and we got our meeting.

Jeff's a very charismatic speaker who has a keen sense of humor. Not all evangelical pastors are cut from the same cloth, and Jeff certainly defies the stereotype. Before his call to the ministry, he was a teenage hippie tripping through California. When he preaches he's captivating, energetic, and funny.

During our meeting, though, he was fairly serious. He wanted to know why it was so important to us that I get a chance to make it big in the NFL. Did I want to succeed for myself, or was there a larger purpose?

I told him we felt like God was opening a door for us, one that would lead to a platform to spread the good news about Jesus. I talked about how we had been humbled many times, and that I simply wanted to use the gifts the Lord had bestowed upon me to glorify him. I told Jeff, "I just want a chance to go out onto the field and show my capabilities." Brenda added, "We've got such a unique story. I think we're going to be the light for a lot of people."

Jeff sensed our sincerity. When we were getting ready to leave he told us to prepare. We took that as a message that we needed to get our lives ready for a transformation because things were about to take off. That meant getting our family in order and becoming the strong parents we'd need to be to get through such a big change.

Perhaps I craved spiritual peace because my work environment had become a bit unnerving. From the first minicamp on, Mike Martz was just *killing* me. He was throwing this whole new, intricate offense my way, and even when I'd do something good, it wasn't good enough. It's no wonder the organization was toying with the idea of bringing in Jeff Hostetler or Paul Justin, because Mike certainly wasn't displaying a whole lot of faith in me.

In May Coach Vermeil called me in and told me, "You're going to be our guy. We believe you can be the backup." Maybe that was only because Hostetler had decided not to sign, but I wasn't about to question it. Because Trent was so familiar with the offense, they told me to expect a lot of reps and game action in the pre-season.

"Coach," I promised, "I won't let you down."

A week or so later Brenda woke me up early one morning to tell me about a vivid dream she'd just had. In it I was the Rams' starting quarterback. Then, shortly thereafter, Pastor Jeff gave a very moving sermon at church that talked about a Bible passage from Ephesians, 3:20: "Whatever you're dreaming right now, dream even bigger, because God is able to do exceeding abundantly beyond all we can ask or think." I started thinking, *What if Brenda is right? What if I do become the starter? It's great that I've made it this far, but why not pray for an even greater reward?*

Brenda turned to me and whispered, "You have to start believing me; you have to trust the Lord, otherwise your dreams won't be realized." She was right; I hadn't asked the Lord to make me the starter because I knew that would have meant Trent getting injured, and you obviously don't want to wish misfortune on anyone, let alone a friend. But what I came to realize during that period was that such a request went beyond the two of us competing on a football field. I didn't rationalize how it was going to happen, but I felt I had to believe God was going to use me in a big way in order for it to happen.

After the sermon Brenda told me, "You're going to be starting by the end of the year; don't leave me hanging."

We discussed our situation with Jeff and his wife, Patsy. Just before I left for training camp in July, after Jeff had finished a sermon and the church had cleared out, he stood with us and whispered a prayer, "God, just open up doors and give Kurt opportunity and favor, and protect him." He stopped and looked up at us, and we were both crying. It was intense—you could just *feel* God's presence.

Then I got to training camp, and I felt another presence—that of Mike Martz chewing me out on an unwavering basis. It seemed like he yelled at me every day, every play, all the time. It was brutal. It was one thing to get berated when I screwed up, but even when I thought I did things exactly the way he wanted, I still incurred his wrath.

Mike thought that I forced things, that I always tried to make things happen that weren't necessarily there. He wanted me to let the game come to me. "Don't do anything stupid to hurt the team," he'd say to me. "It's not about you as an individual; let other people make the plays." He and Coach Vermeil talked a lot about game management and being aware of the big picture. Mike also messed with my footwork. He had me moving my feet in a completely different way from what I was used to, which was frustrating.

The worst part, though, was the disparity in treatment between me and Trent. As Coach Vermeil had promised, we split the reps about evenly, but we sure didn't split the *rips*. I'd do something one day and get yelled at for it, and Trent would come back the next day and do the same thing, and Mike wouldn't say a word. If I threw a pass to a certain guy it was the wrong read; if Trent threw to the same guy his read was right.

Maybe I was paranoid, but this is what I remember: during one of our film sessions, they showed a play where Trent threw the ball behind a receiver on a crossing route. Mike stopped the tape and said to the receiver, "Now, let me tell you why Trent put that ball there. He did it for a reason; he was trying to protect you from getting hit." Later, in the same session, they showed a nearly identical play in which I put the ball a touch behind the receiver. "Come on, Kurt," Mike growled, "you've got to hit him in stride."

Another time at practice I tried to hum the ball to the slot receiver on a sprint-out pass, but the ball got tipped by a defender who had cut underneath. Mike immediately started yelling: "What the hell are you *thinking?*" He had told us to read inside out on the play, meaning to look first for the inside receiver and, if he was covered, to look then for the guys on the outside. So I said, "I read it inside out." Wrong answer. "No, that's not how we read it," Mike barked. "We read it outside in!" Now I was baffled. I looked at John Ramsdell, my quarterbacks coach, and shrugged. "Didn't he tell us to read it inside out?" I asked. Coach Ramsdell nodded yes. Later we went back and looked at our notes from a meeting three or four days earlier, and sure enough, each of us had written down, "Read inside out." Coach Ramsdell said, "Maybe Mike changed it to outside in and neither one of us heard it." Uh, yeah, okay.

I'd had strict coaches before, but I'd never been through anything like this. Trent would tell me, "You've just got to understand, he's testing you." I understood, but that didn't make it any easier. I still felt like an idiot in front of everybody because, believe me, my teammates noticed it.

It wasn't just that Mike was testing me. He was also coaching Trent through me. I could understand that, too. You pay a guy who already knows your offense all this money to be the top dog, you'd better make sure everyone views him as the leader. The last thing you're going to do is make him feel that he's screwing up in any way—or make his teammates feel that he's faltering. You want to make it seem like he's making all the right decisions and throws, so everybody will follow him to the promised land.

The problem was, football players aren't that dumb. Other guys started laughing about the disparity, and it became a source of entertainment in quarterback meetings. Without meaning any disrespect to coach Martz, we tried to make light of the situation. Mike was going to jump on me for something; it was inevitable. When he would start in on me during a film session Gus Ornstein, a rookie free agent quarterback, would look over at me and darn near start laughing. I'd have to bury my head to keep from cracking up. Mike might've seen us for all I know, but if he did he never said anything.

At night I'd call Brenda and say, "I think I'm doing okay, but I got yelled at again." It happened so often I couldn't help but wonder how much of it was really a test to see how I'd react to pressure and how much of it was because Mike really felt that way. Maybe they'd still bring in Hostetler or Justin and I'd be out of a job. I spent a lot of time reading through the Bible, and in the beginning of the book of James I found where it says, "Consider all trials and tribulations as joy"; they test your faith and cause you to mature and persevere. That's one of Brenda's life verses because of all she's been through. I tried to apply it to my situation. I needed simply to put my life in God's hands.

Every so often Coach Martz would pull me aside and give me some praise on an individual basis—just enough to keep my spirits up. And Coach Vermeil would grab me and say, "You know, Coach Martz is just trying to test you by being hard on you. You're doing a great job." It was nice to hear those things, but they seemed like nothing compared to the tongue-lashings I received.

While I was up in Macomb getting my self-esteem bruised, the rest of my family had an incredible experience at a different kind of camp. Zachary and Jesse got to spend a week at Camp Barnabas, a Christian retreat in Purdy, Missouri, that offers activities for special needs children. It also gives their siblings a chance to shed their normal caretaking responsibilities and have some fun of their own, and Jesse loved it as much as Zack. Brenda worked as a volunteer nurse, and the experience touched her so much she called it life changing. When she told me about it I decided to try to help get the camp some exposure. I had no idea how much we'd be able to offer in terms of funding and publicity over the next several months; that was just one of the many blessings that awaited us.

We opened the preseason at home against the Oakland Raiders, and I played the second and third quarters. On my first play Mike called a deep route to Torry Holt, and I was getting a lot of pressure, so I stepped up in the pocket and tried to make the throw. But I got hit as I released, and the ball popped straight up in the air. Fortunately, it got knocked down, but of course I still got yelled at by Mike: "Don't ever throw a ball if you don't think you can finish the throw," he growled. "Just take the sack." I went 12 for 18 in the game, yet the next day Mike harped on three of the incompletions, telling me how stupid the throws were.

Next we faced the Bears in Chicago, and I managed to trigger one of the all-time Mike Martz tantrums. I had moved the team all the way downfield to the two yard line, and Mike called a pass to the end zone. Somebody missed a block, and one of the Bears' players came free and got right in my face. I could hear Mike's admonition from the previous game in my head, and when my primary receiver wasn't open—*Just take the sack*—I went down with the ball. Oops! As soon as I hit the ground I realized I had blown it. Another of Mike's rules is, "Never take a sack in the red zone," the area from the opponent's twenty yard line to the goal line. Now I was in big trouble.

On the next play I threw a touchdown to Justin Watson on a swing pass, but it was called back because of offensive pass interference. I actually had touchdowns called back in each of the first two games; I was beginning to wonder if I'd ever get my first NFL scoring pass. As our field goal unit came out, I froze in my tracks because I was dreading what awaited me on the sideline. I thought to myself, *It would be better to stay out here the rest of the game and play defense, because I'll get less punishment that way.*

As I jogged off I got this silly smile on my face. It was like that nervous, almost giddy feeling you get when you're a kid and you're about to get yelled at and you know there's nothing that can save you. Sure enough, as soon as I reached the sideline, Coach Ramsdell said, "Coach Martz wants to talk to you." Mike was upstairs in the coaches' box, and when I picked up the phone he was screaming so loud that I had to hold it about five inches from my ear. "That's the *stupidest play I've ever seen!*" he screamed. "I can't believe anyone would do anything *that dumb!*" I couldn't even make out the rest; he was *ranting.* And he wasn't done. I heard about that play in the locker room, too, and again the next day when we were watching film.

We broke camp and returned to St. Louis, and, just like that, my initiation ended. Coach Martz called me into his office and came clean. "There's a reason why we've been so hard on you," he said. "We had to get you ready because we know there's a good chance you'll have to play at some point this year. So forget about all the criticism. That's over now. It's time to head into the season and attack it and go from here." Looking back it amazes me how far Mike and I have come from that point. Our relationship now is the best I've ever had with a head coach, and I can't imagine a player and coach having a better one.

Next up was the home exhibition game against the San Diego Chargers, and, man, our team was looking good. Our first-string offense had been impressive in a series of intrasquad drills with the Indianapolis Colts in training camp and the first two exhibition games. Now, against the Chargers, it was on fire. Trent completed his first eleven passes, making him a ridiculous 28 of 32 in the preseason. But on his last attempt, as he was releasing the ball, our world turned cold: Rodney Harrison, the Chargers' Pro Bowl safety, lunged at Trent after being knocked to the turf, and Trent fell to the ground, clutching his knee.

At first I didn't think it was that bad. I figured he had a twisted ankle, or maybe a strained knee. I went over and started warming up, but the more time it took, the more serious it seemed to be. When I finally started paying attention I realized how devastated everyone on our sidelines was. Isaac Bruce was down on both knees, pounding the turf in frustration. I didn't blame him, because I think everybody felt that way. Coach Vermeil says he's never been in a game or practice where players were so visibly shaken. They had good reason to be angry. Nobody knew a whole lot about me, other than that I got yelled at a lot. Trent was supposed to be the guy who was going to turn our team around, and now he was down for the count. Heck, I was upset, too, because I knew how hard Trent had battled for his chance.

Rodney Harrison has the reputation as a dirty player, and some of our guys felt that his hit on Trent was a cheap shot. I didn't see it that way. He had made a couple of questionable hits earlier in the game, but I didn't think this one was malicious because he was crawling into Trent. That said, when you're a veteran starter, why crawl into someone's knees in an exhibition game? It's not about winning a game or making a team in that context. So, though it wasn't a dirty play, I think it could have been avoided.

I went in and threw just one pass, a completion to Torry that I threaded between two defenders. He fumbled, and the half ended. In the locker room Trent told me he had probably torn his anterior cruciate ligament and was out for the season. "Now it's your turn," he said. "Go do it."

"Thanks," I said. "I'll be praying for you."

Then I went to talk to Coach Martz. "That was a good pass you threw to Torry," he said. "I'm not sure it was the right read, but it was a good pass." But the next day, when we went to watch film, I walked Mike through my progressions—which receiver was my first option, which one was my second, and so on—and I was able to tell him everything I did and why, even where the defensive backs and linebackers had moved once the ball was snapped. The game had really slowed down for me, and I had a clear understanding of what I was supposed to do. Mike was impressed; I could see it in his eyes that he was relieved. He said, "Okay, no problem, as long as you had a reason." From then on his whole demeanor changed. I think it kind of hit him that I wasn't just running back there and throwing it up.

The coaches decided to play me just one series in the second half. I guess they were worried that I'd get hurt, too. Everyone was in a daze. When I got home that night I called Trent in the hospital to see how he was doing and to make sure his spirits were up. He was in a pretty good mood, considering. I knew how many hard hours he had put in to become an NFL starter; it had to hurt. But he handled himself with so much class, not only that night but the entire season.

Then I hung up the phone and started stressing. Would they give me a shot to be the starter, or would they bring in Jeff Hostetler or someone else? I stayed up most of the night playing out different scenarios in my head and talking to Brenda. When I got to the facility early the next morning I wondered whether I'd have to swallow another dose of disappointment. I didn't see Coach Vermeil, but after a while Mike Martz called me into a meeting room. "We're going to bring in a veteran," he said. I swallowed hard. "But whoever we sign will be the backup," Mike continued. "You're the guy now." And that was that. He and the other coaches didn't dwell on it. They just went about their business and said, "Let's go play." Their approach never changed one iota, and that helped me.

Later that day, in our full team meeting, Coach Vermeil stood up and said, "Kurt, you're the guy. I expect you to play well." I didn't say anything back, but I had to hold my tongue. I wanted to stand up and say, "Yeah, I expect to play well, too." But obviously I had to prove myself on the field, not with my mouth.

At that point some of my teammates were thinking, "Man, here we go again. Our season's over." In the days that followed a lot of people, even some of the players, would suggest that the franchise was cursed. But their strong reaction to Trent's injury didn't bother me. I liked the fact that they had gotten so attached to him in such a short time. I hoped I could earn a similar degree of loyalty and respect.

Even though our last game was technically an exhibition, it was possibly the biggest game of my life. We had signed Paul Justin as a backup, and now we were headed to Pontiac, Michigan, to play the Detroit Lions in the Silverdome. I knew it was my chance to open some eyes, solidify my position, and give my teammates and coaches a big confidence boost. I played the first half, and we put up points on each of our three drives. When I finally threw my first touchdown pass our equipment manager, Todd Hewitt, asked me if I wanted to keep the ball. I told him, "Nah, don't worry about it. I hope there'll be a lot more to come." I felt great out there. I made good reads and good throws, and we went into the locker room with a 17–0 lead. My night was done; I had made my statement loud and clear.

You could almost hear people exhale. It was like, "Okay, he's gonna be all right. He's what we thought he was, and we're still gonna be good." After the game people were breathing just a bit easier. Coach Vermeil presented me with the game ball—he said, "Who else would get it but Kurt Warner?"—and gave me a big hug as everyone cheered. He was crying, and for the first of many times he said to me, "I love you."

Not everyone was so adoring. The media crunch was huge after Trent's injury, and the questions I was getting, by nature, weren't overly upbeat: "What do you think is going to happen now?" "Can you play as well as Trent?" "Do you believe that you can lead this team?"

What was I supposed to say? "No, there's no way I can do what Trent did. I'll never be able to carry this team." I knew what I really felt, but it would have looked stupid in print: "Darn right I can lead this team. In fact, I think I can be even better than Trent." This was no knock on Trent's ability. As pro athletes, we're conditioned to believe no one else is better; that's our competitive nature.

The questions didn't bug me as much as the way we were written off nationally by everyone—and I do mean everyone. You'd read things like, "The Rams are done. Before I thought they were an 8–8 team; now they'll be lucky if they win four games." A couple of ESPN guys said we were finished without Trent, and that included Sean Salisbury, who used to be a backup quarterback in the NFL. One time on CNN I saw Trev Alberts, the former Indianapolis Colts linebacker who played high school ball in Cedar Falls. Coming out of high school, we had played together in the Shrine game featuring the top players in Iowa, and I thought, *Cool, maybe he'll say something positive about me.* Uncool: he sold us down the river like everyone else.

You'd think someone would have gone to bat for me, if only to be different. Actually, there was one person. Right before the Super Bowl this guy out of Chicago sent me a clip that he had written a week after Trent's injury. It said, "Based on what I saw in the Chicago game, I think the Rams are going to be all right," or something to that effect. Thanks, brother. I needed that.

But for all the skepticism, my teammates did an amazing job of rallying around me. I remember Todd Lyght coming up to me and saying, "You have everybody's support on the team. This whole thing is bigger than one position. No one man can carry the load. We'll try to make your job as easy as possible." Isaac Bruce said something to reporters like, "All Kurt has to do is drive the car and let us be the wheels." That was the way Marshall Faulk and so many others treated my situation, too—just do your thing, and we'll take care of the rest.

A few days after the Detroit game Ricky Proehl, our veteran backup receiver, said something interesting to me: "You're under more pressure now, but you seem more comfortable as the starter than you ever did as the backup." That made sense, because the backup role was out of the ordinary for me. I was used to being in control. Once I became the starter, I actually felt *less* pressure. Now I could just play. They could yell at me all they wanted, but I was the one who was responsible for making the plays—and that's the way I liked it.

One day Coach Vermeil said during an interview, "Kurt Warner will play better this year than any of the five quarterbacks who were number one picks in the draft." Everyone made a big deal out of it, but it didn't seem like such a bold statement to me. I expected myself to play better than those guys because they had never played professionally. Heck, when was the last time a rookie came into the league and really played at a high level? Maybe Dan Marino in '83, and he was an anomaly.

The truth was, I expected myself to play as well as almost any quarterback in the league. And I thought everyone was a little too freaked out about the situation. Trent had been playing really well, and he's a very good quarterback, but the guy had been a starter for only part of one season. He, too, had been a no-name until he got his shot in Washington the previous year and raised some eyebrows because of his solid play. With Marshall Faulk, Isaac Bruce, and a bunch of other weapons, I didn't see why I couldn't do the same.

The whipping boy was about to do some whipping of his own.

CHAPTER THIRTEEN

WHO IS THIS GUY?

We were flying back from Hawaii last February 7, the day after the 2000 Pro Bowl, when a tall, gregarious man ambled up to my father, Gene, and introduced himself. "Mr. Warner," he said, "I'm Chris Berman of ESPN. I just wanted to tell you how great it's been watching your son this season."

My dad was eating it up. Who wouldn't love talking sports with Chris Berman? They exchanged pleasantries for a minute, and then Chris said, "You know, Mr. Warner, this is the greatest single-season sports story in history." My dad furrowed his brow and gave one of those "I'll bet you say that to all the fathers" looks.

"I'm serious," Berman said. "We've all put our heads together on this, and when you consider where you son came from and what he accomplished in one year, this is it."

When I heard about Chris's statement, I had a hard time digesting it. Praise like that is hard to fathom. Part of the problem is that I'm hard to impress because my personal expectations are so lofty. That's not to say I expected to throw forty-one touchdown passes, win the regular season and Super Bowl MVP awards, and set a record for passing yards in a Super Bowl. But I did think I could emerge as a pretty cool success story.

But the best single-season sports story ever? I'll leave that for the historians to debate. What I am proud of is this: were it not for the incredible story of the Rams, who entered 1999 with the worst record of any NFL team in the '90s and exited as the premier team in football, we wouldn't even be having this discussion.

Think back to our season opener against the Baltimore Ravens. If someone had told you the Rams were going all the way, you'd have probably said, "Yeah, all the way to the top of next year's draft." After Trent Green got hurt no one even gave us a chance to break .500. Remember how I said that the only person who didn't write us off was a guy from Chicago? Well, there was one other individual who put himself on the line—hint: he was wearing a blue-and-gold number 13 jersey—because he was blessed with inside information.

Shortly after Coach Vermeil decided to go with me as Trent's replacement I told him, "Don't worry about all the people doubting your decision. You gave me the chance, and I'm going to prove you right."

Even people I thought were in my corner weren't convinced that I could do the job. A couple of days after our season opener, our friend Stacy, one of Brenda's buddies from nursing school, told me proudly, "I've got you on my fantasy football team." I was pumped; I'd never heard of anyone picking me before. "I did pretty well for you in Week One," I said, noting that I'd thrown for three touchdowns and more than 300 yards. She hesitated for a moment, then stared at the floor. "Actually," she admitted, "I didn't start you. I went with Vinny Testaverde." Stacy tried to explain her rationale, but I didn't want to hear it. I said, "I appreciate that you picked me, but you weren't confident enough to actually play me. I thought friends are supposed to have faith in each other." I ribbed her about it all season, too.

My friends over at Nike were even slower to catch on. Before Trent got hurt, when I was the backup, nobody from corporate America wanted to have anything to do with me. I had no shoe deal, no card deal, and no other marketing opportunities. Then when I became the starter the contract proposals—mainly from Nike and various trading card companies—reflected their skepticism. I'm sure they expected that I'd jump at their lowball offers, but they didn't realize two things about me: first, I'm not driven by money or a desire to set up a marketing empire; time with my family is more important. Second, I figured if I proved myself on the field, business would take care of itself.

I was willing to bet on myself and turn my back on the deals. I remember telling one of my agents, Rob Lefko, "I know I'm going to play well. Give me a few weeks and they'll be offering more." Now, I'm not a big gambler—when we went to the ESPYs in Las Vegas after the season, I stayed holed up in my room most of the time—but I was on a serious roll. Every week, as I would have more and more success, the proposal amounts would go up. Way up. From the second to the fifth weeks of the season the offers from the trading card companies increased tenfold. Then it got even crazier. Put it this way: the first offer I got was for $1.50 per card; at season's end, I was signing deals that paid anywhere from $60 to $90 per card.

The shoe situation was similar. I was playing in Nikes anyway, but they hadn't even been willing to give me a token deal before Trent got hurt. After my hot start, they were anxious to bring me into the fold. They told me most of their money had already been allotted to other players but that they could get around it by crafting a deal with a small amount up front and a bunch of money tied to performance incentives. At the time I'm sure they were thinking, *This'll seem like a great deal to him, but there's no way he'll reach most of these plateaus.* I hope the fact that I ended up realizing every one of the incentives didn't hurt the company's bottomline, but I'm sure Phil Knight can afford it.

Even though the coaches displayed a lot of faith in me, I could tell they weren't totally sold, either. One day early in the season Coach Vermeil came up to me and said, "Hey, I've got a Beta machine, we're going to have it sent over to your house so you can watch film at home." I was like, "Yippie—I get to spend less time with my family and more time studying game tapes." Okay, I didn't really say that. But I wish I had been in a position to say no. I watch plenty of film at the facility, and in the past, if I ever felt a need to study further at home, they'd just dub one of the Beta cassettes onto VHS. As far as I know, that's the way it had worked with Tony Banks when he was the starter the previous year. Why did I need all the extra work?

As much as I value film study, I also feel that it reaches a point of diminishing returns for me. Sometimes, when I get too keyed in on what the opposing defense has done in the past, I start over-thinking game situations, rather than just going out there and operating within the flow of our offense. One great thing about Mike Martz is that instead of constantly reacting to what the opponent's doing, he makes the defense adjust to our scheme. That's the mentality I like to take into games.

Our opener was at home against the Baltimore Ravens, a team that turned out to be really good in the second half of the season but was still finding its way at the time. This was a huge game for me, because even though I had quelled some of coaches' anxiety with my performance in the final preseason game in Detroit, the regular season is a completely different story. The speed and intensity increase immeasurably, and I knew it would be a chal-lenge. Still, I felt confident. When I arrived at the stadium, as I was walking through a hallway toward our locker room, I ran into an old friend: Tony Banks, who had signed with the Ravens after the Rams released him. Not only had Tony been beaten out by Scott Mitchell, he had been banished to third on the depth chart, behind Stoney Case.

What a role reversal. Now I was a starter and he was the third-stringer. If he had brought me breakfast, the picture would have been complete. I asked him about his situation, and he said, "I'm going to stick it out and try to work my way through this." He con-gratulated me, and I told him to hang in there. (And he did. By the end of the year the Ravens were one of the hottest teams in the league, and Tony had become their present and future starter.)

Once the game began, two things were abundantly clear: we weren't the same old Rams, and I wasn't going to fold under pres-sure. I threw an early interception to Ray Lewis, my first of two on the day, but I also got into a nice rhythm and made some plays that not everyone can make. We had a 17–3 lead at halftime and cruised to a 27–10 victory. The coaches were impressed. At one point my quarterbacks coach, John Ramsdell, said after a play, "You're unbelievable." Later I went to the phone and talked to Coach Martz, and he said, "Just keep doing what you're doing; you're playing great."

I finished with twenty-eight completions in forty-four attempts for 309 yards and three touchdowns. We ran out the clock at the end of the game, and I kept the ball and started jogging off the field past the area behind our bench, near where we enter the locker-room tunnel. Brenda was sitting about ten rows up, and she came down to greet me. Spontaneously, we established what would become a familiar ritual. I felt like kissing her, so I said, *What the heck?* We kissed, and I gave her the ball because we had both been through a lot to get to that point.

In the locker room Coach Vermeil gave me the same treatment he had after the Detroit game—hug, sobs, "I love you," game ball. I lifted the ball over my head and thanked him for the opportunity, then thanked my teammates for believing in me. "This isn't all I've got," I assured them. "I'm going to get better."

Because of the quirky schedule made necessary by the Cleveland Browns' return to the league, we had a bye on the second week of the season. Brenda and I loaded the kids into our minivan and drove back to Iowa to visit family. As we were cruising up Highway 61, I pointed out that Miller Lite had named me the league's player of the week. "You know what?" I said to Brenda, "it's not going to end now, but if it did end, and that was the last game I ever played, I can still say for that one week I was the best player in the NFL. Think about how far we've had to travel to get to that point. This is it. We made it."

That Saturday night we went to watch my old college team, Northern Iowa, play Central Washington at the UNI-Dome. We were hanging out in the student section, enjoying relative anonymity because I was an old man. All of a sudden I heard my name over the P.A. system. The announcer told the crowd where I was sitting, and from that point on it was a mob scene of autograph seekers. I was caught totally off guard; it was one of the first times my life had been disrupted like that. "We'd better start getting used to it," Brenda said.

Our second game was also at home, against the Atlanta Falcons, our NFC West rivals who had come out of nowhere the previous season to win the conference. But we caught them at a vulnerable time—their star halfback, Jamal Anderson, had gone down with a season-ending knee injury the week before—and they were flatter than my hair. It was a game where everything seemed to flow for us, and we beat them 35–7. I was named the NFC Offensive Player of the Week after throwing for 275 yards and three touchdowns, joining Dan Marino as the second quarterback in the last fifty years to throw for three TDs in each of his first two starts. Amazingly, it wasn't the last time I'd be compared to Marino before the year was done; halfway through the season I was on pace to tie his single-season record of forty-eight touchdown passes.

After that game I remember telling my mom, "We're going all the way." She probably thought I'd taken one too many shots to the head, but I felt that good about our team.

The next week we traveled to Cincinnati to play the Bengals, and the big story was our number three receiver, Az-Zahir Hakim. We won the game by a 38–10 score, and Az accounted for twenty-four of the points himself, with three receiving touchdowns and another score on an eighty-four-yard punt return. The guy was just incredible. With Isaac Bruce, Torry Holt, and Marshall Faulk, we knew we had an explosive offense, but now we had another guy who was virtually unstoppable. I remember I started off the game horribly but ended up 17 of 21, with 310 yards and the three touchdowns to Az. The first one, a nine-yard pass to the corner of the end zone, was the funniest: just as I released the ball, this Bengals lineman tackled me to the ground and, as he sat on top of me, started growling. It was hilarious. He just sat there going, "Rrrrraaaaaah!" like a lion at feeding time. I guess he was trying to intimidate me or something. I said, "Hey, Tarzan, I just threw a touchdown pass. Get off of me."

Now I'd thrown for three TDs in each of my first three starts, something not even Marino had done. The new thing was to compare me to Johnny Unitas, another incredible compliment. I knew Johnny U. was one of the greatest quarterbacks of all time, but until then I hadn't been familiar with his story. It's really amazing how many parallels there are: he came out of nowhere, played semipro ball, and eventually became the league MVP. He even had a flattop.

In the Cincinnati game my passer rating—I won't bore you explaining the formula behind that bizarre statistic—was 158.3, the highest possible for a single outing. The last person who had done that was Jeff Blake in 1995. Still, I'm a perfectionist, and I remember staying up most of that Sunday night thinking about the four passes I missed and what I could have done better. That's normal for me, and I'm usually the first guy at the facility the next morning, because I want to go over the film and correct the mistakes I've made.

Now, at 3–0, our team was getting some national recognition. Yet there was still a current of skepticism in the air because the big, bad 49ers were coming to town, looking to win their eighteenth consecutive game against us.

It's impossible to convey just how big a game this was for us. To be legitimate, to set ourselves apart, we *had* to beat the 49ers. We all knew the history. In 1995, the Rams' first year in St. Louis after moving from southern California, they got off to a 5–1 start before the Niners came to town. Steve Young was injured, but San Francisco, with Elvis Grbac at quarterback, came in and crushed them by a 44–10 score. This time the scenario seemed eerily similar. The Niners, after being blown out by Jacksonville in their opener, had rebounded to beat Tennessee and Arizona, and Jeff Garcia would be subbing for the injured Young.

This was a big game nationally, and people were starting to get wind of my story. *Sports Illustrated* and ESPN, among other media outlets, came to town to do features on me, and my precious anonymity was in the process of being destroyed. I was still enough of an unknown quantity that ESPN's Andrea Kremer, who's as thorough as anyone in the business, approached me after coming to my house for an interview and asked, "Now, who are you?" There were about ten people buzzing around, and she thought I was a member of the camera crew. We had a great laugh about that.

That same week, after one too many calls from enthusiastic Ram fans—not to mention a cousin from my dad's side of the family whom I had never met—we decided to switch to an unlisted phone number. We still got plenty of hysteria every time we checked our e-mail; if I told you what our online address was, you'd never believe me.

It was all so crazy. The night before the 49er game Brenda kept waking up in the middle of the night to pray that we could sustain the success and withstand the madness. She'd nudge me awake and say, "Kurt, pray with me." I was delirious. Finally I said, "How about if I get some sleep and you pray for both of us?"

I'd never been so relaxed going into a game. We had what was probably our best week of practice all season, and late in the week Coach Vermeil gathered us and said, "You guys have been flying around all week, and you're ready to play. This is our time—it's our time to beat the 49ers and get things moving in our direction. Somebody has to step up; why not the Rams?"

If ever I felt the power of the Lord on the football field, this was the day. At the start of church services on Friday night we had joined our fellow worshipers in chanting, "All things are possible!" during the chorus of one of the songs, and that's exactly how I felt once the game began. On our first possession we drove eighty-three yards for a touchdown, which came when I froze their safety with a pump fake and hit Isaac Bruce on a thirteen-yard slant. Three minutes later I connected with Isaac on another touchdown, this time a five-yard fade against a double-zone. Coach Vermeil was impressed: that was the first of two occasions that day on which I threw TDs to guys I'd never gone to when practicing those plays. At one point he came up to me and said, "I can't believe you're so relaxed out there. You're even calmer in big games than you are in the other games. There's a feeling of peace about you."

By the end of the first quarter I had thrown for 177 yards and three touchdowns, the third also to Isaac on a forty-five-yard go-route. It seemed like everything was happening in slow motion. My line gave me a ton of time, my passes were perfect, and my receivers were wide open. I don't think the 49ers knew what hit them; they had no idea what we were capable of until that point. We had taken them out of their comfort zone immediately. It was like a typical 49ers-Rams game, only the roles were reversed.

Isaac Bruce, who had suffered through so many of those defeats, was the guy spearheading everything. He was so pumped up and emotional that he was nearly hyperventilating on the sideline. He ended up with four touchdown catches, and it could have been five; I had him open down the left sideline early in the second quarter, but Lance Schulters, the 49ers' free safety, made a great play to pick off the pass. (Schulters, who was a first-year starter, also intercepted me again in our rematch in San Francisco. When I saw him over at the Pro Bowl I felt at least a little responsible for getting him to Hawaii.)

Like me, Isaac is a devout Christian who isn't shy about expressing his beliefs. But he's also a very private person, and as much as we clicked on the field, forging a personal bond hasn't come as easily. You've got to earn his trust to some degree; he wants to know what you're about before he's going to give up anything about himself. Sometimes, especially early on, I'd get the feeling that he was shutting me out, that I wasn't part of anything with him. But as the season grew he started coming to the midweek Bible study sessions that we held over at my house, and we got to know each other a little. We're now at the point where we've got a good working relationship, and I look forward to us getting closer in the years to come.

The 49ers, to their credit, at least made us sweat, fighting back from a 28–10 deficit to creep to within eight points, 28–20, late in the third quarter. If we were going to crumble in the wake of their mystique, as the old Rams would have, this would have been the time.

Sorry, fellas. Tony Horne, our fifth receiver—one of the self-proclaimed "Warner Brothers"—raced ninety-seven yards with the ensuing kickoff, and that was the ballgame. This was the first time we had really been pressed all season, and Tony and his blockers came through. It became a recurring theme: whenever we got in a pinch someone unexpected would step up and make a play.

We won the game, 42–20, and I finished with crazy stats: 20 for 23 for 323 yards and five touchdowns. After four games I had fourteen touchdown passes—more than all of our quarterbacks had combined to throw the previous *season*. It was a triumph for our team, not only because we ended the losing streak, but also because our performance had revealed our character. That losing atmosphere from the previous year was gone; we were a team that expected to win big games and rose to the occasion.

Suddenly, we were the hottest story in sports. I had thought the previous week was bad in terms of hype, but it was nothing compared to what happened after we beat the 49ers. On Wednesday *Sports Illustrated* came out, and I was on the cover with the caption "Who Is This Guy?" My wife and kids were probably asking the same thing, because it seemed like I was spending more time doing interviews than I was with them.

Our next game was a rematch with the Falcons in Atlanta, and that was probably my toughest week of the season. Now it seemed like everyone wanted a piece of me. I could understand how it was a big story, but at that point it had been told and retold several times and even I was getting bored by it. When you're growing up you always think how cool it would be to see yourself on TV; now I was so sick of myself that I'd reach for the remote. It was hard to stay as focused as I needed to be, and I had a lousy week of practice. I was tired—mentally, emotionally, and physically—and I felt that everybody was trying to pull me in a different direction. After that week I ended up shutting down most of the one-on-one interview requests because I realized how distracting those things could be.

There was one interview request, however, to which I eagerly said yes. I had the good fortune of being asked to appear at a crusade given by the Reverend Billy Graham, a Christian icon whom I admire greatly. He was speaking at the Trans World Dome on the Friday night before our game in Atlanta. I guess he had read or heard some of my comments about what I stood for, and he had someone call the Rams and ask if I could fit it into my schedule. Fit it in? I would have been thrilled just to be in the audience, let alone have a chance to join him onstage.

The thought of meeting him made me a little nervous. Here I was feeling like such a big shot, getting on the cover of *SI* and all, but his presence in St. Louis restored perspective in a hurry. I had my family with me before the show, and we got to meet him for only a couple of minutes because we had been told not to tire him out. He actually knew a little bit about our situation, which was incredibly flattering. We also got introduced to one of our favorite singers, Charlie Daniels; he and Zack sat on a golf cart and pretended they were driving around the inside of the dome.

My appearance was basically a question-and-answer session. The moderator, Cliff Barrows, asked what makes the difference in my life, and I said, "I've been in this place many a time, with the seats packed and people cheering, but I've never been as awestruck as I am now." I talked about how growing up I'd always put my life on one side and relations with God on the other. I knew God was there, but I only called upon him when I needed him or felt compelled to thank him. Eventually, I realized that my life is God, and I need to live every day for him. Then, referring to the *SI* cover, Cliff asked, "Who is Kurt Warner?" I replied that the only secret to my success was Jesus, that "it doesn't have anything to do with how I work out or what I eat or being in the right place at the right time. I was born for such a time as this."

Predictably, in the wake of all the distractions, I didn't play my best game. Thankfully, Marshall Faulk was there to bail me out. We won the game 41–13, but that was deceptive because two of our touchdowns came on a kickoff return (by Tony Horne, again) and an interception return (a ninety-one-yarder by Grant Wistrom, our 267-pound defensive end). I was a very modest 11 of 20 for 111 yards; Marshall, meanwhile, carried eighteen times for 181 yards and added thirty-two receiving yards on three catches.

Marshall put up amazing numbers all year, breaking Barry Sanders's record for total yards from scrimmage and becoming the second back to go over 1,000 yards rushing and receiving in the same season. But unless you're a football player, it's tough to understand just how great he is. There were times when I caught myself cutting short my follow-through after handoffs so I could turn and watch him run. I've never seen a player who can do what he does, both from a mental and physical standpoint. He thinks like a quarterback. You can put him in any situation and he sees the whole field, knows whom he has to pick up and how he can help out, because he's aware of everyone's assignments. He's a vicious blocker who never misses an assignment, and if you split him out wide he runs routes like a receiver. I know I'm rambling here, but I could write an entire chapter about Marshall; he's just phenomenal. When his career is over he may go down as the best multipurpose running back of all time. I know I wouldn't trade him for anybody.

Next we returned home to face the Cleveland Browns—a trap game if there ever was one. We were 5–0; they were 0–5. We had the unstoppable attack; their offense needed a jump-start. But here's where I think our legacy saved us. Since we had been losers for so long, we maintained an incredible focus throughout the season; I think we were paranoid about sliding back into the abyss. We never allowed ourselves to get cocky, and we took a certain pride in sustaining our intensity. So much for a trap: we crushed Cleveland, 34–3, and I was 23 of 29 for 203 yards and three touchdowns.

No one could have called it at the time, but our next game, against the Tennessee Titans in Nashville on Halloween, was a Super Bowl preview. The Titans, coming off three consecutive 8–8 seasons, were 5–1, with an impressive victory over Jacksonville and a lone defeat to the 49ers. They're a fast, physical, well-coached team, and we looked forward to the challenge. We felt like we were a pretty good team but, for whatever reason, the Titans didn't seem to think so.

The night before the game Coach Vermeil, as he always does, addressed us during our team meeting. He started out by saying, "Now, if we lose tomorrow, I just want you to know that we're still in good shape." Guys looked around the room at one another, wondering why he would have chosen those words. Then, a couple of minutes later, he did it again: "If we lose, we're still at the top of our conference and in great position for the rest of the season." And then he said it again. All around the room guys were mumbling to one another, "What's he talking about? Is he doubting us?" No one could figure out why he was talking that way. Usually Coach Vermeil is so upbeat; even when we were lousy, he thought we could beat anyone we played. Now it sounded like he was preparing us for the disappointment of defeat.

The fourth time Dick said, "If we lose," Isaac Bruce, who's a bit of a renegade, actually muttered, "We ain't gonna lose!" A few minutes later Dick awarded a game ball in advance to Kevin Warren, our vice president of player programs. Amazingly, he said it again, "If we don't win this game, this ball can be for next week's victory." Kevin stood up and made a point of saying, "Now tomorrow, *when* we win, I'll be proud to accept this game ball." Guys were really angry; I know I was. Coach Vermeil's speech was all anyone could talk about when we walked out of the meeting, and Isaac was practically in a frenzy. As he said later, "I thought it was Jeff Fisher standing up there." Fisher, of course, is the Titans' coach.

To me it was great that we were so irate. The year before we had gone into games anticipating defeat; our goal had been to keep it close and hope for the best. Now, after six games, we were already at the point where we expected to win every week. Losing wasn't even in our vocabulary, and when Coach Vermeil brought it up guys were offended.

So in addition to proving our worth to the Titans, we were determined to show *our own coach* what we were made of. Before the game Isaac was bouncing off the locker-room walls. I had never seen anyone that hyped up for a pro game—he was screaming and gesturing as we exited the tunnel for pregame introductions, just taking the whole thing personally.

Perhaps we were too fired up, because with 1:24 left in the first quarter, we were already down 21–0. Much of it was my fault: twice I fumbled inside our thirty yard line and the Titans came back with quick touchdowns. We were definitely off our game, and Tennessee had a lot to do with it. Jevon Kearse, their rookie pass-rushing sensation, was in our backfield all day; Fred Miller, our left tackle, was so rattled that he got called for *six* false start penalties on the afternoon. It was every offensive lineman's nightmare, but to his credit he bounced back later in the season. The Titans' crowd was totally into the game. Coach Vermeil later complained that the Titans had pumped in artificial crowd noise, but to me that was a non-story.

I remember seeing some of my teammates and coaches looking at me, wondering how I'd respond. Maybe they were worried that my glow had worn off, that I wouldn't be able to cope when things got rough. Perhaps they were thinking that Arena Kurt had just reared his head. At halftime it was still 21–0, and I could see the rationalizations that awaited us: *When they finally played a good team, they caved. . . . Warner's a dome guy; he can't handle playing on grass. . . . The quarterback's great if you give him time, but knock him around a little and he falls apart.*

That last one bothered me the most. Any quarterback will become less effective when he's getting hit all the time, but I pride myself on a willingness to hang in there and take the punishment. The Titans hadn't rattled me; I had just gotten sloppy a couple of times and held onto the ball too long.

Just before we went back out onto the field, Isaac stood up in the locker room and said, "This game is *not* over. We're gonna turn it around and win this thing. It's gonna take a great comeback, and we're gonna do it." Again, that spoke to the character our team had already established. Nobody ever would have said anything like that the previous year.

Sure enough, we fought our way back into the game. On the second play of the third quarter I hit Marshall on a short pass, and he busted free for a fifty-seven-yard touchdown. Seven minutes later I connected with Isaac on a three-yard scoring pass. Tennessee kicked a field goal to go up 24–14. Late in the game I took us eighty yards for another score—a fifteen-yard pass to halfback Amp Lee, a dangerous third-down specialist who had sort of been lost in the shuffle to that point. With 2:09 left we recovered an onside kick, setting the stage for a fantastic finish. I got us down to their twenty yard line, but our kicker, Jeff Wilkins, uncharacteristically missed a field goal that would have forced overtime. I ended up with 328 passing yards, but the only important stat was that we were now 6–1.

In the locker room we were devastated. You'd have thought we'd lost a playoff game. That was yet another sign that our attitude had undergone a makeover. We were convinced that we had been the better team, and we bemoaned our missed opportunity. But as we got a day or two removed from the disappointment, we began to appreciate the mettle we had displayed. Instead of getting down on ourselves when things went badly, we had shown our character and answered a lot of questions about our team. I think we took a lot from that game, because it was our first true test to see how we'd handle adversity. The fact that we hung in there, I believe, set the stage for bigger and better things down the road—especially the clutch plays in the NFC Championship game and the Super Bowl—because we were able to stay calm in dire situations. On a personal level, I think I also answered the call. A few people came up to me afterward and said, "You showed a lot of character."

Next we went to Detroit to play the Lions, the team we had shredded in our final preseason game. Like us, they had surprised a lot of people. Everyone figured they'd be awful in the wake of Barry Sanders's surprise retirement, but they were 5–2 going into that game, and they ended up making the playoffs.

We came out a little sluggish, but eventually we settled down and got into one of those back-and-forth contests. With six minutes to go we got the ball at our own thirteen yard line, trailing by a 24–19 margin. We put together a long drive for the go-ahead touchdown, and I really felt like I was in command. A couple of times I had to pick up yards by scrambling, which is totally unlike me; I'm slower than a *National Geographic* special. The touchdown came on a two-yard, play-action pass to Ryan Tucker—a backup lineman Mike Martz had inserted as an eligible receiver for that play.

We hit the two-point conversion to go up 27–24, and when I straggled back to the sidelines, exhausted, Marshall Faulk came up to me and pounded his fist against his chest. "That took a lot of heart," he said. This was a big turning point for me, a moment I really held on to all season long. For the first time, I really felt like this was my team and everybody was behind me. Instead of just being the new guy who'd been thrown into a tough situation, I had won my teammates' respect to the point where I was now a leader. Marshall's approval meant everything to me. As the year went on he and I became more and more vocal with each other about what we were seeing on the field, and it really helped me, because the guy understands everything going on around him. By the end of the season, even if he broke off a route or ran it just a little bit differently, I felt like I knew exactly where he would be; we were that in tune with each other.

The Lions had one more crack at us, but our defense was all over them. Charlie Batch, the Lions' quarterback, had been knocked out of the game with a broken thumb in the third quarter, and now Gus Frerotte, the former Redskins starter, was in the game. With a little more than a minute to go, it was fourth and twenty-six from the Lions' twenty-one, and Isaac Bruce came up to me on the sidelines and said, "It's over. It's over."

"One more play," I cautioned. And what a play it was: Frerotte dropped back and unleashed a bomb, and Germaine Crowell caught it for a fifty-seven-yard gain. It was kind of a fluke, but give them credit—great pass, great catch. I knew it had to be killing Mike Martz, because he and Gus hadn't been on the best of terms in Washington the previous season. I started thinking about overtime, but the Lions weren't playing for the tie. Frerotte threw a twelve-yard touchdown pass to Johnnie Morton with twenty-eight seconds to go, and we lost, 31–27.

This time we weren't angry, we were just stunned. Guys were like zombies after that game, not only in the locker room but for the next couple of days, too. I remember lying in bed with Brenda in the middle of the night and saying, "How did we lose that game?"

Now the skeptics were out in full force. Halfway through the season, we had played just two teams with winning records and lost to both of them. But we were hardly demoralized. We felt that we should have won both of those games, and we still believed we were a very good team.

Things were a little tighter than usual in the week leading up to our next game, a division clash with the Carolina Panthers at home. Right off the bat, Carolina drove down and scored a touchdown to go up 7–0, and it felt like a giant vacuum cleaner had sucked all the oxygen out of the Trans World Dome. We needed to answer before things became really tense, and we did: I hit a pass to Marshall that he turned into a big gain, and then I found Isaac coming across on a post for a twenty-two-yard touchdown. The crowd roared—it was almost like an extremely loud sigh of relief—and then Todd Lyght ran back an interception fifty-seven yards for a touchdown, and we were rolling. We got another defensive TD, on a Mike Jones fumble recovery, and walked off with a 35–10 laugher.

That launched a seven-game winning streak, which earned us home-field advantage throughout the playoffs and completed one of the great turnarounds in NFL history. It was one of those magical convergences that happen every so often in sports, and to our credit we enjoyed the journey nearly as much as we did the prize. For the most part our players truly liked and got along with one another, and just about everyone found a way to help the cause.

There were so many unsung heroes, guys like Jeff Robinson, a converted defensive lineman who made a successful transition to tight end. Well, mostly successful; he still retained many of the idiosyncrasies that you'd expect from a madman who once chased quarterbacks for a living. After beating Carolina we went to San Francisco for a rematch with the 49ers, who by now had slipped to 3–6 and didn't scare anyone. Their defense played really well this time, but ours did also, and we won, 23–7. Late in the game I was trying to run down the play clock, and Jeff went in motion across the backfield. Just as he started jogging across the line, he tripped on his own shoelaces and fell flat on his face. It was hilarious. I was barely able to take the snap from center and hand off to the back. Jeff bounced back up and tried to make his block, but it was hopeless. I give him credit for laughing at himself, though; when he got back to the sidelines he bowed to all the fans who were razzing him.

And that wasn't even his most embarrassing moment. Later in the year, at the end of a blowout victory over the Bears in St. Louis, Jeff got into it with Chicago's Ty Hallock, and one of the officials stepped in to restore order. The official got a little carried away, though, and ended up grabbing Jeff around the ankles and tackling him to the turf. Tackled by the ref! Then, for good measure, he threw Jeff out of the game. We had a lot of fun with that one.

Jeff could sure dish it out, though. Back in training camp, he used to simulate cracking a whip whenever I walked by as a comment on my status as Mike Martz's whipping boy. Later, he changed my nickname to "Elliott Ness" because they said I was so bigtime that I was "untouchable." Eventually the guys took to calling me "Superhero" because they thought I carried myself differently as a starter. Sometimes I'd show up a couple of minutes late for prepractice stretching because I had been doing an interview, and Paul Justin and the other guys would say, "Anytime you want to get started, Kurt. It's up to you." Whenever the guys tried to push my buttons, it seemed like Jeff was always the ringleader. He'd get on me about my calves, or lack thereof, and make fun of my mannerisms on the field. He and some of the other guys had my routine down pat: I'd walk up to the line, pat the center on the side, wipe my hand on my hip, throw the pass, and adjust my helmet. A couple of times in practice I saw guys standing behind me and mimicking my behavior.

Fortunately, they never got too personal; I was hearing enough of that stuff from everyone else. The postgame kissing routine, and the overall attention generated by my story, had turned Brenda into something of a celebrity. Between her striking hairstyle and, shall we say, expressive outfits on game day, she had become quite a target. Brenda would go on-line and check out what people were saying about her in the chat rooms, and some of it was pretty brutal: *Her hair's too short and her fingernails are too long. . . . Too bad he got married in the Arena League. . . . She looks like a lesbian. . . . What'd he do, marry his mother?* Most of that stuff, I'm sure, is a product of jealousy, so I try not to take it that seriously. Personally, I love the way Brenda dresses. She's hip and different, and she wears outfits that a lot of other people are afraid to wear. Then again, I think she could wear a bathrobe and look great.

My own wardrobe choices also triggered a fair amount of controversy. During TV interviews I always wore T-shirts bearing Christian messages. Back before anyone knew who I was, Brenda used to wait until those shirts would go on sale at the Christian bookstore near our house and buy them for me as a treat. Once I started wearing the shirts on TV, boxes from Cross-Eyed and other companies began arriving at the Rams' facility with enough shirts to last me every day of the year. It was a great way to underscore my faith, but it also caught the attention of the people at Nike because they were hoping I'd give them some exposure, too. So they sent a bunch of Nike hats over to the Rams, assuming I'd wear them on the sidelines during games. It was a nice gesture but I don't wear hats. I never have, other than when I played baseball as a kid, because I have a small head and they make me look like a big goof. People are always trying to get me to wear this cap or that, and I'm always saying no. It's like asking me to wear a G-string; you'd be better off saving your breath, because it's not going to happen.

When I didn't wear the Nike hats someone from their office called wanting to know what the deal was. Back before I signed my contract with Nike, I had told my agent to make sure they knew I wouldn't wear hats—though I doubt my agent even told them, because it hardly seemed relevant at the time. "I don't wear hats, remember?" I told the person from Nike. Finally I said, "Look, if it's a problem, we can just forget the contract and I'll pay you back the money and move on." *That's* how much I hate hats. When they realized I was that adamant, they backed off.

Speaking of caps, one of my proudest moments from the '99 season came the night before our rematch with the Carolina Panthers in early December, when Coach Vermeil took off his hat to me. Amazingly, we had a chance to clinch our first division title since 1985 in only the twelfth game of the season. The Panthers, thanks to George Seifert's coaching and some inspired play, had jelled into a pretty formidable team, and now they had us at their stadium. The night before the game, during our team meeting, Coach Vermeil said, "We're on the brink of being division champions, and the pressure is on us to finish the job. How will we handle the pressure? I hope we'll all be like Kurt Warner, because you can't handle pressure—on or off the field—any better than this guy has all year." Then he simulated tipping his cap and smiled in my direction; it was a real thrill.

The next day we went out and seized the moment, scoring the game's first three touchdowns and holding on for a 34–21 victory. I completed 22 of 31 passes for a season-best 351 yards. I threw for three touchdowns to run my season total to thirty-two, breaking Jim Everett's team record. There was a lot of emotion that day. Coach Vermeil and our owner, Georgia Frontiere, were teary-eyed on the sidelines, and some of the veterans like Todd Lyght and D'Marco Farr who had never been in that position were just elated.

What I remember most about that game, though, was the hit I took from Carolina's Kevin Greene in the second quarter. He came through on a pass rush and slammed his helmet into my sternum, and for a second I thought he had collapsed both my lungs. I stayed down on the grass for a while, and once I realized it wasn't serious—just the wind knocked out of me—I walked off the field. By rule I had to sit out a play, and it was the only one I missed all season because of injury. Before anyone knew what was happening, I ran back onto the field and told my backup, Paul Justin, he was out of the game. He didn't want to leave, and I should have listened to him: on the next play I threw an interception.

Two days later, I was in L.A. for a taped appearance on *Wheel of Fortune,* and who did I see on the set but Kevin Greene? My first instinct was to run to my dressing room, but he turned out to be a great guy. Right off, he wanted to make sure that I didn't think his hit was a cheap shot. Some people have accused him of being a dirty player, but I think he's just a guy who's superintense and plays hard every snap. The *Wheel of Fortune* experience was a lot of fun. Zack and Jesse came with me to L.A., which gave us a chance to spend a little quality time together, and I raised more than $23,000 for Camp Barnabas.

The next Sunday we went to New Orleans to face the Saints for the second time in three weeks. We had beaten them 43–12 in St. Louis, and now we had a chance to close out our division schedule with an 8–0 record—and become the first team ever to do so after failing to win a division game the previous season. This time, as our team gathered at the hotel the night before the game, Coach Vermeil decided to skip the meeting and make it a players-only affair. I hadn't made a speech since the Arena League, but I decided to get up and address the team.

"We've got a chance to do something special," I said. "This opportunity is precious—ask Ricky Proehl, who's been in the league ten years and has never been in a playoff game." Then I talked about Todd Collins, our middle linebacker, who went to the Super Bowl with New England following the '96 season. "They were a young team that kept their nucleus together, but they never made it back," I continued. "You never know how often these chances will come along. We all know we've got something special going here, that we've got the chemistry and the talent to do some great things, but there's no guarantee we'll be in this position again. Let's make sure we take advantage of this opportunity."

My message seemed to hit home with the guys—we won the game 30–14—but one person who didn't need any extra motivation was Marshall Faulk. New Orleans is his hometown, and he basically took over the Superdome, with 210 combined yards (154 rushing, 56 receiving) and two touchdowns. The next week it was our opponents' words that fired us up: the New York Giants were in the playoff hunt at that point, and some of them talked about how they planned to take it to us physically. They suggested that we were soft, that they were going to smack us in the mouth and see if we could handle it.

The whole thing was silly. First of all, it's not like we were going to get intimidated by their yapping. If you're a player who gets rattled by words, chances are you won't be in the NFL for long. Second, all that talking does is rile up your opponent. All week we were saying to one another, "Yeah, that's right, keep talking; we'll see what you guys say on Sunday." Believe me, we were ready to play—we whipped them 31–10, and it could have been so much worse. We stood up to them physically, and we let them know about it, too. Early in the fourth quarter we had a 17–3 lead when I fired a short pass to Az Hakim, who wove in and out, broke about three tackles, and burst into the clear for a breakaway touchdown. When he got to the five yard line he turned around and backpedaled into the end zone. Our coaches weren't thrilled with that last part, and it's not the type of thing I usually approve of, but in this case it was an exclamation point—our way of getting the last word. Besides, you have to know Az; he's such a character, and he's got that little touch of arrogance in him that can really spark a team.

Now, with home-field advantage sewn up, we had two meaningless games to close out the season. We beat the Bears at home, 34–12, and then we went to Philadelphia to face the Eagles, the team Dick coached from 1976 to 1982. This time, at our Saturday night team meeting, I couldn't believe who stood up to give the speech: Smokin' Joe Frazier. He talked about believing in yourself, never giving up, and never selling yourself short. "A lot of people didn't give me a chance because of where I came from," he said, "but I believed in myself, and that was all that counted."

Obviously, I could relate. Less than two years earlier, Al Lugenbill was begging NFL teams to give me a workout. Now I was the NFC's Pro Bowl starter, the league MVP, and, with thirty-nine touchdown passes, on the verge of joining Dan Marino as the only players to have thrown forty or more in a season.

I had a plan for number forty, too. I wanted Ricky Proehl to catch it, because he's an unheralded player who, despite being our fifth-leading receiver, hadn't reached the end zone all year long. Nine other guys on our team had caught touchdowns, including a backup lineman, Ryan Tucker, and I hoped to make Ricky the tenth.

Alas, it didn't happen. In fact, of all things, my fortieth touchdown came on a shovel pass—to Marshall, who caught it at the eight yard line and did all the work. Then, in the third quarter, I had a chance to hit Ricky on a play that might have gone the distance, but I blew it. He was wide open down the middle and probably would have scored if he'd caught it in stride, but the ball got away from me, and he had to make a diving catch at the fifteen. On the next play I threw a touchdown pass to Torry Holt, giving me forty-one for the season and tying the game at 24. I was done for the day, and so was our team: we lost, 38–31, to finish the season 13–3.

Afterward I was a little bummed out, more about the missed opportunity with Ricky than the outcome. I remember thanking my receivers for helping me achieve so much during the season, and getting Ricky his touchdown would have been a great show of appreciation for a guy who's as unselfish as they come. He's a classic role player and a great model of what the NFL should be: a dogged, hardworking player who's willing to do whatever you ask of him.

Not many people realize this, but Ricky was our team MVP in '98, and then he became a forgotten man with the return of Isaac, the addition of Torry, and the emergence of Az. But he kept making plays for us—of his thirty-three receptions, twenty-five were for first downs—and he never complained about his role.

When I messed up my last chance to get him a touchdown, Ricky, true to his nature, didn't sweat it. Looking back, I shouldn't have, either.

In three short weeks, we'd make up for it in a big way.

CHAPTER FOURTEEN

BELIEVE IT OR NOT

They were coming from all directions, doling out steady doses of physical punishment, and suddenly the idea of playing quarter-back in an NFL playoff game didn't seem so appealing. "We've got him, baby!" the amped-up defenders yelled to one another. "He doesn't want to be out there. He's not looking at his receivers; he's looking at us. He's got happy feet."

Thankfully, they weren't talking about me.

It was the third quarter of our divisional playoff game against the Minnesota Vikings, and our defensive players were the ones doing the yapping about Vikings quarterback Jeff George. He was coming apart in the din of the Trans World Dome, throwing passes off his back foot and flinching in the face of our pass rush. Meanwhile, we were unleashing an offensive outburst that would stamp us as the team to beat. Suddenly, after a season of cautious praise and underlying skepticism, the St. Louis Rams were bona fide Super Bowl favorites. And Minnesota, everyone's trendy upset special? Despite entering the game as one of football's hottest teams, the Vikings totally unraveled. The lasting images were of Jeff George fumbling a third-quarter snap and watching innocuously while our defense recovered; of Randy Moss, in a totally classless move, squirting an official with a water bottle as time ran down; and of Denny Green's team trudging off into an uncertain future after a 49–37 defeat that wasn't nearly as close as the score indicated.

If the Vikings were stunned, they weren't alone. Though we were seven-point favorites, a lot of people thought we would meet our match in Minnesota, which had started to resemble the powerful unit that went 15–1 in '98 before losing in the NFC Championship game. Many fans and experts believed the Vikings' high-powered offense, with George zinging the ball to Randy Moss and Cris Carter, was capable of keeping pace with ours.

But you don't know how a quarterback will react to big-game pressure until it happens, especially when some of that pressure comes in the form of a relentless pass rush. George, who had taken over for Randall Cunningham six games into the season, gave more ammunition to the critics who say he'll never come through in a truly big game. Meanwhile, in my NFL playoff debut, I was fortunate enough to play one of the best games of my life.

Oddly enough, I was a bit of a mess leading up to that performance, and there was a lot of concern, even from my teammates and coaches, that I might be buckling under the stress. The fact that I stood up to the challenge was, in my mind, yet another example of how my faith in the Lord guides me through times of great tension. Afterward, when I thanked God for the victory, I'm sure a lot of people cringed, because they think he doesn't care about who wins a football game. Before I address that very loaded subject, let me give you a sense of my mind-set going into what at that point was the biggest game of my life.

By virtue of our conference-best, 13–3 record in the regular season, we earned a bye in the first round of the playoffs. That meant we would play our first game in St. Louis against one of three opponents: Detroit, Minnesota, or Dallas. After the Lions lost to Washington on the first Saturday of the playoffs, we knew we'd face the winner of the following day's game between the Vikings and Cowboys.

I'm not going to lie to you; I wanted Dallas to win that game. Outscoring the Cowboys didn't seem like it would be a problem, but the Vikings scared me, because we could put up 40 against them and lose. Their offense was so explosive, and it was really in a rhythm. The Vikings were playing as well as anybody at that point—they'd won eight of their ten games after Jeff became the starting quarterback—and I thought they'd represent our biggest challenge of the season. If anybody was in position to knock us off, I felt they were.

So, on the first Sunday of the playoffs, I sat in my living room, watched every play of the Dallas-Minnesota game, and rooted my lungs out for the Cowboys. Just like the old days. But the Vikings won, and now I had another week to prepare for a game I was already itching to play.

Man, was I antsy. I was worn down from a week's worth of practice and media scrutiny, not to mention a quick trip to New York to appear on *The Late Show* with David Letterman. I know I brought that last bit of tension upon myself, but the offer was too good to refuse: Brenda and I not only got our first-ever visit to New York, but the producers also paid for our pastors, Jeff and Patsy Perry, to accompany us in the name of spiritual support.

I had put off the Letterman appearance a couple of times during the year, but with the first-round bye, our schedule allowed enough time to squeeze it in right after the regular season ended. We covered all the Big Apple basics: shopping, checking out the lights of Times Square, paying thirty dollars for a bad haircut, getting treated rudely by a waitress at a midtown deli. The show was fun, too. Lauren Bacall was one of the guests, and I got to meet her briefly before the taping. She said, "I'm a big fan," and that was really cool, to have a legend like that even know who I was. Brenda was convinced she was flirting with me, which would have been *really* flattering, but I think that's just my wife's vivid imagination at work.

Anyway, the highlight of the taping was when David Letterman and I went out onto the street outside the midtown theater where the show is taped and tried to throw footballs into a wood chipper. It was pouring rain, and as soon as we got back inside the production assistants were all over me like they were bellhops and I was Donald Trump. "What shirt size do you wear?" they asked, panting. Because my shirt had gotten all wet, they were going to go out and buy me a new one to wear home on the plane. "Give us the shirt you have on," one of them told me, "and we'll have it dry cleaned and sent back to you." I thought it was hilarious. I had agreed to go outside in the first place, and it wasn't like the world was going to come to an end. But I guess they must be used to dealing with guests who *do* freak out when their shirts get wet. I said, "Don't worry about it; it's just a shirt," and one of them responded, "We'll run over to wardrobe and bring back two shirts, and you can pick which one you want."

The trip to New York was hectic, but in a way it was good, because it got my mind off football for a while. I was going crazy waiting for that game to get under way. I'm not one of these people who like to overprepare; once I get a sense of the opponent's strengths and weaknesses and what we're trying to do offensively, I feel confident that I'll be able to perform effectively come game time. We had game-planned loosely for the Vikings, as well as the other prospective opponents, during the bye week, and by the next Monday I was ready to play. I could tell some of my teammates felt the same way, too. As the two-week stretch wore on, our practices became more and more sluggish, and I was particularly bad. In our last couple of practices, I wasn't very crisp or accurate, and people were starting to get concerned.

Right after practice on Friday, two days before the game, Marshall Faulk came up to me as we were walking off the field and asked, "How are you doing? Are you all right?" He didn't come out and say, "I'm asking these questions because you've been stinking up the place," but I'm pretty sure that's what was going through his head. I just kind of laughed it off and told him I felt great. The truth was, I didn't know why I hadn't practiced well. I think I was just tired of waiting. But I was confident I'd be sharp on Sunday.

Marshall wasn't alone in his concern. A couple of other teammates told me, "Just relax and go out there and play your game," and I could tell the coaches were worried. Coach Vermeil said something in the paper about the fact that I hadn't been as sharp during the latter practices. I'm sure people were thinking, *Uh-oh, is he going to crack under the pressure?* And, given my lack of NFL playoff experience, maybe they had reason to be a little uneasy. A lot of quarterbacks can look like world beaters when things are going well, but when the intensity rises and the hits get more ferocious and constant, some have been known to go to pieces.

That's why I'll never forget a comment that Mike Martz, my offensive coordinator, made to reporters in the days leading up to the game. Mike, you'll recall, spent the first several months of our relationship treating me like his personal piñata. But now, at a time when I really appreciated it, he gave me a huge vote of confidence. Mike said he couldn't wait for the playoffs to begin because he felt that I and some of the other leaders on the team play our best under pressure. That stuck in my mind, because I've always felt that I'm at my best when my back's against the wall, when people tell me I can't do something. That goes not just for sports but for everything in my life.

I couldn't wait to go out and stand up to the pressure—the Vikings' pass rush, their shifting coverages, and, most notably, John Randle's mouth.

Randle is the Vikings' perennial All-Pro defensive tackle and resident stand-up comic. Okay, he's a three-point-stance comic, but who's quibbling? Not only is Randle a motor mouth when he's on the field, he's a free-flowing fountain of information, a man who takes such pride in his trash-talking craft that he researches arcane details about his opponents' past. First he studies the playbook, then he devours the opposing team's media guide. Randle's rants aren't so much mean and nasty as they are disarmingly silly; his idea is to throw you off your rhythm by getting you to focus on things that have nothing to do with the game.

I knew Randle could have a field day with me, given my unorthodox past. But, alas, most of his chatter during our game escaped me. He did most of his talking from the sidelines during time-outs or when he was up at the line of scrimmage and we were still in our offensive huddle, and it was so noisy in the Trans World

Dome that I couldn't make out a lot of what he was saying. I'd hear bits and pieces: "I'm gonna get you . . . Look out, 13!" He mentioned that I'd been a third-stringer and said something about the Hy-Vee, but nothing that really stood out. Only a few guys all season tried to talk trash to me—Randle, the guy in Cincinnati who growled at me, Tampa Bay's Warren Sapp, and Chicago's Mike Wells—and I don't know what they were thinking. Do they really believe someone at this level will be intimidated by words or noises? When that stuff happens I just laugh.

Of course, by the end of the game, Randle wasn't saying much. The best way to silence a defender is to score touchdowns, and at times it seemed like we could do that at will. After the Vikings drove down for a field goal to open the game, I was anxious to run our first play because I knew we had a chance to hit it big. Mike Martz had told me on Saturday that we would open with Act 6 388 F-Drag, and I spent most of the night before the game going over various scenarios as I lay in bed. If the Vikings came out in a Cover-2 defense—basically, a two-deep zone in which the safeties provide inside help to the cornerbacks—I felt like we'd get a touchdown.

Sure enough, when we took over on our twenty-three yard line with 9:13 remaining, I got the look I wanted from Minnesota's defense. The first thing I did is to read the front-side safety, Robert Griffith, to make sure he was playing two-deep. We had seen on film that the Vikings often blitzed their front-side cornerback in that situation, leaving Griffith as the only person to cover our front-side receiver. In that case the front-side receiver, tight end Roland Williams, essentially would run Griffith away from the play, leaving the free safety, Anthony Bass, alone in the deep middle. If so, he'd have a daunting decision to make, because Isaac Bruce and Torry Holt would be coming at him full speed on post patterns from left to right—Isaac from the slot, and Torry from the far left. First Bass would have to worry about stopping the run, because there was a play-fake to Marshall at the start of the play.

I loved our chances as I took the snap, and the play developed perfectly. I faked a handoff to Marshall, their corner blitzed and got picked up, Williams gobbled up Griffith, and Bass, even though he chose to run with Isaac instead of Torry, couldn't get there in time to stop him from catching the ball in stride and bursting free up the middle. Seventy-seven yards later Isaac was in the end zone, doing the Bob and Weave with our other receivers, and the Vikings' defenders were wondering what had hit them.

We could have blown them out then and there, and it's my fault that we didn't. After I hit Marshall on a forty-one-yard pass to make it 14–3, we had a chance to score another touchdown early in the second quarter. But I underthrew Isaac on a deep pass that should have gone the distance, Jimmy Hitchcock intercepted it at the four yard line, and Jeff George drove them ninety-six yards for a touchdown. Later, after I fumbled away the ball at the Vikings' forty-seven, they put together another scoring drive. So we went into halftime down 17–14—it was only the third time we had trailed at home all season—and wondering how we could possibly be behind.

Nobody panicked, because we knew we were capable of so much more. "We're going to keep doing what we're doing," Mike Martz told us in the locker room, "because they're not stopping us, we're stopping ourselves. We're going to go out and put a lot of points on the board in the second half."

Leave it to Tony Horne to cut right to the chase. Horne, our number five receiver and return ace, fielded the second-half kick-off at the five yard line, faked a runback to his right, and then abruptly cut back left, fooling everybody en route to his third return for the touchdown of the season. Every time we needed a big play in '99, it seemed like Tony was there to make it. Just as he had bailed us out of tense situations and scored momentum-changing TDs against San Francisco and Atlanta in October, he gave us the lead for good against Minnesota. The guy was just amazing this year, and yet on a personal level the season was a struggle for him. In the wake of his heroics against the 49ers and Falcons, he was suspended for four games by the NFL after violating the league's substance abuse policy.

The suspension hit us hard, but it was even harder for him, because he felt like he was letting his teammates down. None of us really saw it that way. He obviously had some problems to work through, but we all make mistakes. Tony's a great kid who works really hard, and sometimes it takes a crisis situation like that to open your eyes and set you straight.

At our Bible study sessions we prayed for Tony all the time. We actually tried to get him to come to Bible study during his suspension, when he was isolated from all other team functions, but he never was able to make it. Still, we kept him in our prayers, and when he returned we welcomed him back with open arms. I was one of the first people who saw him in the locker room the day he got back, and I just gave him a hug and said, "Hey, glad to have you back. If there's anything you need, we're here for you—just let us know." I think he was excited to hear that and happy that we weren't holding the suspension against him.

Even though losing Tony possibly hurt our team, and definitely cost him individually, those weren't the primary issues. In our eyes the most important thing wasn't getting Tony back on the football field but helping him to get his life in order. Knowing Tony's character, I think he understood the ramifications of the suspension, and he didn't need us to make him feel any worse about it.

It was great that Tony got to be a hero against the Vikings, and he had plenty of company. One thing that made the '99 Rams so special was that everybody on the team understood and accepted his role and managed to make a contribution at some critical juncture. It wasn't about "me, me, me," it was about the team, and everybody was happy to play his role and be part of the special thing we had going. Robert Holcombe and Amp Lee made key contributions out of the backfield. When we lost Keith Lyle, our veteran safety, to a shoulder injury in November, Devin Bush stepped in and came up with big play after big play. With Ernie Conwell recovering from a serious knee injury, Roland Williams came through with a big year at tight end. When Orlando Pace, our All-Pro left tackle, got thrown out of a game against the New York Giants, Ryan Tucker held down the fort. And Ryan also came up big against the Vikings, catching a pass off a tackle-eligible play late in the third quarter for his second touchdown of the season.

By then our second-half explosion was in full force. After Tony's touchdown return, we scored on four out of our next five drives to go up 49–17 before the Vikings started putting up points in garbage time. It seemed like everything we did worked, and the Vikings' defensive players were totally out of sorts. I remember them getting very confused, trying to cover two players with one defender or leaving a receiver totally wide open. Our plays weren't necessarily that complicated, but we kept them so off balance they didn't know where to line up or how to stop us.

As usual our offensive line allowed us to dominate by winning the war up front. It wasn't like they were a bunch of bullies, either. I don't know if, from an athletic standpoint, our line was the most talented in football, but I believe our group was the smartest and best disciplined. Even though the linemen might not have made every block, they were always in great position and picked up the right guy. That was a key factor in my success, because the linemen didn't allow any defenders to run free, and that gave me time to read and get rid of the ball quickly. It was the same with their run blocking; they were intelligent enough to be in the right position, and they always blocked the right guy. With our gung-ho offensive approach and gifted skill players, sometimes all it took was a quick block to get Marshall through a hole or to allow me to get the ball to one of our receivers in stride. In my mind, we had the best line in the league.

Some of the credit for the line's play has to go to Jim Hanifan, the assistant coach in charge of that unit. Hanny is one of those classic characters who add spice to everyday life in the NFL. He's a former head coach of the St. Louis Cardinals who has a million stories and always has a cigarette burning, though he tried to quit smoking late in the season after he was hospitalized and diagnosed with a clogged artery. Here's what happened: Hanny was at Rams Park late one night when he started having chest pains, and Coach Vermeil called 911. An ambulance arrived, and by that time, I guess, Hanny was feeling better. The guy is such a joker that when he was walking out to meet the paramedics he fell over and pretended to go into cardiac arrest. Everyone rushed over to help him, and he got up and started laughing. I'm sure the paramedics didn't think it was so funny, but that's Hanny. He ended up undergoing angioplasty, and he was back at work shortly thereafter.

As great as our offensive line was against the Vikings, our defensive line deserves a lot of credit, too, because its relentless pass rush got into Jeff George's head. Even though Jeff ended up with impressive numbers—he was 29 of 50 for 424 yards and four touchdowns, compared to my 27 of 33 for 391 yards and five TDs—he definitely didn't look like a championship-caliber quarterback. A lot of people thought Denny Green was crazy over the off-season when he tried to bring in Dan Marino to replace Jeff, but I could understand his thinking: Marino has proven he can hang in there in big games when things get really tough. I guess Denny doesn't think the same applies to Jeff George, because he ended up going with Dante Culpepper as his starter for 2000, and Jeff signed with Washington as a backup to Brad Johnson.

To Jeff and his teammates' credit, they went down fighting, scoring three touchdowns against us in the final five minutes. But those points were pretty much cosmetic, and Randy Moss, their second-year receiving star, managed to put an ugly exclamation point on the defeat. With just over two minutes remaining, Moss went out for a pass and apparently thought interference should have been called. He walked to the sidelines, grabbed a Gatorade bottle, and squirted water on the field judge, Jim Saracino, earning a fifteen-yard penalty. I didn't even know about it until I went home and watched Sportscenter. It looked ridiculous, especially when Moss tried to hide behind some of his teammates after the fact.

I couldn't believe what I was seeing. I don't think there's any place for that stuff, and I hate to see people do it and give the league a bad name. There are always going to be mistakes and calls that you don't agree with, but you've got to know how to handle your displeasure and move forward. There are a lot of things you see in sports nowadays, like spitting in faces or celebrating after routine plays, where people do things in the heat of battle that they probably regret afterward. What Randy did was totally uncalled for; he was later fined $40,000 by the league, and I think the punishment was appropriate. A few weeks later, at the Pro Bowl, I got an up close and personal view of Randy Moss—but I'll get to that later.

I don't think it was any coincidence that Isaac Bruce jacked up his game against Moss and Cris Carter in the playoffs. Isaac is such a competitor, and he believes he is the best receiver in football. The previous two seasons, when he was battling hamstring injuries and dropped from the ranks of elite receivers in a lot of people's eyes, it just killed him. That Minnesota game gave him a chance to make a huge statement, and he delivered, ending up on the cover of the following week's *Sports Illustrated*.

Isaac also sparked a lot of controversy about religion and sports, and some of the biggest names in the sports media, like *SI*'s Rick Reilly, took him to task for statements he made around that time. The issue came to the forefront in early December after Isaac and his girlfriend were involved in a scary car accident. They had attended a University of Missouri basketball game in Columbia and were heading eastbound on Interstate 70, back to St. Louis, when the left rear tire of his Mercedes blew out and the car skidded out of control. Isaac, who wasn't wearing his seat belt, took his hands off the steering wheel, raised them into the air, and screamed, "Jesus!" The car flipped twice and landed upright in a roadside gully, and though the airbags didn't deploy and the vehicle's roof collapsed, Isaac walked away uninjured and his girlfriend suffered only a small gash on her forehead.

Among other things, Isaac suggested that a man who showed up at the scene and offered to call an ambulance may have been an angel. He insisted that anyone in a similar situation can prevent himself or herself from being harmed by yelling "Jesus!" When pressed by Rick Reilly during an interview a few days before the Super Bowl, Isaac claimed that some of the other people killed or injured in high-profile tragedies, including Derrick Thomas, Payne Stewart, and the kids at the Columbine High School massacre, would have escaped harm if they'd simply screamed out Jesus' name.

I know that given an opportunity Isaac would have been able to clarify his position. I wish Rick Reilly had interviewed me for that story, because I would have given him a viewpoint that might have added to the dialogue. For despite what some people in the media think, not all Christians see everything the same way.

I never feel comfortable speaking for anyone else, because I only know what I believe. Each individual has a unique relationship with God. However, because I've been very open in stating my beliefs, I understand that I'll inevitably be asked to answer for the statements of other Christians. And I welcome the questions because I believe it's important to get that kind of dialogue into the public realm, especially since spiritual faith is an issue people in the media are often eager to ignore.

In my mind, even when an article is skeptical about an athlete's Christian beliefs, it's still better than nothing at all being written. At least that stimulates discussion and allows people to draw their own conclusions. I think faith needs to be an issue, in sports and in every other realm. To avoid it and disregard it on a consistent basis is ridiculous. I do get frustrated at some of the media coverage, in part because some reporters will shy away from any statement I make about spiritual beliefs, as if they have nothing to do with what I am about or why I have succeeded. Also, it bothers me that sometimes the subject is made into a mockery. People say, God couldn't care less about a football game. There's no way he helped you throw a touchdown pass. But unless you know and understand God's power in my life, I think it's impossible to appreciate its impact in all that I do.

Let's look at some of the controversial questions surrounding faith and sports and address them, one by one:

Does God care about a football game?

Of course he does. He loves people so much that he cares about everything and anything they care about. I'm not saying that a football game is the most important thing to him or that he's controlling the outcome. But to say that he doesn't care about how I perform and whether I succeed is ridiculous. He is a part of every facet of our lives, and he cares about everything you could possibly do, even things that seem trivial.

Are some decisions and acts more pertinent to glorifying his kingdom than others? Sure they are. Does he care about winning a football game more than he does curing a sick person? No, he doesn't care about it more, but he does care about it. He is so powerful and so intricate that he can be a part of every bit of our lives and guide us in the direction that he wants us to go in one area without sacrificing his attention to another area.

Does God care more about one athlete's success than he does another's? Does the team with the most Christians win?

That's a silly way to frame the debate. It's not about winning or losing, anyway; the issue is a lot bigger than that. It has to do with what God wants to accomplish on this earth and how he can best achieve that goal. If God's purpose was to have somebody win a bunch of football games, then he'd have it the way he wants to have it. But when you look at the big picture, you look at how you can glorify God in every situation—after a win, loss, or tie; in injury, in prosperity, or whatever. Could I pray to win and then go out and lie on the football field and expect us to score more points than the other team? Of course not. We still make the choices and use our talents and gifts, but ultimately he can have as much or little control as he wants to have. I'm not going to read too much into things and say that he wanted me to win the Super Bowl more than he did, say, Hardy Nickerson, a devout Christian who played for the Tampa Bay Buccaneers. That's not what it's about, anyway. As much as I loved winning a championship, that's not my focus. Instead, my focus is on taking every bit of prosperity that he gives me and using it for the bigger purpose of glorifying his kingdom.

Were the Rams a team of destiny?

That's a term that gets tossed around a lot, and I may have helped fuel that perception when I said a few games into the season that "the Lord has big plans for this team." What I meant was that I believed God would use the situation, whether it was inside our locker room or in front of millions of people after winning the Super Bowl, to glorify his kingdom. I do believe that he had something special in store for our particular team because of the strong Christian base we had and the ability we had to touch a lot of lives. But there was no way to know the scope of his plan until it played out.

So many times we try to view things from a human standpoint, but we need to step into God's shoes. It doesn't have to be this or that. Normally, you'd say God doesn't care about football games. Humans try to make it all cut and dried, but we can't understand the extent of his scope.

If God doesn't necessarily care who wins, why thank him publicly after a victory?

Again, this is bigger than winning and losing. I'm not just thanking God for the victory, I'm thanking him for everything he does in my life. It's my opportunity to profess in front of everybody that I live my life for Jesus. If someone were to put a microphone in front of me after I'd just lost a big game, I'd thank Jesus in that context, too. I go home and thank him every day when I walk off the field healthy. A lot of times we don't thank him enough for expectations that aren't met. If we hadn't won the Super Bowl, for instance, it would've been crazy for me not to thank him for all that he had done throughout the season. When I thank him after a game I'm thanking him for every bit of influence, guidance, wisdom, talent, understanding, and protection he gives me in every situation.

What about when athletes thank God for touchdowns?

I thank God for everything that happens, on and off the field, so why exclude our trips to the end zone? If I throw a touchdown pass to Isaac, does it mean the Lord had an angel grab the football and put it into Isaac's hand? I don't know. What I do know is that

*Entering the Arena: Running onto the field
at a Barnstormers home game*

*What a difference three years and a Super Bowl make:
The Barnstormers retire my jersey*

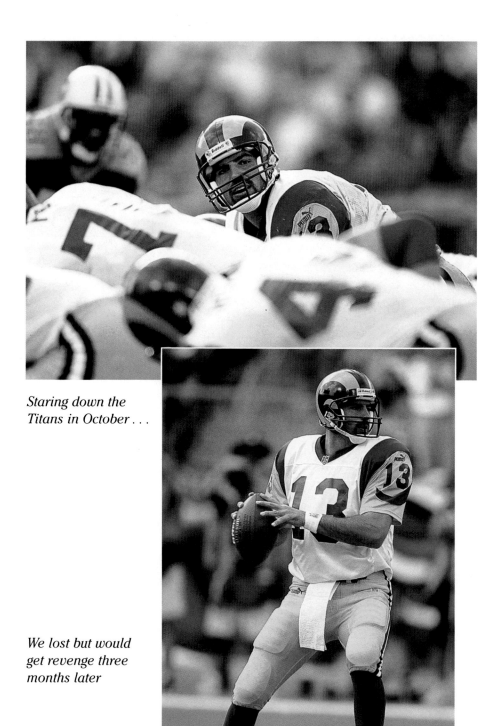

Staring down the Titans in October . . .

We lost but would get revenge three months later

Ready to break the 49er jinx at 3Com Park

Gutting it out against the Buccaneers in the NFC Championship Game

*Super Bowl XXXIV:
Driving for our
first touchdown in
the third quarter
against the Titans*

Not freakin' out: Hanging in against Jevon "The Freak" Kearse

With a great offensive line . . .

. . . I had time to find the open man

"I'm going to Disney World!"

With Coach Vermeil who always believed in me

The greatest feeling a football player can experience

www.whymilk.com

M.V.B.
(Most Valuable Beverage)

Want to win? Milk has 9 essential
nutrients active bodies need. Which is just
enough to help anyone beat the odds.

God has given me the physical gifts to make the throw and has put me in situations to learn and grow and gain wisdom as a football player. I believe he allows me to get focused by my trusting him with all sorts of things, on and off the field, that are beyond my control. I think the peace that comes over me when I do that makes it easier for me to relax and concentrate. I believe he can give me clarity to see what's going on and to know where to throw the ball. He has given me the gift of being able to throw with accuracy. I'm convinced that God has prepared me for the opportunity to be successful on the football field through the different people he's placed in my life, the work I've put in, and the different experiences I've had. It's not just about stepping onto the football field and saying, "Lord, help me throw a touchdown pass." It's about the whole process and the whole preparation period, in football and in life. He doesn't necessarily take personal charge of each and every pass I throw, but to disregard that notion entirely and say that God can't throw a touchdown pass is ridiculous, in my mind. He can do anything he chooses to do.

Isaac Bruce said he felt a twinge in his hamstring before the Vikings' playoff game, but after praying for healing he was able to run without any problems. A few years back Reggie White tore his hamstring but returned for the playoffs, saying God had healed him. Mark Brunell said the Lord would cure a serious knee injury in the '97 preseason then came back to play a few weeks later. Can Christian athletes defy medical science?

Absolutely. Can God heal somebody? There's no question in my mind. Can he cure anything from a pulled hamstring to a serious illness at the drop of a hat? Certainly. If I were in a situation similar to Isaac's and felt a twinge in my hamstring before a game, I'd react the same way he did. As it is, I go into every game asking for protection. A lot of people ask for protection when they fly on an airplane or drive in a car, and then when they arrive they don't regard it as miraculous that they didn't get into an accident. Who's to say that it wasn't divine intervention that allowed them to get to their destination safely? And who's to say that it wasn't divine intervention that cured Isaac or Reggie White or Mark Brunell?

Obviously God doesn't heal everyone every time they pray. I don't pretend to know why he answers yes to some prayers and no to others. I do believe that God wants to use whatever hardship and obstacles we encounter in life to push us to greater heights of faith and trust and to draw each of us closer to him. He says in the Bible that we should consider trials and tests as joy because they give us a chance to see where we're at, to test our faith, to mature, and to learn from the struggle. In my case there were so many roadblocks on my drive toward the NFL—let alone toward the Super Bowl—that I did a whole lot of growing. Then, when the Ultimate Game was finally in my line of vision, the Lord gave me one doozy of a challenge: the Tampa Bay Buccaneers, owners of the best defense in football.

The Bucs came to St. Louis for the NFC Championship game as fourteen-point underdogs, supposedly the largest non–Super Bowl spread in NFL postseason history. But we knew we were in for a struggle. Just as people around the country hadn't given us enough credit throughout most of the season, we now felt they might be giving us too much respect after our dismantling of the Vikings. It's funny how that switch happened almost immediately. As we came off the field after beating the Vikings, I saw a sign in the stands that read, "We still haven't beaten anybody." That epitomized our whole season; no matter who we beat, skeptics always picked apart the caliber of our opponent after the fact. The Vikings came in as the hottest team in the league, but we destroyed them, too. Maybe the reason our opponents all seemed so flawed in retrospect was because we were that much better than everybody else.

The good news was that Tampa Bay's conservative offense didn't figure to put up too many points against our defense. The bad news was that the Bucs' defense was capable of controlling the game. When I watched them on film, the thing that stood out was their speed. Not only were they fast at every position, they were so good up front that they didn't have to blitz to get pressure on the quarterback. In terms of scheme, they weren't the most complex defense in the world, but they were so good at sticking to their assignments and capitalizing on mistakes that it presented a huge challenge.

After the Minnesota game our offensive coordinator, Mike Martz, had become the league's hottest assistant coach—and with good reason. He probably could have had his pick of several head-coaching jobs after the season, so the Rams acted swiftly, signing him to a lucrative contract extension that promised he'd succeed Coach Vermeil no later than 2002. Even given all our history, I was greatly relieved. I had grown so comfortable with Mike that I used to tell him if I'm going to be here you better be here too.

Mike seemed capable of toying with any defense we faced. But as we started preparing for the Bucs, I knew we'd approach this game with a much different philosophy. To beat Tampa Bay, it was all about being patient. We felt that if we could put up, say, three touchdowns on them quickly we might be able to put them away. But instead of going for broke, Mike felt we had to pick and choose. We could still be aggressive, but only at the appropriate times. A lot of teams got into trouble by getting too greedy against Tampa. With the Bucs' speed and talent, they were always capable of making a game-turning play, as was the case in their playoff opener against Washington. The Redskins were in control of the game in the second half, but one turnover set the stage for Tampa's two-touchdown comeback victory. We had to be careful not to fall into that same trap.

The game began with one of those horrific sequences that, if you were hooked up to PlayStation, would have caused you to press the restart button. After the Bucs kicked off, we took over at our twenty-three yard line, and Mike called a screen pass to Marshall. I dropped back and tried to dump the ball off, and Steve White, the Bucs' defensive end, reached up, deflected the ball, and intercepted it at the twenty. It was one of those flukish plays; he looked like he was locked up against Orlando Pace, and I thought I could get it around him. But he made a great play, and Tampa kicked a field goal to go up 3–0.

We got the ball back at our twenty after a touchback, and the ensuing drive was like a microcosm of our afternoon. We moved the ball down the field, but at key moments we weren't as concise or crisp as we had been all season. A lot of that was their doing, too; whereas we might be able to get away with a sloppy route or an incorrect read against other teams, the Bucs were so good that they were able to capitalize on any little imprecision.

After twelve plays, only one of which went for greater than twelve yards, we had a first and goal at the Tampa seven. I went back to pass and had Isaac open on a flat route, and I threw a low pass that he catches for a touchdown ninety-nine times out of a hundred. This time, however, he failed to haul it in, and I was kicking myself for not throwing it a little higher. Then, after an incompletion to Roland Williams, we had a busted play on third down, and I fumbled while trying to run up the middle. Fortunately, Marshall recovered at the six, and Jeff Wilkins nailed a game-tying field goal.

The little things were killing us, and it was mighty frustrating. On the first play of the second quarter, a bad snap led to a safety when Tampa's rookie quarterback, Shaun King, batted the ball out of the end zone. Now we led 5–3, but we missed a forty-four-yard field goal on our next drive, and we failed to extend the lead before halftime. When the Bucs nailed a go-ahead field goal on the first drive of the third quarter our sideline became a tense and nervous place.

At that point we trailed 6–5, and I think I started pressing a little bit, trying to make things happen that weren't necessarily there. No one said anything to me, but I got the feeling that if we were going to win the game, it was going to be on my shoulders. The Bucs had done a good job of bottling up Marshall Faulk, and they were disrupting our receivers' timing just enough to throw us off of our game. Mike Martz was getting especially frustrated, because for the first time all year his scheme looked vulnerable.

Az Hakim, our speedy number three receiver, was suffering from cramps and dehydration and sat out much of the second half, and that took us a bit out of our game plan. Mike couldn't run a lot of the plays we had practiced with our four-receiver sets, and he wasn't thrilled about adjusting on the fly. We talked via the head-sets and reassured each other that our time would come. "Don't force anything, and stay patient," he told me. "It's only going to take one play to win this game, and when the opportunity arises, we'll take our shot."

On our first possession of the third quarter we drove to Tampa's fourteen, but a holding penalty pushed us back to the twenty-four. After two incompletions I tried to throw a ball near the goal line to Ricky Proehl, who had become the number three receiver in Az's absence. But there was a miscommunication; I didn't think he was going to go as deep as he went, so I anticipated his turn and ended up underthrowing him. Hardy Nickerson, Tampa's great middle linebacker, jumped up and made a nice play to intercept it at the two. It wasn't necessarily anyone's fault: Ricky was just trying to get us a little closer to the end zone, and I released the ball before I could adjust.

Then, early in the fourth quarter, I threw my third interception of the game. This time I was looking for Torry Holt inside the Bucs' forty-five, but Brian Kelly stepped in front and snagged it on the run. This was an example of how a subtle adjustment can change the game. Torry is coached to cut underneath the defender no matter what; even if the defender is sitting and waiting on the inside route, Torry has to cut straight across and go in front of him for the play to work. But Kelly, the cornerback, made a great play and cut off Torry before he could get underneath. I'm pretty sure Torry, who was a rookie, will never let that happen again, but it was a case of him getting outfoxed by a crafty defender. So even though Torry broke free on a skinny post and I put the ball where I wanted to put it, Kelly's position was such that he was able to make a play on the ball.

Now lips were puckered and hearts were pounding. Kelly

returned the ball to our forty-two, but our defense held—again. We went three plays and out, and the Bucs got the ball near midfield with 9:20 to go. Inside the dome it was tighter than spandex on Orlando Pace, our three-hundred-twenty-pound Pro Bowl left tackle. Still, I didn't panic. Everybody said after the game that the Bucs had finally found our weakness and shut us down, but that really wasn't the case. We threw for 258 yards and moved the ball with regularity, but it was like they had an invisible force field between us and the end zone. I knew we could break on through.

With eight minutes to go our defense made a play that gave me the opening I needed. Shaun King threw a pass to Warrick Dunn, and Dre Bly, our nickel cornerback, intercepted it and returned the ball to the Tampa forty-seven. As I entered the huddle I told my teammates, "Okay, this is it. We've got to go down and make it happen right now. This is when we have to make a play to seal the deal."

I could feel the energy level pick up. A field goal would give us the lead, but we wanted the touchdown. With 4:50 to go, on third and four from their thirty, we called our second time-out and assessed our options. The play, Smoke Right H-Choice, was designed for Marshall Faulk, who was lined up in the backfield. He figured to have single coverage, and he could basically do whatever he wanted to get open. It was a high-percentage play, and there was no reason to question the call.

Yet when I got back onto the field, as I waited for the TV time-out to end, I started feeling a little nervous: what if they blitzed and I didn't have time to get Marshall the ball before he broke out of his route? Marshall would be the "hot" receiver on the front side. However, we'd throw it to him quickly in the event of a blitz. If the blitz came from the backside, there would be a sight adjustment on the left. And since Az Hakim was out of the game, the outlet receiver would be Ricky Proehl, who'd be lined up wide left.

As we stood on the field waiting to huddle, Ricky and I hatched our plan. Normally in that situation the best route for him to run would be an inside slant, because it would allow me to get rid of the ball quickly. But the Bucs' defenders are so smart that we thought they might allow for that possibility and sit on the slant. Then we would be playing right into their hands.

"What if I were to run a hitch?" Ricky asked, describing a route in which the receiver runs a five-yard hook and turns to the inside.

"Yeah," I answered, "or we could go for it all and run a fade."

"What do you think?" Ricky asked.

Hmmm. I paused for a moment, then thought to myself, *We didn't get here by being wimps.* "Let's go for it," I said, offering a slight smile. "We need a big play, so what the heck? If they blitz, go deep, and I'm coming to you."

Sure enough, the Bucs blitzed their free safety, Damien Robinson, and I knew it was do-or-die. Our protection called for the linemen to slide over and pick up the blitzer, freeing up one of Tampa's defensive ends. I knew he'd be unblocked, so I'd have to make a five-step drop and get rid of the ball quickly.

On a fade route, the receiver drifts toward the corner of the end zone and, while keeping the defender to the inside, looks for the ball over his outside shoulder. The safety blitz left Brian Kelly singled up against Ricky on the left side, and though Ricky had a step on him, the coverage was pretty tight. Not that I had time to quibble. I felt the pressure and released the pass, trying to put the ball high enough so that Ricky would have a chance to make a play. I knew this was a gamble, because it was probably the only time we'd gone to Ricky on that kind of play all year long.

The ball felt good as I released it, and I remember looking up and seeing him jump up and get it. I didn't realize how great a catch it was until I saw the replay, which showed how Ricky shielded the ball from Kelly and hauled it in with his left hand. My only concern at the time was whether he was in bounds, and when I heard the crowd roar and saw the official raise his hands, I went nuts along with everybody else.

You had to admire the Lord's touch on that one. Here's Ricky Proehl, the ultimate team guy, who goes all season long without catching a touchdown pass and never complains. Then, with our team facing elimination, he comes through with the catch that takes us to the Super Bowl. It was such a testament to his character. The guy was written off at every stage of his career, told that he's not good enough or fast enough to play at this level, and he kept fighting and fighting until he made one of the biggest catches in playoff history.

The game wasn't over, though. The Bucs stopped us on the two-point conversion and, down 11–6, got the ball at their own twenty-three with 4:44 remaining. They had a first down at our twenty-two with 1:25 left, but then Grant Wistrom sacked Shaun King for a thirteen-yard loss. On the next play Bert Emanuel made a diving catch at the twenty-three yard line. Or was it a catch? The officials called it incomplete because it hit the turf, and we had to sweat out a long replay review before the call was upheld. On fourth and twenty-three from the thirty-five, King took one last shot to the end zone that our defense batted down, and I got to end the game with a kneel-down. As time expired, Isaac came over and asked if I was going to keep the ball. I thought about giving it to him, but I'm a stickler for tradition: I jogged to the corner of the end zone, kissed Brenda, and handed it to her.

It was a special moment for us, but the old-guard Rams were the ones who seemed truly touched. The game had been a struggle, but now none of that mattered. The Rams—the Rams!—were going to the Super Bowl, and the scene in our locker room was just surreal.

Up to that point our attitude had always been to keep pressing ahead and to focus only on what was in front of us. Now the Ultimate Game was in our direct line of vision. It was just amazing to realize where we had come from and how far we had traveled to get to that point. It was too much to fathom, like we didn't really understand what had happened. Guys like Todd Lyght and Keith Lyle and Isaac, who had suffered through so much losing, were walking around in a daze. Nobody knew what to do or what to say; you could just tell from their demeanor that they were ecstatic about the opportunity and were looking forward to it—because it really is something to savor. You think about guys like Dan Marino, who ended up retiring after last season without having won a championship. He made the Super Bowl in his second season and lost, and even though he set all kinds of records and was in the playoffs almost every year, he never got another chance to play for the biggest prize.

I remember Todd Lyght, our veteran cornerback, approaching me on the field and thanking me for getting us to the Super Bowl. I thanked him right back, not only because the defense had carried us against the Bucs, but because of his inspirational play throughout the season. A Ram since '91, he had lost more than ninety games throughout his career, and there had been some humiliating moments. Once, when the Rams were in Anaheim, they hosted a Monday night game against the 49ers, who as usual were kicking their butts. As the game wound down, the Rams' crowd was so weak that the stadium was filled with chants of "Beat L.A."—from the Niners fans who had come down from the Bay Area. Going into the '99 season, based on the way things had been, I'm sure Todd was thinking, *My contract is up after this year, and then I'm out of here.*

Now, unbelievably, St. Louis was the place to be. And tomorrow, with a bounce in our step, we were heading to Atlanta.

CHAPTER FIFTEEN

JUST ANOTHER GAME

To tell the inside story of my Super Bowl experience, we have to go back to the sleepless night I spent at the Crowne Plaza Ravinia hotel in Atlanta on Thursday, January 27, 2000. I accomplished many firsts during our victory over the Tennessee Titans at the Georgia Dome, but here's one that slipped through the cracks: I'd be willing to wager that I was the first-ever Super Bowl MVP who spurned his wife's amorous advances three nights before the game, then stayed up until dawn worrying that his roommate hadn't made it back to the hotel.

No wonder Paul Justin, my friend and backup, started calling me "Mr. Mom" in the days leading up to the game.

It sounds so silly now, but at the time I was genuinely concerned for Paul's safety. Brenda had arrived along with the rest of the wives on Thursday, and after she and I went to dinner she tried to lure me back to the hotel where family members were staying, a few minutes away from the Crowne Plaza. Believe me, she can be very persuasive, but I managed to resist. My first four days in Atlanta had been mighty hectic, what with the media attention and constant barrage of activity. Though it wasn't very romantic of me, I wanted to spend some quality time alone with my game plan.

"I really need to get some sleep," I told her as we said good-bye.

What a joke that proclamation turned out to be.

We had a curfew that night, but it was one of those wink-and-nod curfews: if you were a veteran and had a reasonable evening planned, and you let one of the coaches know, it was cool to stay out as late as you wanted. It also happened that there was an ice storm in Atlanta that night, and local authorities were warning people to stay off the roads. So when I got back to the room and Paul wasn't there I started to get a little stressed. I tried to call him on his cell phone a couple of times, but I kept getting voice mail. It wasn't like "P.J." to blow off curfew without letting me know, and even though I figured he was probably staying at his girlfriend's hotel room, my mind started spinning and I spent the next several hours tossing and turning in bed.

Each time I heard the slightest noise I'd sit up and think, *Here's Paul.* But curfew came and went, and I kept stirring and worrying that he'd been in an accident. I don't know why I was so nervous. Maybe I was practicing for my daughter's first date, or perhaps I was just keyed up for the game.

Finally, around 3 A.M., I couldn't take it anymore. I called Paul's cell phone again—no answer. I called Kevin Warren, our vice president of player programs. He said he'd try to track P.J. down. I called Marci Moran, our community relations manager, and told her to try to get hold of Paul's girlfriend. She said she'd see what she could find out. I called Brenda and woke her up. "You've got the biggest game of your life in less than three days," she said. "Get some sleep, you goofball."

But I couldn't sleep. It just wasn't like Paul not to call. Finally, around the time it was getting light, I managed to doze off for an hour or so. At around 7:30 I threw on some clothes and hurried down to the team breakfast, but he wasn't there, either. I asked around to see if anyone had heard from him, but nobody had. Now I was really concerned. I walked into our quarterbacks meeting, and who should enter the door right behind me but, you guessed it, Paul Justin.

"Where were you?" everyone asked in unison.

"Geez," P.J. said, "will you guys relax?"

First I was relieved, then I was peeved. He had indeed spent the night at his girlfriend's, and he had notified only our quarterback coach, John Ramsdell. "Hey, thanks for calling and letting me know where you were gonna be," I said sarcastically. "I was up all night, but it's no big thing. I don't have anything that important to do on Sunday or anything."

"Hey, dummy," he shot back, "I've been alive thirty-one years, and somehow I've managed to survive. I don't need someone to wait up for me." Looking back, I have to laugh at his reaction. The guy has a knack for off-the-cuff jokes and putting things into unique terminology. All season long in our quarterback meetings, we joked that Paul should put his wit and wisdom into book form and call it *The World According to P.J.*

Paul and I weren't really angry at each other, just annoyed, but the ribbing continued for the next several days. At one point P.J. said, "That's it—you've got a new nickname." And from then on he addressed me as "Mr. Mom."

Rooming with Paul had been my idea. The team offered me a solo room in Atlanta, but Paul and I had stayed together on the road all year, and I had grown to enjoy our conversations. We have a lot in common, especially in terms of our backgrounds. He played in the Arena League in 1993, and before I hit it big with the Rams he was probably that league's greatest success story. We used to sit there and swap tales from our respective Arena days, like the time Paul, while playing for the Arizona Rattlers, threw an interception against Dallas and got so angry he ran down the defender and squared up to slam him into the wall. But the defender stopped at the last moment, and Paul went headfirst into the padding. Fortunately, he wasn't paralyzed, but he did experience a tingling sensation throughout his spine and a season's worth of embarrassment. More than most of our teammates, Paul and I truly appreciated the NFL lifestyle, from the charter flights to the sweet Nike bags we got at the Super Bowl. One of our pet expressions was, "Gotta love the pros!"

I thought having a roommate might keep me loose, but the truth was, I didn't have a whole lot of fun in the week leading up to the game. Not only was I being dragged from interview to appearance to practice to meeting to function to obligation, none of my teammates thought to include me in his plans. As you know, I'm no party animal, but it would have been nice to go to dinner and hang out with some of the guys. But I was like the pretty girl guys are afraid to ask out because they assume she's so popular, so she sits home alone. On my first couple of nights in Atlanta it was me, Dan Patrick, and the Bible, kicking it in my hotel room.

Coach Vermeil had taken the 1980 Eagles to the Super Bowl, where they had lost to the Oakland Raiders, and he told us one of his regrets was that his players had been too tight going into that game. "There's going to be a lot of craziness—a million things to do, people pulling and tugging at you, and media attention unlike anything you've experienced before," he told us early in the week. "Just try to enjoy it. Don't get caught up in everything that you have to do, because the more you fight it, the tougher it's going to be. Just take everything in stride, enjoy the fact that you've gotten to this point, and try to concentrate on football."

I tried to take his advice, but with only a one-week break between the conference championship game and the Super Bowl, rather than the usual two weeks, everything was a blur. I remember lying in bed with Brenda in St. Louis a few hours after our NFC Championship victory over Tampa Bay and talking about how far we had come. "This is what it's all about, the culmination of everything God has had in store for us all these years," I told her. "We tried to stay faithful, and he brought us to the point that we had dreamed about. We're in the Super Bowl. And now that we're here our lives will never be the same."

The next morning I grabbed a couple of suitcases and did some power packing: a couple suits and a pile of sweats and jeans and T-shirts. Regrettably, I didn't pack any cold-weather gear, and the Super Bowl host city was anything but Hot-lanta that week. There was ice, snow, and plenty of chill. Thankfully, a letterman's coat came in my Nike bag, and I ended up wearing that all week long. The joke was that everyone on the team was wearing identical coats because we were all in the same boat.

The cold weather made it a little tougher to concentrate at practice, and the whole routine was different because we were operating out of a hotel room rather than our own facility. We didn't have the normal amount of film-watching sessions, so it was on each of us to review tapes on his own as the week progressed. The assistant coaches stayed back in St. Louis and put the game plan together then flew out on Tuesday night. Normally we would spend Monday breaking down film from the previous game, but we didn't even watch our victory over the Bucs because of time constraints.

When Mike Martz introduced the game plan to us on Wednesday, I could tell he was excited. After holding us back in the Tampa Bay game, he felt we could air it out against Tennessee, because the Titans were likely to blitz and create one-on-one matchups we might be able to exploit. I spent a lot of time that week talking strategy with Paul Justin and John Ramsdell, our quarterbacks coach. Whereas Mike was in charge of the big picture, John was great about the specifics and nuances of our scheme, everything from footwork to understanding reads to breaking down blocking assignments. As the week wore on Mike Martz got more and more fired up about the plan, because playing aggressively against single coverage is our strength. "For this game," he told us, "we're not holding anything back. We're not going to sit back and let these guys bring the game to us; we're going to attack them and play the way we played all year."

I hadn't played my best against Tampa, and I knew that if I went into the Super Bowl and played an average game, we probably wouldn't win. The comforting thing was that when we looked at film of our defeat to the Titans in October, we became more and more convinced that it hadn't been so much a case of what they did to us but of what we didn't do. We moved the ball throughout much of the game, and had we not missed a throw here or a block there we could have done some serious damage. That gave us a lot of confidence.

The problem was, I didn't want to think too much about the game, especially in the early part of the week. I was also getting tired of talking about it, though I did have a lot of fun at Media Day at the Georgia Dome on Tuesday afternoon. I got asked the same questions over and over by various waves of journalists—"What do you think of Steve McNair?" "What was it like working at the Hy-Vee Supermarket?" "Did you ever imagine you could be in this position?"—and I had to be careful to answer them in similar fashion so that people wouldn't think I was inconsistent. The MTV people bulled their way to the front and loudly shouted out a couple of questions that, to my surprise, were about my faith, rather than whether I thought Ricky Martin was cooler than Kid Rock or something like that. At one point somebody from the Cartoon Network asked me which cartoon character I would support for president, and I said, "Bugs Bunny, of course, because he's the leader of the Warner Brothers."

It was all very exciting, but the mob scene, especially at our hotel, made things difficult. I ordered a lot of room service, and at one point I sent Paul down to the lobby to get me a chocolate bar, some change, and other supplies. Just my luck, he ran into Mike Martz in the elevator and he said, "You'll never believe what Kurt is making me do." Paul was so riled up that when he got back to the room, he said, "What am I, your girlfriend?"

"Yeah," I joked, "but just for this week."

On a few occasions I really wanted to take a walk without being hassled, so they sent a security guard to guide me through back rooms and service entrances. When I got really ambitious I had the same security guard take me to a nearby mall in search of a haircut. But it wasn't as simple as it sounds. Every place we tried was a hair salon, and none of the hairdressers did flattops. I ended up having to go to a place in another part of town the next day to get the flattop, if you could call it that.

Things mellowed out in the latter part of the week, and one of the more enjoyable functions I attended was the Miller Lite NFL Player of the Year press conference at the downtown Hyatt Regency. I ended up winning the award, which was a little weird for me because I don't drink beer, but they donated $30,000 to

Camp Barnabas, so on balance it was a good thing. Some of the other nominees like Peyton Manning and Stephen Davis were there, and it was neat to meet and talk to them. Everyone assumes that I know all the other prominent players in the league, but since I was such a nobody until '99, I've been pretty isolated from that crowd. So I'm still sort of excited when I meet a guy like Peyton Manning, who I'd been watching since his freshman year at Tennessee.

We had plenty of spiritual support in Atlanta. Jeff Perry, my pastor, came out to lead our Bible study session on Wednesday night. On Sunday morning we got another surprise. Henry T. Blackabee, a well-known evangelist from the Atlanta area, had come to St. Louis in October and led our pregame chapel session before we played Carolina. At that time he talked about the importance of staying faithful and obedient and said, "God is looking for a group of men with clean hearts." Noting that the Super Bowl was in his hometown, he promised he would come speak to us again if we made it that far. Sure enough, on the morning of the game he was there to lead our chapel service at the team hotel. He reiterated some of his earlier comments and pointed out how he had watched us grow.

Late in the week I got a message that blew my mind: it was from the Reverend Billy Graham, asking me to give him a call. Man, was I thrilled! I called my own pastor, Jeff Perry, to rub it in, because Jeff might be the biggest Billy Graham fan on earth. The fact that the Reverend Graham called me—and that I was able to meet him in October when I spoke at his St. Louis crusade—drove Jeff nuts. Jeff has done some relief work in Kosovo with Franklin Graham (Billy's son), but he has never gotten to meet the legend himself. It's a running joke between us; Jeff's always complaining to the congregation that "one person among us got to meet Billy Graham but didn't even introduce him to his pastor." On Friday I left Dr. Graham a message with my cell phone number, but it was off most of the time and we never ended up talking. Still, I really appreciated the gesture.

The weather turned even lousier on Saturday, and we were advised to stay off the roads, so our walk-through at the Dome was canceled. Coach Vermeil was livid, but it was the best thing that could have happened to me. Walk-throughs are pretty useless, and I used the time to take a long nap, which I definitely needed after the sleepless night I'd spent waiting up for Paul.

On Saturday night Mike Martz invited me to come down to one of the meeting rooms so we could watch a little extra film together, and we reinforced our belief that we could catch the Titans in some matchups that would be pretty appealing to us. That night I talked on the phone to my mom, and she said, "Kurt, you're going to be in the Super Bowl tomorrow. You've dreamed of this forever. What are you thinking?" I said, "Mom, it's just another game. It's another game that I've got to play."

"Are you going to think that when you take the field tomorrow?" she asked.

I laughed and admitted, "Probably not."

Later Saturday night, after going over my plays, I said my prayers and got an okay night's sleep. After breakfast on Sunday I went back up to the room and tried to take a nap, but it was futile. Every once in a while I'd pop on the TV and watch the pregame shows, just to see how they were hyping the game. I didn't get any tips or anything, but it was interesting to watch other active players like Cris Carter give their thoughts on the keys to the game and analyze it from every angle. It may have been the first time in my life that I watched one of those shows before a game that I would actually be playing in, and it was kind of fun.

I always take the last bus over to the stadium, because I hate waiting around. When I got there I sat by myself. I prayed for peace, calmness, clarity, and protection, not only for me but for players on both teams. I usually claim Psalm 91, which is about the Lord watching over us and protecting us. Then I got dressed and went out to the field to warm up. I had some lively conversations with media members like Al Michaels and Matt Millen and Ron Jaworski, who played quarterback for Coach Vermeil's Eagles and always likes to grab the ball from me before games and throw a warm-up pass to one of the receivers. His arm is pretty weak these days, but it's his way of trying to do his part for Coach Vermeil. He seemed to believe that if he didn't throw that ball during warm-ups, we'd have no chance of winning. All I can say is, Thanks, Jaws: your game ball will be arriving shortly.

Later, I saw The Freak—Jevon Kearse, the Titans' amazing rookie pass rusher, whom I had met briefly before our first meeting in October. I congratulated him for his season and said, "It's the start of a great career."

"Talk about a great year," he answered in that ultralow voice of his, and we laughed, shook hands, and wished each other well.

As game time approached, I made a conscious effort to stay as calm as possible. If my teammates could see that I was unfazed by the drama, they'd keep things in perspective as well. The first time I really noticed the excitement was when we went into the tunnel before pregame introductions. Some of our more animated players, guys like Roland Williams and London Fletcher, were yelling and screaming and pounding everybody on the shoulder pads. Marshall Faulk and Isaac Bruce and I took a step back and told one another, "It's on our shoulders. We need to go out and take control." Coach Vermeil saw us and came over, and the four of us had a group hug before they started calling names.

Todd Collins, our linebacker who had played in the Super Bowl with New England three years earlier, had told me that there was nothing like running out of the tunnel before the Super Bowl and knowing there were tens of millions of people getting ready to watch you play. "It's the biggest adrenaline rush you'll ever experience," he said. My heart rate definitely picked up when they called my name, but it wasn't as dramatic as I had expected it to be. I was ready to go, but I wasn't freaking out.

Then the Titans kicked off, and the coolest thing happened: after all the hype, after all the emotional peaks and valleys, a football game broke out. It was an important football game, to be sure, but it was just football—the same game I'd been playing since I was a kid. Once that ball is kicked you forget about all the insanity that preceded it, and you dig in and do what you've been trained to do for years. And that's a comforting feeling because it allows you to get a handle on what had seemed like a daunting situation.

Right away, I could tell I was on my game. On our first drive the Titans blitzed five times, and I connected on my first two third-down passes, to Isaac for seventeen yards and to Ricky Proehl for eleven. On third and nine from the Tennessee seventeen, Blaine Bishop, the Titans' excellent strong safety, got in my face on a blitz, and I threw it up to Torry Holt in the end zone. We felt he was grabbed on the play by Dainon Sidney, but there was no call, and we blew our field goal chance when the snap slipped out of the hands of our holder, Mike Horan.

A pattern had been established. The Titans kept blitzing us, I kept hitting the open man, and we kept bogging down near the goal line. We had the ball five times in the first half, and each time we got inside the twenty yard line. We didn't turn the ball over, yet we came away with only nine points—no touchdowns, three field goals, and two missed field goals. The Titans, after missing a forty-seven-yard field goal on their first series, did nothing on offense, but the halftime score was just 9–0.

It should have been much, much more lopsided. Tennessee played good defense in the red zone, but we had our share of blown chances. Midway through the second quarter, I threw a pass to Torry at the goal line that he very nearly caught. Blaine Bishop made a nice defensive play, but Torry had a shot at it; instead, we settled for our second field goal.

Then, right before halftime, we drove down and had first and goal at the ten. On first down we motioned Marshall out of the backfield and split him out as a fifth receiver, leaving only the five linemen to block. Tennessee sent six defenders—their strength against our strength—and Anthony Dorsett, the free safety, was the unblocked man. I had Az Hakim open for a touchdown, but I got clocked by Dorsett as I released it and the pass came up short. As I lay on the ground I felt a shooting pain in my ribs, on the right side just under the breastplate. I knew it was bad—every time I moved or got hit it felt like a knife tearing through my flesh—yet I had no choice but to play through it.

After another incompletion, to Isaac, we set up a play on third and goal that definitely should have been a touchdown. This one was my fault. It's a play in which we have four receivers, two on each side. The outside guys run hitch routes, and the inside guys flare out to the corners of the end zone. We got press, man-to-man coverage, which is what we wanted, and Marshall picked up the blitzing defender. Ricky Proehl, who had broken from the inside, was wide open in the corner of the end zone. But I sensed the pass rush and stupidly hurried the throw. I tried to anticipate where Ricky would be and threw it too high, and he could only get a hand on it. It's uncharacteristic of me to bail out early like that, and I should have had more faith that Marshall would pick up the blitzer, because Marshall almost never misses. Had I waited a split second longer for Ricky to come out of his break, we would have had the touchdown, but instead we had to settle for Jeff Wilkins's third field goal and a 9–0 halftime lead.

As I walked off the field toward the locker room, two things bothered me: first, though we were clearly outplaying the Titans, we were also playing right into their hands. All season long they stayed in games they seemed to have no business being in, and they'd stick around and stick around and eventually wear down their opponent. If we could get them into a situation where Steve McNair had to pass and Eddie George's running would be less of a factor, we'd be in good shape. But the fact that they were within nine points was a concern.

Second, and more important, I was a physical wreck. Not only was the pain in my ribs excruciating—technically, I had strained cartilage—but my left elbow was banged up. I'd sustained what we call a "stinger," which is like a jolting numbness that comes from temporary nerve damage. Every time I made contact with a certain spot of my elbow, my left (nonthrowing) hand would go numb.

Beyond that, I was exhausted. I had thrown thirty-five times, more than I do in some *games,* against the most aggressive defense in football. At the time I had no idea how many passes I had thrown; I might have said twenty-five, but thirty-five? No way. All I knew was I needed a rest, so I found a spot on the training table and lay there trying to conserve energy.

The medical people examined me and asked if I wanted to take a painkilling injection for my ribs. I told them no because I was concerned it might mess with me from a mental standpoint, and that was the last thing I needed. "I'm fine," I told the doctors. "I just want to go out and play." Todd Lyght, our veteran corner-back, was on a table next to me, getting treatment for a strained groin, and he asked, "Kurt, man, are you gonna be okay? Can you finish this game?" I told him not to worry. I was getting annoyed by all the questions. I was hot and sore and tired and soaked with sweat, and I just wanted to get out there and finish the darn thing.

Only another quarterback could really understand what I was going through, and when Paul Justin and Trent Green entered the room, I gave them both a nasty, tormented look they knew well. "Hey, man, suck it up," Paul barked. "In thirty minutes you're going to Disneyland." He and Trent thought it was hilarious; I just stared back at them like a zombie. I drank a little water and hoped that halftime, which was much longer than usual, would end, already. Mike Martz came over and said, "We're not going to change anything. We're going to stay aggressive and keep going at them." Right before we went back out for the third quarter, Coach Vermeil told the team, "Play smart. They cannot stop us unless we stop ourselves by not executing. They can't cover us." I later learned that he was concerned enough to run down Paul Justin before we took the field and tell him, "Make sure you're warmed up; Kurt's not doing too well right now."

After all I'd been through to get to that point, it would've taken a whole lot more than pain and fatigue to keep me from finishing the job. The Titans got the ball first and drove to our twenty-nine, but Todd Lyght saved us by blocking Al Del Greco's field goal attempt, which would have brought Tennessee to within six points. This was getting too close for comfort. We needed a cushion, and as I jogged back onto the field I was determined to get us one. Once again we moved the ball; a thirty-one-yard pass to Isaac got us down to their twenty-six.

Then came one of the scariest moments I've witnessed on a football field. I dropped back, went through my reads, and found Ernie Conwell, our 265-pound tight end, in a seam between defenders. He caught the ball and bulled his way to the ten, where two Tennessee players converged—Anthony Dorsett from behind and Blaine Bishop from the flat, where he'd been covering another receiver. Bishop, who weighs 200 pounds, is a big hitter, but this hit was *too* big. It was a helmet-to-body collision with Ernie, and after they hit the ground, Blaine didn't get up.

At first it didn't seem like anything serious, but as Blaine lay there, facedown and motionless, it became a very frightening situation. There are so many vicious hits in football, and you never really know when something ominous will happen. Just like that, a player could be paralyzed or even locked in a life-threatening situation. Once a guy goes down in that fashion, you stop thinking about the game and your only concern is his safety.

I wanted to go to Blaine and grab his hand, to see if he was all right and to say a prayer and let him know we were thinking of him. But the officials wouldn't let me near him. They said, "Stay back. Stay away from him." So I did the next best thing: I went a few yards away from him, knelt down, and said a prayer alone. I asked the Lord to heal him and get him back onto the football field.

Blaine stayed down for several minutes, and at one point Coach Vermeil gathered us as a team and asked that we observe a moment of silence to pray for him. I looked at Ernie Conwell, and I could see he was taking it hard. Ernie's probably my best friend on the team. Our families go to church together, and we share a lot of the same values. He's a hard worker who's in it not for the money but to touch people's lives from a Christian standpoint, share the gospel, and be a model teammate. He's also one of the nicest people I know, a guy who would do anything for you. I know that if I were in a time of need, no matter the circumstances, he would drop everything and be there in a heartbeat. To be in that position, making a big catch in the Super Bowl, he had to overcome incredible obstacles. Midway through the '98 season he suffered one of the most gruesome knee injuries imaginable, and it was doubtful he'd be able to make it back at all. At first it took him twenty minutes just to scale the staircase at his townhouse on crutches, but he kept working hard. Now, after signing a long-term contract with the Rams following the '99 season, he finally has some security, and I look forward to being his teammate for years to come.

Ernie and I bowed our heads as the doctors carefully loaded Blaine onto a stretcher and into an ambulance. Now, here's the weird thing. As quickly as you turn off the game when someone gets seriously hurt, you turn it right back on when they leave. After the ambulance drove off I had to switch right back into football mode and trust that the Lord would look out for Blaine's safety. Once the game ended a couple of people told me he was okay—he'd suffered a severe concussion and a sprained neck but no permanent damage—and I was extremely relieved. For now, though, I had to try to get us a touchdown.

Two plays after the injury time-out, on third and goal from the nine, we split three receivers to the right, with Torry Holt alone on the left. The Titans blitzed, and my sight adjustment to the backside was Torry coming to the middle on a slant. I had to throw it quickly, because one of the blitzing defensive backs was unblocked, and Torry caught it in front of Dainon Sidney for the score. Touchdown—finally! I had promised to do the Bob and Weave in the Super Bowl, but this didn't seem like the time; I was more relieved than anything. After the extra point we had a 16–0 lead, and I thought we could finish them off on our next possession.

But like everyone else, I guess, I misjudged the Tennessee Titans. I knew they were a very good team with a lot of heart; I didn't realize they were a *great* team with enormous heart. After that touchdown they had every reason to quit, especially with Blaine Bishop, their biggest hitter and emotional leader, lying in an ambulance. Instead, they cranked up their energy level and toughness and gave us the fight of our lives—not to mention the most stirring Super Bowl finish in history.

Jeff Fisher and the Titans' assistant coaches changed their entire offensive game plan, going back to what they do best— Eddie George's running, Steve McNair's scrambling and high-percentage passes to the tight ends—and pounding our defense into submission. Instead of trying to get back into the game with big plays, they just kept chunking away, and our defense started to get tired. Really tired. Tennessee finally got on the board with fourteen seconds left in the third quarter, when Eddie George bulled in from a yard out. We stopped the two-point conversion, and the lead was 16–6.

Then, for the first time all day, the Titans' defense stopped us. On third and sixteen from our thirty-one, I overthrew Torry on a deep pass, and we punted. The Titans responded with another methodical drive. This time Eddie George went two yards around right end for the touchdown, and now it was 16–13 with 7:21 left in the game.

Things were a little testy on our sidelines. At one point, while Tennessee was moving the ball, Coach Vermeil came up to me and started talking about my mechanics. "Your arm is down lower, your delivery is lower, and you're throwing off your back foot," he said. "Get that arm up." This was the last thing I wanted to hear. I can handle criticism about making reads or whether I'm picking up the defensive coverages, but the last thing I want to mess with at that stage is my mechanics. I'm not going to start tinkering with my drops or the way I throw; I just go out and play and react. I get so focused and into what Brenda calls "The Zone" that I just tune out stuff like that. I stared right back at Coach Vermeil. Actually, I stared *through* him, like I was looking through the back of his head.

"I don't want to talk about it anymore," I finally said. "I just want to play."

Marshall ran for two yards to start the next drive, and then Mike Martz sent in a play that could have given us some breathing room. It was a formation that isolates Marshall on a slant route so he can do some serious damage. But I couldn't get the ball to him, because Jason Fisk batted it into the air at the line of scrimmage. I was pressured into another incompletion on third down, and we punted again. This time they took over at their forty-seven, and I started getting a sick feeling in my stomach.

On Tennessee's next drive, Billy Jenkins nailed Jackie Harris after a catch and forced a fumble, but the Titans recovered. A few plays later they tied it up on Al Del Greco's forty-three-yard field goal with 2:12 to go, setting up the classic climax I've already described.

A chill ran down my spine. I thought about where I was and how hard I had fought to get here. There had been so many trying moments, so many times I wondered if I'd ever have a chance to tap my athletic potential. I got blown off by Hayden Fry, sat on the bench for three years at Northern Iowa, was virtually ignored at Packers camp, cleaned up shattered mayonnaise jars at the Hy-Vee, nearly short-circuited my Arena League career before it began, lost my future in-laws in a tornado, missed a Bears tryout because a scorpion turned my throwing arm into a whoopee cushion, got hazed mercilessly by Mike Martz. . . . The list goes on and on. Now, because of my perseverance and faith, I had been rewarded beyond my wildest dreams. I had a chance to do my thing with the whole world watching, and no one could take it away from me. I might succeed—or, then again, I might fail—but as I jogged back onto the field for the biggest play of my life, I realized that wasn't really the point after all. I sneaked a glance at Brenda, so radiant in her electric blue sweater. I thought of my kids and my friends and my family and my relationship with God and realized, more than ever before, how truly blessed I am. When I lined up over center and snatched the football, I felt a power I'd never known surging through the leather and into my veins.

Everything was sharp and clear and brilliant: I dropped back, saw Jevon Kearse charging toward me, and threw deep down the sidelines as I got slammed to the turf. Isaac came back to catch it—my only completion of the fourth quarter, by the way—and then he was gone into a mass of flashbulbs and gyrating body parts.

A few minutes later Mike Jones stopped Kevin Dyson on our one yard line as time expired, and the ramifications of the triumph began setting in: I was the Super Bowl MVP, and my 414 passing yards had broken Joe Montana's single-game record. Darn right, I was going to Disneyland—actually Disney World, for those of you scoring at home—and there was nothing Mickey Mouse about it. But I was humbled by the magnitude of the moment. That's what my faith does for me; it keeps me grounded and focused on what's truly important in life.

Three hours later I was celebrating the achievement with most of the people closest to me, at the Rams' victory party in a Crowne Plaza Ravinia ballroom. Eventually, a smaller group of us went back up to my room, and we prayed together and recounted some of the game's more exciting moments. Then, at about 2:30 A.M., the last of our visitors filed out. Now it was just Brenda and me—alone at last. The kids were back home in St. Louis with a baby-sitter, the rest of the world was asleep or talking about the game, and I lay down in bed beside the woman I loved feeling like the luckiest man on earth.

I closed my eyes and turned to kiss her. And then . . . click, the sound of our door opening. In stumbled Paul Justin, in full cele-bration mode. He turned on the light and saw us. "Oh, geez, you guys, I'm sorry," he stammered. "I really should've called."

For the first time all season, I was sorry I had a roommate.

In three hours I had to be at the downtown Hyatt Regency for the winning coach and MVP press conference. Brenda slept for a while, and P.J. and I sat up and chatted like young pals at a slum-ber party while Sportscenter blared in the background. We talked about the game and his plans for next year—he ended up signing with the Dallas Cowboys—and about life in general.

"Have you ever thought about what it would be like to play another position?" he asked.

I considered the question. "And not have the ball in my hands? And not be in total control of the situation?"

He nodded.

"Not be the *quarterback?*" I said. "No way. I couldn't do it."

We both started laughing. For the first time in days I fell asleep, peacefully, without worrying about what lay ahead.

CHAPTER SIXTEEN

HUDDLE UP

On the night of February 14, at the end of a two-week whirlwind that took me from the Super Bowl in Atlanta to Disney World in Orlando to the victory parade in St. Louis to the Pro Bowl in Hawaii to the ESPYs in Las Vegas, my miracle season came to an abrupt and frightening end. It happened shortly after I attended ESPN's gala awards show, where I was honored as the NFL Player of the Year and Breakthrough Athlete of the Year and rubbed elbows with some of the most amazing athletes on earth. You talk about sports-schmoozers' heaven, this was it: Michael Jordan, Jerry Rice, Evander Holyfield, Michael Johnson, Tiger Woods, all of them casual and down-to-earth and treating me like an equal. While all of us award winners were mingling backstage, Pete Sampras came up and introduced himself to *me* and he said he was moved by my story.

Needless to say, that kind of stuff didn't happen when I was the quarterback of the Iowa Barnstormers.

Later that night, when Brenda and I retired to our hotel room, we were feeling pretty high on life. After all of our struggles and trials, we had finally made it. Today I was the league and Super Bowl MVP; tomorrow a big contract, a book deal, and major national endorsements were waiting in the wings. I stretched out on our king-sized bed, and Brenda called home to return a message from our friend Kim, the woman who was watching our kids. Kade, our younger son, who was sixteen months old at the time, had been limping around for the past several days, and Kim had taken him to the doctor to get it checked out.

"What? Are you sure?" Brenda asked. I could tell from her voice that something was wrong. When she hung up the phone she gave me the news: Kade had stopped walking altogether, and the doctor's appointment had been a disaster. They wanted to do some blood tests on him, but without me or Brenda there he refused to be held down. The doctors thought the leg might be fractured, but they also weren't ruling out the possibility that it was something more serious. The next call we made was to the airlines, and we moved up our flights to the first thing the next morning.

It was time to get out of the fast lane and go home.

This wasn't the first time my ability to keep things in perspective had been tested. When you go from being a fringe player with a listed phone number to a sudden celebrity whose garbage is examined by the men in charge of collecting it, there are times when your view of reality becomes a bit skewed. If you're not careful, you can lose touch with the drive and the values that helped propel you to great heights and begin to believe that the world orbits at your behest. The universe becomes the *you-niverse,* and you forget what you were striving for in the first place.

That's why my faith is so important to me. Lord knows, I'm not perfect. Selfishness is a huge root of all evil, whether it's greed or just getting caught up in your own little world, and I'm certainly not immune to such struggles. I believe that the closer I get to God, the easier it is for me to avoid those temptations and establish a comfort zone where the focus isn't always on me.

Staying grounded has been a constant challenge. Certainly, having people tell you how great you are is part of it, but the fight against self-absorption began long before I emerged from the shadows of anonymity. For so many years, at so many stops on my unorthodox career path, people doubted my abilities. To overcome their skepticism—and the long odds against me—I had to maintain an incredible degree of faith in myself. Other than Brenda, my parents, and a few others close to me, nobody thought I could do what I ended up doing. Every single day was a struggle to prove the experts wrong, and that struggle often seemed futile.

When you get into that position, whether it's in football or any other aspect of life, two things happen: you feel incredibly isolated, and you cultivate an extremely powerful sense of self. Each of those qualities carries its own set of evils. You have to be careful not to become a self-obsessed, bitter, resentful, antisocial wreck.

This is where faith plays an integral role for me. It's great to believe in yourself, but in my opinion, you have to believe in something more as well. For me, becoming a Christian wasn't just a transition that made me a better person. It also made me *feel* better as a person, and specifically, it made me feel less isolated. Before, it was me against the world, or my family and I versus everyone. But once I accepted Jesus and committed my life to him, I had a community of brothers and sisters who believed in a common cause. It was an extended family, like a football team, only the goal wasn't to defeat an opponent but to share in a love and ecstasy that, in my mind, dwarfed everything else in importance.

In 1993 Nike aired a memorable commercial in which Charles Barkley declared, "I am not a role model." His view was that children should look up to their parents and teachers rather than professional athletes, and thus he had no responsibility to serve as a positive example. I understand what he was saying, because athletes in our culture are glorified to insane proportions. But to me the issue isn't whether we should or shouldn't be role models, because it's really a moot point. The reality is that we are role models, and there's no getting around that fact. So, to me, the question then becomes, What should we do about it?

I embrace my status as a role model bigtime, and it has nothing to do with athletics. I want to be a role model for Christ in everything that I do. Living my life for him, and showing people the beauty of that reality, is my mission in life. It's my agenda, the reason why I felt it important to write this book and share my story. Whether I'm a Super Bowl champion or a regular guy stocking groceries at the Hy-Vee, sharing my faith and glorifying Jesus is the central focus of my time on this earth.

The fact that I now have a podium, I believe, is no coincidence. The Lord didn't plan for me just to play football games and come home and hide in my closet. He prepared me for this over a long period of time—in lower-profile locker rooms and the grocery store and Amsterdam, through all the personal tragedies and in spite of all the people who doubted me along the way. He didn't want me just to throw touchdown passes so I could feel good about myself and then die.

So when someone says, "Just because I'm an athlete doesn't mean I should be a role model," I think it's crazy. Maybe you shouldn't be a role model just because you're a football player, but how can you shirk the responsibility of being a role model in general? I believe we all need to be role models. So, don't look up to me just because I play football. Look up to me because of what I stand for and what I believe in and who I am and the way I live my life. Emulate me because of the person I am. If you want to copy the way I throw a pass or handle adversity on the field, I think that's great. But that's not what a role model is. It's about the whole role.

As I said, no one is perfect, and I certainly don't claim to be. But I'm extremely confident that I won't show up in the news one day acting in a highly irresponsible manner, turning my back on my faith and my values. There's no secret life of Kurt Warner, because that would go against everything I believe. Character shouldn't be measured by what you do when millions of people are watching. It should be judged by who you are when you're alone in your private space and there's no image to maintain, as well as by the way you deal with things in your day-to-day life. I've had my share of struggles and hard times and sins, but I will say this: with me, what you see is what you get. My heart is my heart, and it's on my sleeve, and I'm not scared of standing up for a lifestyle and a faith that I believe are right. You're not going to spend time with me and come away doubting my sincerity or thinking I'm somebody different behind closed doors. You may not choose to view me as a role model, but you won't call me a faker or a hypocrite.

It helps me to hold myself up as someone who lives his life for Jesus, because it makes me more accountable and keeps me on my toes. I also believe that the way to become influential is by gaining credibility, and the only way to do that is to walk the walk as well as talk the talk.

That said, I'm not so naive as to believe that everyone who says he or she is a strong Christian will always behave in an exemplary manner. It does bother me when people claim to be strong Christians without making any effort to hold themselves to the standards Christ taught. I know plenty of athletes, even some people who have been my teammates, who talk about Jesus and his importance in their life then go out and hit the bar scene and turn their backs on the values their faith teaches. Again, I try very hard to be unbiased and nonjudgmental, but when so-called hypo-Christians try to have it both ways, it undermines the credibility of worshipers who are sincere in their faith.

I'm sure many nonbelievers view athletes proclaiming their faith in postgame interviews as a cliché, but that's not something I spend much time worrying about. I guess my view is that if saying "Thank you, Jesus" after a game is a cliché, then I'm happy to be part of the process, because that's the way I want my life to be defined. I'm going to stand up on every mountain—or podium—and shout Jesus' name and praise him for everything that happens in my life, and if that makes me a cliché, then I'm proud of it.

Many Christian athletes seem timid about enunciating their love for Jesus, perhaps because they think it will turn off the public and cost them endorsement money. While I respect the fact that everyone has different beliefs, I'm personally very eager to share my views with anyone who will listen. Just as I pride myself on hanging in there against a fearsome pass rush, I'm determined not to flinch when people mock or shout down my views. My role model in that regard is my wife. When Brenda was a teenager in Waterloo, Iowa, she literally had to fight for the right to voice her faith. Classmates would call her "Jesus Freak" and "Holy Roller" and knock her down in the halls and throw punches at her simply because of her beliefs. She was kicked out of junior high school parties because she was dragging everybody down. Friends would say, "It's fine if you believe that stuff, but when you're with us, could you just not talk about it?" Brenda replied that her relationship with God wasn't like a coat that she could put on or take off. But eventually people accepted her for who she was and even started respecting her for not backing down from her principles.

For all the fuss people have made about my story in the wake of my achievements with the Rams, Brenda's story, in my mind, is far more compelling. I can see why people have been moved by my journey, because it was such a drastic change to go from being an overlooked outsider to a guy triumphing in front of millions of people. But it's still hard for me to understand the amount of excitement it has generated. For one thing, I always expected to do well if I ever got the chance, and I had faith that the Lord would lead me to a place where I could glorify his name. Second, if you look at the big picture, my highs and lows haven't been as dramatic as a lot of other people's peaks and valleys. Compare my story to Brenda's: sure, I had to work at a grocery store and play Arena football, but she had to cope with her child's mental and physical disabilities and endure her parents' sudden death. Yet her faith was strong enough that she pressed ahead, raised a family, and has not lost sight of what's truly important in life. You tell me which story is more intriguing; I don't think it's even close. And obviously there are thousands of others like Brenda we never hear about who have triumphed in the face of circumstances far more daunting than getting passed over by a few football teams.

Still, the NFL is the NFL, and people have been touched by my sudden rise. I don't have any problem with that, but the interest has caused a rather drastic change in our personal lives. Before this happened we were utterly anonymous, and while we've certainly reaped many benefits of our sudden celebrity, we were totally unprepared for the madness that would accompany our fame. In the face of all the hoopla, it has been a constant struggle to protect our close-knit family and carve out the space we desire.

I don't want to sound like one of those rich, famous people who whine about the invasion of privacy that inevitably follows fame. I'm happy to be a public figure, and most of the time I gladly sign autographs and politely interact with fans. But some of the things that have happened to me since I became a prominent player are downright ridiculous. For instance, I love the fact that people know who Brenda is and feel some sort of attachment to her. But when she goes to pick up medication prescribed by her gynecologist at the pharmacy and there's a note from the pharmacist asking if I can sign some items, I think that's crossing the line of decency.

Similarly, while I eagerly give money to all sorts of charitable causes, I had to shake my head when a woman hand-delivered a letter to Brenda asking that we buy her a new wheelchair—with X rays of her curved spine enclosed for authenticity. Once when I was leaving a supermarket, a woman asked if I would *follow her home* so that I could sign a shirt. When I'm stuck in traffic, even on the freeways, people will leave their vehicles and run back across the road to ask me for autographs. Also, when I feel the need to visit a restaurant restroom, people often follow me in and ask me to sign various items. I feel like saying, "Do you mind if I wash my hands first?"

Brenda has witnessed garbage men removing bags from our trash cans and bringing them to the front of their truck, apparently so they could examine the contents. Considering that Kade is in disposable diapers, I don't even want to think about what treasures they might have unearthed.

A couple of months after the season ended, we loaded the kids into the van late one night and drove up Highway 61 to visit family members back home. As we crossed the border from Missouri to Iowa and the speed limit changed from 65 to 55, I got pulled over by a state trooper for speeding. He was nice enough to give me a warning, and then he said, "Can I just ask one favor of you?" I said sure, thinking he wanted an autograph or something. Instead, he asked me to get out of the car, walk backward about twenty feet, then turn and wave. "We've got the video cameras mounted in the squad car," he explained. "I'd love it if you could wave to my son, because he'll never believe I pulled you over."

Most of this stuff is harmless, but it does wear on me. If I politely decline to sign an autograph for whatever reason, and someone is pushy or rude, it really sours me on the whole experience. I sometimes feel that even when people are nice enough to help us out they have ulterior motives. For instance, as we were leaving for the Pro Bowl, some police officers drove us onto the tarmac so we could board our flight without being besieged by autograph seekers. Obviously, we were very appreciative, but when we got back to St. Louis an officer whispered into my ear, "Our chief's here, and it's against policy to have you sign anything, but we left a bag of stuff in your car." The bag was full of memorabilia and other things the cops wanted me to sign.

Again, I don't want to portray myself as an object of pity, but at times I feel as though my entire life has become a transaction. Even when I visit my parents and other relatives in Iowa, there's always some friend they want me to talk to or some stuff they want me to sign, and it bothers me because around them I just want to be the same person I've always been. I understand that my relatives want to share in my success because they've been a part of the triumph, and I want them to be able to reap the rewards. But it upsets me when I bring my kids to their grandparents' house and instead of all of us being able to hang out in a relaxed fashion, commitments have been made to sign autographs for this person or that person, or people come to the house who are in awe of the situation and we can't be ourselves. It's so tough to carve out time together as a family, and my hope is that when we get that time we can spend it being a family, not talking about football or appeasing other people.

The bottom line is, I get sick of talking about myself all the time. I'm not a guy who likes to be the center of attention or be bombarded with compliments, and though I'm flattered that other people are interested, it doesn't make me especially comfortable. Besides, I can't help but scoff at people's sudden desire to take care of me. Six years ago Brenda was on food stamps and I was making $5.50 an hour. Yet now that we have more money, everyone wants to shower us with gifts. We get free T-shirts, free gear, deals on cars and cell phones, and all kinds of other perks. I always tell Brenda that the rich get richer, and it's true: a few years ago we were eating ramen noodles and peanut butter and jelly sandwiches for dinner, and now that we can go out to a restaurant and afford to buy anything on the menu, a lot of times they won't even bring us a check.

Not only do the rich get richer, the rich get spoiled, and that's a trap we're determined to avoid. During my first year with the Rams there was a Disney ice show at the Kiel Center in St. Louis, and the team got some free tickets that they offered to the players. So Brenda and I took the kids, and it turned out the seats were in the upper deck. Oh, well; we were still happy to be there. But a couple of other players came to our section, saw where the seats were, and went ballistic: "I can't believe our tickets are so bad. We're out of here." And some of them actually walked out, went outside, and bought tickets that allowed them to sit down low. We were just so thrilled to be in the building, especially for free, and we've vowed never to lose touch with that feeling.

Some of the things that get thrown our way are hilarious. During the '99 season, after our loss to Detroit, one newspaper's account of the game contained a line cracking that I had been subpar in the first half because I had missed my weekly viewing of *Third Rock From the Sun.* I think the writer was trying to make a joke—like, I had been playing so well that I must be an alien, and now I had come back to earth—but in Hollywood they took it quite literally. A few weeks later I got a big box of stuff from the sitcom's producers, and mixed in with the cups, hats, T-shirts, posters, and videotapes was a note from John Lithgow saying, "Thanks for being a fan." I'd probably seen about five minutes' worth of *Third Rock* in my life, but it was a nice gesture.

Then there was the big national TV commercial I turned down because I refused to shave. As I've said, I absolutely hate shaving, and for years my only resistance against facial hair has come in the form of an electric beard trimmer. Sometimes I have a goatee and sometimes a scraggly scruff, but I simply will not use a razor. So, when the folks from Edge shaving gel called—they're the ones who did those funny ads with Tim Duncan and David Robinson a couple years back—and offered me $150,000 for a TV spot in which I'd shave, I had to say no. As I told Jay Leno on a *Tonight Show* appearance after the '99 season, since I refused to shave for my own wedding, it wouldn't have looked too good if I broke down and shaved for Edge. Besides, I'm not going to be one of those public figures who will do anything for money, because if I want to be a strong Christian role model, my integrity is paramount. Now here's the crazy thing: a week after I turned down the commercial, my agent called and said, "Now they want you even more, because you stuck to your principles and didn't just take the money and run." So the folks at Edge decided to try to figure out a new idea in which I could appear in the spot but wouldn't have to shave.

Sometimes I have to roll my eyes at the special treatment we receive. People who wouldn't give us the time of day before I became the starter now act like we're the best thing since squeezable ketchup bottles. Before every school year we have a meeting with the district's special needs administrators to set up Zachary's IEP, which stands for Individual Education Program. It's where you determine the curriculum and resource breakdown for every special needs child—how many minutes will be devoted to which disability and what kind of computers and other specific learning aids can be obtained toward that end. In 1998, when I was a third-string quarterback, Brenda wasn't satisfied with the first meeting and asked for another one. And another one. And another one. There were fifteen meetings in all over the course of the school year, and it took almost until the end of the term to get everything that we had requested. Brenda can be *very* persistent, and you can imagine how well liked she was by the school district.

Needless to say, we no longer have a problem getting them to listen to our concerns about Zachary's educational needs. If we say, "Hop on one foot," they ask, "Left foot or right?" Recently, in fact, we got a letter from the school district asking if Brenda would be part of a board made up of parents to aid in the resolution of such disputes.

And, at our most recent IEP meeting, one of the teachers brought items for me to sign. I understand that things have changed, and it's great that Zachary's educational opportunities have improved as a result, but it makes me wonder, *What about all the other kids whose parents aren't star quarterbacks?* I know exactly what kind of struggles they go through each and every year, because Brenda has been fighting these battles for Zachary since he was three.

Of all the things I love about Brenda, her strength and independence are what strike me most. There's a part of me that never gives up, and Brenda is even more that way. She won't take the easy way out to avoid confrontation, and when it comes to her children, she'll fight with everything she's got. I know she believes in this family and our faith, and she'll go to the wall to defend it. For that reason, she's an incredible source of strength for me. She also protects me when I need to be protected. One of my character flaws, if you want to call it that, is that I'm very easygoing and want to be the good guy all the time. Brenda is vigilant about preserving our family's space, and with the way our life has changed in the past year, that's a difficult job.

My family is everything to me. I'd give up anything or everything that I had to in order to take care of Brenda and the kids and to act in their best interests. Everything I do, I want them to be part of. No decision is ever made without considering how it will affect my family. Brenda and the kids are the ones who have been my support system throughout my unlikely path to NFL stardom, the ones who have allowed me to fulfill my dream.

The term *family man* is tossed around a lot, but I'm one person who truly fits that description. When I get done with practice or playing a game, I would love to hang out with the guys and social-ize, but I don't believe that's where I need to be. Especially during the season, there are so few hours that I can spend with my family that I can't squander those opportunities. When I travel to do an autograph-signing session or attend an award banquet or make an appearance, my family needs to be with me. Shortly after the Super Bowl a producer from *Live with Regis and Kathie Lee* called my agent to try to book Brenda and me on the show. We agreed but asked that they pay to fly our kids to New York for the taping. When we were told that it wouldn't be possible to pay for all our flights, we declined the invitation.

Somebody once said that they never see me out by myself—that I'm always with my family—and I loved hearing that. No mat-ter what great things have happened to me in my career, Brenda and the kids are still priority number one, and I want them to experience everything right there alongside me.

I don't want to be a father who's not around to influence my kids in the manner I feel is necessary. I want to influence them by being with them and sharing those experiences and teaching them along the way. Brenda and I have discussed the idea of get-ting a nanny, and while we realize there will be times when we'll need help, we always decide against any sort of permanent arrangement. The bottom line is that we do not want anyone else raising our kids. That's the reason we made the decision to have Brenda stop working and stay at home. We feel that we absolutely must be the primary influences in their lives—not TV, not school, not their friends.

My success has put a lot of strain on the family, and that's not really fair to Brenda and the kids. It makes me mad when they bear the brunt of my celebrity, and while I think they've done a good job of trying to keep our intrafamilial reality as normal as possible, it is a concern. Sometimes I tease Brenda because she seems to get as much airtime during games as I do. There have been some pretty comical moments, like the time she had a doctor's appointment and one of the other patients said, "Oh, my gosh, do you know who you look like?" Brenda was about to acknowledge that yes, she was indeed *the* Brenda Warner when the woman blurted, "Alice, from *The Brady Bunch!*"

As I've stated earlier, Brenda has been called much, much worse. I try to let her know that none of that stuff is true in my eyes, because it can be pretty hard for someone who's not used to it to endure that kind of criticism. I think a lot of people are envious of her position and try to find a way to knock her down as a result. They can say whatever they want, but at home she's my queen, and that's never going to change.

When I talk about my family, I often get so emotional that I start to cry. Zachary, for all of his struggles, is the sweetest, most good-natured kid I could ever imagine. He has more fun with life than anybody I've ever met. There are times when I have to repeat things over and over because that's the way his brain processes things, but he also comes up with thoughts that are pure and amazing and captivate me in a totally unique way.

Things that we take for granted—getting dressed, walking up and down the stairs, eating our meals, reading a book—aren't easy for Zachary. His whole life is a challenge, but he never backs down from anything. He's curious and asks a lot of questions, sometimes more than we want to answer, but once he learns, he learns. His memory is exceptional, and there are so many things we can learn from him. When he runs around and stumbles, which happens many times each day, he gets right back up and moves on. The vigor that he has for life, the joy that he exudes, and the excitement he gathers from little things that we all take for granted—all of that is a constant reminder to us that we need to thank God for giving us such a special child. He still attacks life with the same positive attitude that he did when I met him seven years ago, and we learn new, wondrous things about him on a daily basis.

Each September 6, our family celebrates "Zachary Day." The date falls on the anniversary of his accident, but we put a positive spin on it. We view it as a day that was a turning point for him, one that has affected our life in a tremendous way, and one that sets him apart. It's our way of letting him know that he's an incredible child and that we're so proud of everything he's accomplished since the accident, when nobody gave him a chance to do much of anything. We thank God for having faith in us and trusting that we'd be able to raise this special child and make his life fulfilling.

Then there is Jesse, our singing, dancing performer of a daughter. Not only is Jesse incredibly talented and intelligent, she's also a warm, giving person who makes me immensely proud. The patience and selflessness she displays in helping her brother on a daily basis are breathtaking, and she possesses an amazing amount of maturity and perceptiveness. Fortunately for her—and, many would argue, unfortunately for me—she is very beautiful. Many boys will want to date her in a few years, and I have no problem with that—provided I can come along to supervise.

Jesse and I have our share of clashes, partly because we're very alike. I've got a real laid-back sense of humor and like to kid people good-naturedly, and I think she's the same way. We tend to make light of things and not let people take themselves too seriously, and sometimes we get under each other's skin. But I couldn't ask for a better daughter, and I have no doubt that she'll grow up to be an amazing woman with exceptional grace and kindness.

Kade shares his siblings' sweetness, and he already has an active sense of humor that blows us away. Thankfully, his leg injury turned out to be okay, but not until after we endured several months' worth of uncertainty. He went through a pair of casts and many tests, including one that showed slight abnormalities in his white blood cells. Ultimately, doctors removed some bone marrow to check for leukemia, and to our great relief the results came back negative. Now, we pray, he's back to being what he was before: a walking, unceasing, thrashing machine. Our not-so-little guy—he weighed thirty-five pounds at twenty months—is built like a lineman and eats like one, too. He's a fun-loving, adventurous kid, and I look forward to seeing him grow up . . . and up . . . and up.

Sometimes I get frustrated with my older kids because they don't realize how good they have it. I hate to be the guy who says, "When I was a kid, I had to walk five miles through the snow with holes in my shoes to get to school," but Brenda and I did have it much tougher growing up, and our children don't understand. I can't change the fact that we have money now, and I certainly want them to reap the benefits of our good fortune, but I'm strict and old school when it comes to parenting. I want our kids to have proper values, to understand the importance of hard work, and to grow into people who not only enjoy life but also serve as positive influences in society.

As the madness around us swells, I'm committed to retaining some sense of normalcy. Just as I insist on doing the same things that got me to this level, like showing up early in the morning at Rams Park for off-season workout sessions, I also want to cling to what's left of our former reality. There's a rock outside our home with the words "The Warners' House" painted on it. I know I probably should have removed it by now, but so far I've resisted. On a symbolic level, I like the idea that it's still out there, as anchored and unambiguous as it ever was.

There was a light rain falling in Orlando on the morning after the Super Bowl, and as I sat atop a float carrying me through the wonderful world of Disney, I was amazed at how many people were willing to brave the conditions in order to shake my hand. But from my two companions, I got no love. Try as I might, I couldn't get Mickey or Minnie Mouse to say a single word to me, which, of course, would have been against company policy. Yet unlike Nancy Kerrigan six years earlier, I was genuinely happy to be part of the pageantry.

Later that day I was back in St. Louis, doing the Bob and Weave for 100,000 fans who had gathered downtown for our victory parade. I told the masses that I'd had enough of the whole "He used to work at a supermarket" angle, that it was time instead to start focusing on our quest to repeat as champions. The next day my family and I flew to Hawaii, and during a stopover in San Francisco we sat in an airport lounge watching CNN and heard an announcer say, "Coming up, we'll give you the lowdown on Dick Vermeil's future."

Some of the people in the lounge turned to me and asked, "What do you think he's going to do?" I told them I thought Coach Vermeil would come back to coach another year, because I couldn't see how he would decide to retire without even gathering the players to discuss his plans. The possibility that he wouldn't be back had never even crossed my mind.

Then the commercial break ended and the announcer said that Coach Vermeil was going to retire. I sat there staring at the screen, dumbfounded. Things were happening so fast, and now I had lost the coach with whom I'd shared a special relationship, the guy who put his neck on the line by having faith in me after Trent Green got hurt.

The more I thought about it, though, the more sense it made. He deserved to go out on top, and I was happy for him, because he had turned things around and answered all the critics who said he couldn't be successful in today's game. He proved that he could do it his way and make it back to the pinnacle of his profession, and now it was time for him to move on to the next chapter of his life. The fact that Mike Martz was chosen to succeed him eased the pain, because there would be a large degree of continuity and carryover. It's not like I'd have to learn a new offense or adjust to a completely different regime, and my relationship with Coach Martz had grown to the point where I felt extremely comfortable.

Once we arrived in Hawaii everything was great—with one exception. As fun as it was to rub elbows with the NFL's best players, one of them, Randy Moss, wasn't particularly pleasant. Even after his ref-squirting incident in our playoff game, I was willing to give him the benefit of the doubt and try to get to know him. But he never seemed real interested in talking. Everyone else was pretty friendly, but Randy was just a little more standoffish, a little tougher to get to know. He has been through a lot in the last couple of years. He entered the league with a checkered reputation and then made a huge splash; maybe putting up a wall is part of his coping strategy. He came off as being a little bit arrogant, as someone who had proven everything he needed to prove.

I could see if someone like Cris Carter or Tim Brown copped an attitude because those guys have proven themselves year after year, but Moss was the only one strutting around like he owned the island. This was his second Pro Bowl in as many seasons, and he acted like he was King Kamehameha. He had little desire to hang out with any of the other players. I talked to a lot of the other first-time Pro Bowlers, and none of us could understand what his deal was. Some of them knew Randy, and they said, "We don't understand what makes him tick or why he does what he does."

Not only did he treat practices as a joke, he also blew off the team photo, which I thought was pretty bizarre. I had seen him earlier in the day at the stadium, where we had practiced, but when it came time to gather for the picture he was nowhere to be found. We waited and waited and waited, and finally we took it without him. I don't know why he would do something disruptive like that, but I guess he had his reasons.

I don't know what the circumstances were or what was going on in his head, but he just came off like he didn't have to be out there, that none of it was important to him. To his credit, he showed up on Sunday and had a great attitude—and caught nine passes for 212 yards and a touchdown to earn MVP honors. He actually was fun to play with, too. Early on, he took the liberty of changing one of his routes without informing me, and when we got back to the sideline I asked him what had happened. He told me why he did what he did, and I said, "Well, I want you to do it the way you're supposed to, because how else will I know where you'll be?" He said he was fine with that, and from then on things were very smooth. He was very open to suggestions and to making the proper adjustments and doing whatever he needed to do to get the ball.

Before and even during the Pro Bowl I was a social butterfly, getting to know a lot of prominent players I'd admired from afar. By the second quarter I was done for the day, and I had nothing to do but strike up conversations. I had a lot of fun with Warren Sapp, the Tampa Bay Buccaneers' awesome defensive tackle, who three weeks earlier had been talking trash at me and trying to tear my head off during the NFC Championship game. Before that game someone had showed me a quote from him in which he said he looked forward to hearing the crunch when he broke my leg. Obviously, there was a little bit of showmanship involved there, and we got along great in Hawaii. He actually did the Bob and Weave after Aeneas Williams ran back an interception for a touchdown because, he said, "I was representing the NFC."

A few weeks later things finally began to calm down, and I was back in the weight room, doing all the little things to get ready for the next season. Obviously, there will be a lot of pressure on the team—and on me in particular—to live up to the standards we set in '99. I'm sure many skeptics believe that I was a one-year wonder who'll come crashing down to earth, and I look forward to trying to prove them wrong and winning another championship.

Will I ever have another season like the one I had in '99? That's tough to say. It's not very feasible to think that I'll be able to put up those kinds of crazy numbers every year, and I know that in 2000 everyone will be gunning for me. But I do expect myself to play well, and I expect to do a lot of the same things I did in '99. The bottom line is winning football games, and I believe I'll continue to play well enough, and consistently enough, to keep the Rams at or near the top of the league. I'm realistic enough to know that you don't win Super Bowls and throw forty-nine touchdown passes every year, but I promise you I won't fade into oblivion, either.

A lot of people wonder how it could have taken the NFL so long to uncover my talents, especially since the league spends millions of dollars each year on scouting and player development. The only reason I can think of is that I didn't get many chances to play. In college, I started only my senior season, and I barely touched the ball during my brief time with the Packers. The NFL never really paid any attention to the Arena League, and I just slipped through the cracks. I don't think it was a case of a lot of scouts seeing me play and writing me off because I didn't have the skills. They just missed me entirely, which is pretty funny considering that their job is to scour the earth for hidden talent.

I find a bit of humor in the fact that so many people have jumped forward to proclaim they knew all along that I was a good player. They have to be biting their tongues as they speak, because they weren't bold enough to give me an opportunity to prove myself. At every stop, even after NFL tryouts, all I heard was positive feedback. Sometimes I'd even ask people how they thought I could improve, and they couldn't come up with anything. They just told me to wait by the phone and, of course, they never called.

It would have been very easy to feel sorry for myself or become bitter or walk away from my dream, but I believed in my talents and kept battling, and I guess that makes my story worth telling. It seems to have moved people, and that's incredibly flattering.

"You've been a true inspiration to me," Billy Jenkins, our starting strong safety, told me after the Super Bowl as I was waiting to be interviewed atop the victory podium. "I've been watching you, and everything you do is inspirational, from the way you take everything in to the way you always keep the faith." To hear that from another starter was very touching, especially from a guy like Billy, whom I admire and who has been in the league longer than I have. Before I became the starter Billy was always the guy the coaches held up as someone to emulate. An undrafted free agent who worked his way into the lineup, he's an underrated overachiever who never has gotten the respect he deserved. He's a big hitter who isn't afraid to smack someone in practice, and even in '99 when they brought in another player to take his place, he kept working hard and managed to keep his job. To hear him say that I was inspirational was pretty gratifying.

Whatever your situation in life is, I hope my story is of some value to you. No matter how discounted you might be, if you stay true to your principles, believe in yourself, and keep working hard, good things eventually will happen. You might not get the tangible rewards you were counting on at the start, but there's joy in the journey as well as the destination. If you're willing to put yourself and your dreams on the line, at the very least you'll discover an inner strength you may not have known existed.

If I've done anything by beating the odds, I hope it's that I've spread a positive message to people who otherwise might not be listening. I view my struggle as analogous to that of David against Goliath. David was a guy nobody ever gave a chance to, a man who came out of nowhere to display an incredible amount of power and control. He couldn't have slain Goliath without an unyielding faith in God, and he wasn't just trying to help himself, he was also working to uplift his people.

I know I do a lot of preaching, but even if you don't share my beliefs, please understand my intentions. I live my life for Jesus, and my goal is to share him with as many people as possible. I'm not asking you to believe what I believe so I can feel better about myself. I just want everyone to get a piece of the action, to get invited to the greatest party there is. If you take that step, it doesn't mean you'll be perfect or won't have your struggles during your time on earth. But, in my view, it does guarantee you salvation, and it's my belief that it can never be taken away from you. If that comes off as heavy-handed, please don't take it as a personal attack. I come from a good place, and I want to spread the peace and joy I've achieved through my faith to as many people as I can.

Whatever you believe, and whatever path you choose, I hope my story can be of some use to you. And if you ever see me struggling—on the football field or in life—please don't worry too much. With the right values, a loving family, and an everlasting faith, I know I'll have the strength to fight through any adversity. Remember, with God, all things are possible.

The book might be finished, but my story is far from complete.

Believe me, the best is yet to come.

ACKNOWLEDGMENTS

To Momma—Brenda, my wife and best friend: your undeniable faith in our Heavenly Father has been a path for me to follow. Your unconditional love and support have been my inspiration to live life to the fullest. Your incredible faith in me has been unmatched. Without you I would not be the football player, the person, the husband, or the father that I am today. You complete me! I will always love you.

To the three greatest earthly gifts the Lord has ever given me, my three children, Zachary, Jesse, and Kade: you have truly taught me how to love, each in your own way. Z.T., with your unconditional feelings for those you come in contact with: you don't care what people look like or where they come from, only how they treat you—a lesson for all of us and one that you remind me of every day. J.J., I appreciate your sacrifices and unselfishness on a daily basis. I don't tell you enough, but you are the most incredible little girl I have ever met. Don't *ever* change. Kader, by being my first infant, you have taught me how to love unselfishly—to love through the sacrifices we make for others, learning how to put others always before ourselves. You have all taught me so much, not only about being a good father, but also about being a good person. You are all special blessings, each in your own way, and you make me proud to call myself "Dad." I love you.

To my extended family, you are the greatest. I could not have done any of this without you. Know that my successes are your successes. There would be no Kurt Warner if it weren't for the role that each of you played in my life. Thank you for shaping me into the man I am today.

Mom, thank you for your love, strength, and sacrifices over the years. I know that times were not always easy; you did *great.* Your support has been second to none, and I thank you for the values you instilled in me.

Sue Warner (Mom)

The Warners and the Hawleys

Pops, know that I could not ask for a better father. Though times were tough, you never lost sight of our relationship. I would not change anything in the past to sacrifice what we now have. The greatest compliment I have for you is that I hope as I get older I can have the same relationship with my children as you have with me. Mimi, thanks for all the love over the years. You welcomed us with open arms and always loved us as your own. Your kindness will always hold a special place in my heart.

Gene and Mimi Warner (Dad and Stepmom)

To my bros, Matt and Matt, what can I say? Words cannot express what you mean to me. You are my biggest fans and greatest friends. I can't think of a time that we weren't together. Know that I think of you often and will cherish the memories we have shared. My life would not be the same without you. You are the best.

Three Musketeers: Matt, Matt, and Kurt

Matt and Amber Warner

To Mike Silver, for your special gift of writing. You truly have made this a book that will influence many lives in a positive fashion. Without your unique talent to entertain and inform, I don't feel this book would have the same reach. But, most important, I appreciate your friendship. This is what I will cherish the most.

To Gregg Lewis, for your unique vision to display the true essence of who I am. Your input and sensitivity made a difference. Thanks for your love and devotion to our Lord and Savior.

To Mark Bartelstein and Associates (especially Mark, Rob, and Julie) for all of your hard work and determination on my behalf. Your belief in me has made all the difference and it has been truly appreciated. You have helped to make a crazy year very enjoyable. Thanks for everything.

To all the friends, teammates, coaches, acquaintances . . . that the Lord has placed in my path along the way. You helped to shape my story through your love, teaching, and opportunities. You believed in me when no one else would, and to you I will always be grateful. Thank you.

Jen and Larry Carney (Brenda's parents)

To my fans, whom I thank for your continued support. I hope that my story can positively influence your lives in some small way. For with a strong belief in God and yourself, truly all things are possible.

Most important, I thank my Father in Heaven for the most incredible gift I have ever received—your son, Jesus Christ. Without this there would be no story. To my Lord and Savior Jesus Christ, for your unyielding grace and love: you have shown me the true essence of how to live. I hope that I can in some way make you look down and be proud of who I am here on earth. To the Holy Spirit for your strength and guidance in all that I do: with you inside me, there is nothing that I cannot accomplish for my Heavenly Father. Thank you for opening my heart to the Father's will for my life.

—Kurt Warner,
August 2000

ACKNOWLEDGMENTS
FROM MICHAEL SILVER

I owe so much to the following individuals:

Leslie, my sublime wife, without whom none of this would be possible. Honey, you rock, and your strength keeps it all together. I love and appreciate you so much.

Natalie and Greg Silver—I can't put the ferocity of my love for you into words, but I'll be trying, forever. And Dr. J., my first baby.

My family—Mom, Dad, Elizabeth; the Silvers, the Goyettes, and the Tourgemans; my beautiful nieces and nephews. You all dominate on a daily basis. Much love to Uncle Sonny, Aunt Laura, and the Fingerotes and Johnsons.

Kurt and Brenda Warner, for trusting me from the start and never once pressuring me. And for letting me buy a meal once in a while. Thanks also to Zack, Jesse, Kade, Gene, Mimi, Sue, Matt, Matt, Chach, and the rest of the Warner entourage for making this job easy.

The eclectic and electric ensemble that made this book happen: "King" David Hirshey and the HarperCollins gang; Steve Hanselman and Gideon Weil, keeping it cool in the City by the Bay; Gregg Lewis, with the pinch-hit grand slam; John Sloan and the Zondervan clan; Sloan Harris, from ICM to the front lines; and Rob Lefko and Bartlestein & Associates, who braved the early storm.

The folks who provided the heavy lifting: Jill May, for flawless transcription at warp speed; Josh Elliott, for checking facts and untold acts of inspiration—dude, you've got a great . . . future; Kate Arnold, for the spot; Smoothie Steve Restino; Gordo Taqueria, for bringing the heat.

Interview subjects Mike White, Todd Lyght, Paul Justin, Kevin Warren, Ike Bruce, Ernie Conwell, Dick Vermeil, and Jeff Fisher; Jeff and Patsy Perry (thanks for the Old Testament plugs); John Madden and Steve Young.

The *Sports Illustrated* empire: Bill Colson, Norm Pearlstine, Mark Godich, the other Powers That Be, and the fiercest football lineup this side of St. Louis—Peter King, runs pretty but gets the tough yards; Dr. Z, the legend who can still wing it; Austin Murphy, when he's on, it's over; Dave Fleming, all about the cheddar; and Jeff Chadiha, gets stronger as the game goes on.

The spirit of St. Louis: Michael MacCambridge, tour guide; Bob Costas, man on the high road; Rick Smith, Duane Lewis, William Bryant, Miranda Walker, Marci Moran, and the other helpful folks at Rams Park; Bernie Miklasz, Jim Thomas, Elizabethe Holland, Jeff Gordon, Howard Balzer, and the St. Louis media for raising the bar.

The many people who helped get me here: Rick Telander, guru and warrior; Mary Redclay, for teaching me how to write; Janet Pawson, for stellar career guidance; Worm—I still love you, bro; Slick Vic, Dickie, J.B., and the friends who make this business fun; Mike Fleiss, pop culture shaman; Greg, Kristen, Leila, Bob, and all my Oaktown playas and playettes; Rachel and Lauren Wallock, M & M and all the good friends we've lost along the way; those of you who honor me by allowing me to call you friend and say, "Whassup . . ."

A special thanks to Dr. Mary Jones, Dr. Jim Policy, and the other awesome healers at Children's Hospital and throughout the East Bay.

—Michael Silver,
August 2000

CAREER STATISTICS

College: Gateway Conference offensive player of the year in 1993, his senior season at Northern Iowa. He led the conference in total offense and passing efficiency—passed for over 300 yards four times and was named two-time Gateway player of the week. He became a starter senior season and graduated with a degree in communications.

Arena Football League 1995–1997: Passed for 10,164 yards and 183 touchdowns in three seasons with the Barnstormers and led Iowa to two straight Arena Bowl appearances. He holds all of the Barnstormers individual passing records. **1995:** In his rookie season in the AFL, he threw for 2,980 yards and 43 touchdowns and finished second in the league in passing yards. **1996:** Completed 259 of 422 passes for 3,336 yards and 61 touchdowns and was named first team All-Arena Football League, rushed for 7 touchdowns, and led the Barnstormers to the Arena Bowl. **1997:** Led the Barnstormers to an 11–3 record and their second straight appearance in the Arena Bowl. He completed 65 percent of his passes for 4,149 yards and 79 touchdowns, only the third quarterback in the history of the league to pass for over 4,000 yards. He was named the Arena League's weekly MVP four times. **2000:** Barnstormers retired his #13 jersey—the first in team history.

NFL Europe 1998: Started all ten games for the Amsterdam Admirals. He led the league in passing yards (2,101), attempts (326), completions (165), and touchdowns (15).

NFL

Regular Season Passing

Year	Team	G-S	Att.	Com.	Yards	Pct.	TD	Int.	LG	Sacks-Yds.	Rating
1998	RAMS	1–0	11	4	39	36.4	0	0	21	0–0	47.2
1999	RAMS	16–16	499	325	4,353	65.1	41	13	75t	29–201	109.2
Total		17–16	510	329	4,392	65.0	41	13	75t	29–201	107.9

Postseason Passing

Year	Team	G-S	Att.	Com.	Yards	Pct.	TD	Int.	LG	Sacks-Yds.	Rating
1999	RAMS	3–3	121	77	1,063	63.6	8	4	77t	3–24	100.0
Total		3–3	121	77	1,063*	63.6	8	4	77t	3–24	100.0

* Broke Joe Montana's Super Bowl record with 414 passing yards in Super Bowl XXXIV.

Single Game Highs

Att.	46 @ Tennessee (10/31/99)
	Playoffs 45 vs. Tennessee (Super Bowl XXXIV) (1/30/00)
Comp.	29 @ Tennessee (10/31/99)
	Playoffs 27 vs. Minnesota (1/16/00)
Yards	353 @ Carolina (12/5/99)
TD	5 vs. San Francisco (10/10/99)
	Playoffs 5 vs. Minnesota (1/16/00)
300-yd. passing games	9, Last vs. Chicago (12/26/99)
	Playoffs 2, Last vs. Tennessee (Super Bowl XXXIV) (1/30/00)

In the preceding chapters, you've read some of the highlights of my life—the challenges and the breakthroughs. Every sentence and chapter leads me to this central point: Jesus changed my life . . . and he can change yours too. Simply pray this prayer:

Lord Jesus, you know everything about me. Please forgive me for all the wrong things I've ever said or done. I know that you died for my sins and rose from the dead. Please come into my life and be my Lord. Help me to follow you always. Amen.

". . . If you confess with your mouth Jesus as Lord, and believe in your heart that God raised Him from the dead, you shall be saved; for with the heart man believes, resulting in righteousness, and with the mouth he confesses, resulting in salvation."
(Romans 10:9–10, NASB)

—Kurt Warner,
St. Louis, July 2000